Also by Sara Miles

How to Hack a Party Line

Opposite Sex: Gay Men on Lesbians,
Lesbians on Gay Men (coeditor)

Directed by Desire: The Collected Poems
of June Jordan (coeditor)

Take This Bread

Take
This
Bread

A Radical
Conversion

Sara
Miles

BALLANTINE
BOOKS

New York

Copyright © 2007 by Sara Miles

Published in the United States by Ballantine Books,
an imprint of The Random House Publishing Group,
a division of Random House, Inc., New York.

BALLANTINE and colophon are
registered trademarks of Random House, Inc.

ISBN 978-0-345-48692-9

LIBRARY OF CONGRESS CATALOGING-IN-PUBLICATION DATA

Miles, Sara
Take this bread : a radical conversion / by Sara Miles.
p.   cm.
1. Miles, Sara.   2. Christian converts—United States—
Biography.   3. Church work with the poor—United States.
4. Food relief—United States.   I. Title.
BV4935.M525A3 2007
277.3'083092—dc22
[B]   2006048971

Printed in the United States of America
on acid-free paper

www.ballantinebooks.com
www.saramiles.net

3 4 5 6 7 8 9

Book design by Barbara M. Bachman

For Katie,
my blessing

Contents

Author's Note   x i

Prologue   x i i i

Chapter 1
The Family Table   3

Chapter 2
Pilgrimage   1 0

Chapter 3
Standing the Heat   1 4

Chapter 4
Cooking with My Brother   2 4

Chapter 5
War Years   3 5

Chapter 6
First Communion   5 4

Chapter 7
Crossing   6 5

Chapter 8
Histories   7 4

Chapter 9
Crossing II   9 1

Chapter 10
Seeing More   9 8

Chapter 11
"Good Works"   109

Chapter 12
A Different Everyone   119

Chapter 13
Church of the One True Sack   130

Chapter 14
Gleaners   141

Chapter 15
Faith and Politics   159

Chapter 16
Words and Acts   169

Chapter 17
The Desert   179

Chapter 18
Manna   198

Chapter 19
Misfits   207

Chapter 20
Cooking with My Brother II   218

Chapter 21
Rites   227

Chapter 22
Multiplying the Loaves   242

Chapter 23
Sunday Dinner   250

Chapter 24
The Cost of Faith   261

Chapter 25
The Heavenly Feast   267

Acknowledgments   281

This book is a work of nonfiction. Some of the names in it, and a few identifying details, have been changed to protect privacy.

The conversations recorded in this book took place over a span of thirty years and in several countries. I took notes and checked quotes for all my formal interviews, but often I worked from memory. To the best of my ability, I've tried to reconstruct events, chronology, and dialogue accurately, but there are inevitable errors and omissions.

To use a religious analogy: This book is not the Bible imagined as inerrant and historically definitive. It's more the Bible I believe in—that is, a human compilation of stories told in different voices, edited and rearranged over many drafts to suggest truths not always fully understood.

One early, cloudy morning when I was forty-six, I walked into a church, ate a piece of bread, took a sip of wine. A routine Sunday activity for tens of millions of Americans—except that up until that moment I'd led a thoroughly secular life, at best indifferent to religion, more often appalled by its fundamentalist crusades. This was my first communion. It changed everything.

Eating Jesus, as I did that day to my great astonishment, led me against all my expectations to a faith I'd scorned and work I'd never imagined. The mysterious sacrament turned out to be not a symbolic wafer at all but actual food—indeed, the bread of life. In that shocking moment of communion, filled with a deep desire to reach for and become part of a body, I realized that what I'd been doing with my life all along was what I was meant to do: feed people.

And so I did. I took communion, I passed the bread to others, and then I kept going, compelled to find new ways to share what I'd experienced. I started a food pantry and gave away literally tons of fruit and vegetables and cereal around the same altar where I'd first received the body of Christ. I organized new pantries all over my city to provide hundreds and hundreds of hungry families with free groceries each week. Without committees or meetings or even an official telephone number, I recruited scores of volunteers and raised hundreds of thousands of dollars.

My new vocation didn't turn out to be as simple as going to church on Sundays, folding my hands in the pews, and declaring myself "saved." Nor did my volunteer church work mean talking kindly to poor folks and handing them the occasional sandwich from a sanctified distance. I had to trudge in the rain through housing projects; sit on the curb wiping the runny nose of a psychotic man; stick a battered woman's .357 Magnum in a cookie tin in the trunk of my car. I had to struggle with my atheist family, my doubting friends, and the prejudices and traditions of my newfound church. I learned about the great American scandal of the politics of food, the economy of hunger, and the rules of money. I met thieves, child abusers, millionaires, day laborers, politicians, schizophrenics, gangsters, and bishops—all blown into my life through the restless power of a call to feed people, widening what I thought of as my "community" in ways that were exhilarating, confusing, often scary.

Mine is a personal story of an unexpected and terribly inconvenient Christian conversion, told by a very unlikely convert: a blue-state, secular intellectual; a lesbian; a left-wing journalist with a habit of skepticism. I'm not the person my reporter colleagues ever expected to see exchanging blessings with street-corner evangelists. I'm hardly the person George Bush had in mind to be running a "faith-based charity." My own family never imagined that I'd wind up preaching the Word of God and serving communion to a hymn-singing flock.

But as well as an intimate memoir of personal conversion, mine is a political story. At a moment when right-wing American Christianity is ascendant, when religion worldwide is rife with fundamentalism and exclusionary ideological crusades, I stumbled into a radically inclusive faith centered on sacraments and action. What I found wasn't about angels or going to church or trying to be "good" in a pious, idealized way. It wasn't about arguing a doctrine—the Virgin birth, predestination, the sinfulness of homosexuality and divorce—or pledging blind allegiance to a denomination. I was, as the prophet said, hungering and thirsting for righteousness. I found it at the eternal and material core of Christianity: body, blood, bread, wine, poured out freely, shared by all. I discovered a religion rooted in the most ordinary yet subversive practice: a dinner table where everyone is welcome, where the despised and outcasts are honored.

And so I became a Christian, claiming a faith that many of my fellow believers want to exclude me from; following a God my unbelieving friends see as archaic superstition. At a time when Christianity in America is popularly represented by ecstatic teen crusaders in suburban megachurches, slick preachers proclaiming the "gospel" of prosperity, and shrewd political organizers who rail against evolution, gay marriage, and stem-cell research, it's crucial to understand what faith actually means in the lives of people very different from one another. Why would any thinking person become a Christian? How can anyone reconcile the hateful politics of much contemporary Christianity with Jesus's imperative to love? What are the deepest ideas of this contested religion, and what do they mean in real life? In this book, I look at the Gospel that moved me, the bread that changed me, and the work that saved me, to begin a spiritual and an actual communion across the divides.

Beyond any single moment of epiphany, my conversion was a long, complicated, and often unconscious journey. When I left the home of my atheist parents, I had no reason to think I was looking for God: I just knew I wanted to experience meaning and connection. The material world was my ground: bodily experience the context in which I searched for knowledge and love, political and moral purpose. I looked in all kinds of places, often extreme: in the heat and exertion of restaurant kitchens, in poor people's revolutions and in war zones, in engaged journalism and passionate politics, in love affairs with men and women, in the birth of my child. Something was tugging at me. It drew me from individual experience to collective experience, crossing lines each time—lines of family, of nation, of people unlike me—to find intimate human connection. I saw people betray their friends and sacrifice for strangers; I saw people suffer and starve; I saw people transcend their own limitations to nurture others and become part of communities. Everywhere I saw bodies, and food.

Food and bodies had always been wrapped in meaning for me: They were my way of understanding the world. But it would take decades to have these accumulated experiences make sense in a narrative, much less one I'd call Christian. It took actually eating a piece of bread—a simple chunk of wheat and yeast and water—to pull those layers of meaning together: to make food both absolutely itself and a sign pointing to something bigger. It turned out that the prerequisite for conversion wasn't knowing how to behave in a church, or having a religious vocabulary or an a priori "belief" in an abstract set of propositions: It was hunger, the same hunger I'd always carried.

Holy communion knocked me upside down and forced me to deal with the impossible reality of God. Then, as conversion continued, relentlessly challenging my assumptions about religion and politics and meaning, God forced me to deal with all kinds of other people. In large ways and small, I wrestled with Christianity: its grand promises and its petty demands, its temptations and hypocrisies and promises, its ugly history and often insufferable adherents. Faith for me didn't provide a set of easy answers or certainties: It raised more questions than I was ever comfortable with. The bits of my past—family, work, war, love—came apart as I stumbled into church, then reassembled, through the works communion inspired me to do, into a new life centered on feeding strangers: food and bodies, transformed. I wound up not in what church people like to call "a community of believers"—which tends to be code for "a like-minded club"—but in something huger and wilder than I had ever expected: the suffering, fractious, and unboundaried body of Christ.

It may seem crazy, at this point in history, to assert that any religion—much less Christianity, the religion of our contemporary empire, of the powerful and intolerant—can be a force for connection, for healing, for love. It may seem deluded to assert that people can still be fed with this ordinary yet mystical bread, so besmirched and exhausted and poisoned by centuries of religious practice, in ways that will change our own real lives, not to mention the world, for the better.

But this is my belief: that at the heart of Christianity is a power that continues to speak to and transform us. As I found to my surprise and alarm, it could speak even to me: not in the sappy, Jesus-and-cookies tone of mild-mannered liberal Christianity, or the blustering, blaming hellfire of the religious right. What I heard, and continue to hear, is a voice that can crack religious and political convictions open, that advocates for the least qualified, least official, least likely; that upsets the established order and makes a joke of certainty. It proclaims against reason that the hungry will be fed, that those cast down will be raised up, and that all things, including my own failures, are being made new. It offers food without exception to the worthy and unworthy, the screwed-up and pious, and then commands everyone to do the same. It doesn't promise to solve or erase suffering but to transform it, pledging that by loving one another, even through pain, we will find more life. And it insists that by opening ourselves to strangers, the despised or frightening or unintelligible other, we will see more and more of the holy, since, without exception, all people are one body: God's.

This theology isn't mine alone. It comes from conversation with other believers, tradition, and Scripture; books and prayer and liturgy. It comes, even more, from my years outside church: from unbelieving and unbelievers, from doubt, from questions that still echo unanswered for me. Faith, for me, isn't an argument, a catechism, a philosophical "proof." It is instead a lens, a way of experiencing life, and a willingness to act.

As the Bible says: *Taste and see.*

Take This Bread

Chapter 1

The Family Table

—

My mother nursed a grudge against Christianity for more than fifty years.

Like my father, she was the child of ministers and missionaries, descended from long lines of preachers, evangelists, and soldiers of the Lord. My father had been born in the mountain provinces of Burma to American Baptists, and my mother carried in a laundry hamper across the ocean to Baghdad, as part of the United Mission in Mesopotamia.

Today's struggles between liberal, ecumenical Christians and fundamentalist evangelicals played out as well in my grandparents' times, as they had for generations before. Throughout the nineteenth and twentieth centuries, some missionaries from America believed it was their duty to rescue the foreign poor from hunger and illness; others focused on winning souls for Jesus. Either way, the ambitions of the missionary movement were inextricably linked with those of empire: In the words of a triumphalist hymn, "From many an ancient river, from many a palmy plain, / They call us to deliver their land from error's chain."

Between the world wars, a call had gone out to "evangelize the world in one generation," and it set fire to small-town churches. All over Ohio and Nebraska and Massachusetts, in little Reformed and Baptist and Presbyterian congregations with no plumbing, dirt-poor farmers contributed dimes to support "our missioners" and sent their children off to China, Japan, Ceylon, Burma, Turkey, Syria, Congo, to "lift the multitudes ignorant of Christ's love," as one evangelist put it, "into understanding of God's fatherly purpose for them."

For a smart, ambitious girl, becoming a missionary was not just about duty and responding to God's will: It meant adventure and escape and, in a strange way, freedom from gender roles. Missionary work was a break from the previous generation's religion: Instead of putting on gloves, going to church, and reciting prayers, a young woman could travel alone across the world, tasting danger and testing herself far from the constraints of home. Girls who had obediently bowed their heads in pews became, abroad, imbued with new authority: white, foreign, representatives of a powerful country and a mighty church. And though teaching children and caring for the sick in a strange country might be lonely and grueling, faith, for these young women, meant hurling their own bodies into action, "joining the band," as my grandmother wrote, of the brave and the true.

My father's mother, Margaret, was the child of a New England artist and transcendentalist; her own mystical passion for God propelled her into missionary work. A slight woman, she kept a daily journal as she began her arduous ten-day journey, by pony, through the mountain passes of the Shan Province to her new home in a clearing hacked out of the jungle. With her husband, Max, a painfully shy doctor, she set up a medical mission in what's now called the "Golden Triangle"—the humid, unbelievably remote part of Burma where my father was born. They worshipped in "a bare little room, roughly made of dark, unfinished brown wood," as she wrote in a tract published by the American Baptist Foreign Mission Society. "The women wear silk skirts of green or rose or silvery grey with a Chinese pattern; their black hair is smoothly coiled and decorated with flowers. Some of the men who have been down country wear the Burmese *loonyi*, a skirt like a woman's of brilliant silk, and on their heads a bright silk scarf, knotted at the ear. They are all barefooted, as is the preacher. . . . The babies are allowed to crawl about the floor and offer remarks of their own, and dogs may stay if they behave."

Margaret had few illusions about the relative enlightenment of her own culture. "The problems of our little Shan church seem delicate and difficult, and our responsibility is very great, for the Shans still lean dangerously upon the missionaries. We hear ourselves constantly mentioned in their prayers— the three 'mamas' and the great teacher who have come so far to help them—come from the wonderful country of America, a sort of earthly paradise where everyone is wealthy, and everyone is happy, and everyone is good. Would you feel flattered in our places, or would you feel deeply humiliated, as we do?"

It was a sentiment that my mother's mother, Helen, would have echoed. She was drawn by the Social Gospel of the time, seeking justice and an end to war through the teachings of Jesus. The brilliant daughter of an impoverished Ohio minister, Helen served at a mission school for girls in Japan, where she met and married my grandfather David, a Christian teacher with a burning desire to right wrong. "Imperialism and exploitation," he wrote, "spheres of influence, trade barriers, unequal distribution of the world's goods, starvation in the midst of plenty, slums with gold coasts next door, poverty supporting luxury: These are marks of an unChristian world."

After completing work together for the divinity degree—a degree Helen was not awarded, because of her sex—my grandparents went to Iraq in 1929 with the United Mission in Mesopotamia, traveling through Lebanon and Syria, eating with tribal sheiks in tents, visiting the Kurdish north, and nursing my mother through various fevers in a Baghdad home overgrown with roses. One of my mother's first memories was of lying in her crib, listening to the group of British and American missionaries stationed in Baghdad singing the hymn of their calling: "Shall we whose souls are lighted with wisdom from on high, / Shall we to men benighted the lamp of life deny?"

In the baby book she kept for my mother, Helen wrote the homey details of daily life amid the exotic. "You were thrilled at eating dinner in a 'Maskus hotel' and sleeping in a big bed. The next morning we started on to Baghdad, where our new home was to be. It was a miserable trip, thirty-one hours in length. During the two days of our stay in Damascus, it had rained almost continuously. Sometimes the desert becomes almost impassable because of rain, and often cars will get stuck in the middle of the desert for two or three days or even a week. We set off with trepidation."

Returning home, the young minister and his wife took a church in Baltimore and began to integrate it. As difficult as it may often have felt to be a missionary in a strange land, it was unspeakably harder to anger and disappoint white Americans of their own class and background, but they persisted, moving to Missouri, then New York, joining with the prophetic left wing of the American church in a battle for civil rights that would last their lives. Both sets of grandparents grew more firmly rooted in

the ecumenical movement, fighting the conservative and evangelical forces of their day.

But for Matthew and Betty, the children of these Christian
activists, the church was neither an adventure nor a calling.
While my parents cherished memories of stars in the desert, ele-
phants, tropical rainstorms, and dates, the repressed, small-town
American churches both families returned to when their children were young were suffocating.

"I hated the 'You have to be good because God says so,' " recalled my mother. "I hated being preached at. Everything was
about guilt." Even before she was a teenager, my mother had decided she didn't believe in God, rejecting what she called "the
whole unbelievable, illogical concept" that her parents assumed
was the obvious truth. She didn't believe in angels, she didn't believe in heaven, she didn't believe that dead people would come
magically back to life. Horrified as a child by pictures of the crucifixion, she couldn't stand the "blood" of the Lord's Supper and
refused to pretend the grape juice her father poured reverently
into little cups was anything but grape juice. "You'll grow up and
see," my grandmother told her. It was inconceivable to Helen—
or to my father's parents, who had written out prayers for him to
recite each day since he was four years old—that anyone raised in
a Christian home would ever choose, really, to leave the faith.

My mother and father left as soon as they could, falling in
love at a progressive secular college when my father returned
from occupied Japan, where he had served as an army translator.
The two of them understood each other profoundly: Though
proud of their parents' social activism, they'd emerged from
their missionary childhoods with a deep unease about what mission historian William Hutchison called "Christians' supposed
'right,' anchored in a revelation acknowledged only by Christian

believers, to displace other religions and effect a spiritual conquest of other nations." My mother still smarted from the basic intellectual affront she'd felt as a child when told to repeat aloud things she felt were untrue; my father, a sociologist, couldn't accept believers' claim that they were entitled by God to pressure complete strangers into accepting one culture's version of religious truth. Like so many of their generation in the post-Holocaust world, my parents felt the concept of God was finished, a pointless relic. Why would you have to believe in God to do good—and how could you justify the terrible evils done in God's name? They married and moved to the twenty-three-dollar-a-month cold-water apartment in Greenwich Village where I was born. My parents never opened Bibles again, and we grew up with my mother railing, in an extremely ecumenical way, against the very idea of faith.

She rolled her eyes equally at the crusades of Billy Graham, Jews for Jesus, and the Maharishi Mahesh Yogi. She was infuriated by White House prayer breakfasts and politicians who mentioned God. My mother granted that many ordinary believers were sincere, but remained incredulous about their credulity: "Honestly," she'd say, "How in the world can they believe that stuff?"

I certainly didn't. I had loved my grandparents but been incurious about their faith: Like wearing ironed white shirts or reusing waxed paper to wrap sandwiches, religion just seemed another thing that old people did. So even when one grandmother marched with the NAACP for civil rights, then another got arrested protesting at a military base, I didn't connect their surprising activism with the obscure rituals they practiced on Sundays.

Those rituals—the hymns, the piety, the claustrophobic niceness of church ladies, the bland boiled dinners every

Sunday—had ruled my mother's childhood. She could not swallow it. Instead, she and my father taught us how good it tasted to escape convention, to eat garlic, to travel fearlessly. They loved good food, books, and music; they raised us with boundless love, liberal politics, and secular morals: "Different people are different" was the maxim we absorbed. They hated the Vietnam War and let us go to demonstrations; the upheavals of the 1960s were thrilling rather than threatening to them. My parents never went to church—not on Easter, not at Christmas—and didn't have friends who did; our Sundays were for reading the *New York Times*, listening to Vivaldi on the record player, eating artichokes and mussels, aioli and lemon ice.

My parents went to foreign films, took us to Europe to visit friends, and taught us to read between the lines of a newspaper, but they skimped, to say the least, on religious education. I had a book of Greek myths, with extravagantly colored pictures of gods and goddesses in flowing robes, but no idea who Abraham or Isaiah or Mary were. "Some people," my father said to me once, as if patiently explaining the customs of a faraway tribe, "believe that Jesus was a god." He paused. "And some people think he was just a very, very good man. A teacher." In our modern, professional circles, where only the Italian kids from the neighborhood went to church, and the Jews just believed in psychoanalysis, our family didn't stand out. My parents' atheism proclaimed *this* world, in its physical beauty and fascinating human complexity, as what mattered. We believed them. My sister, Ellen, loved music and books; my brother, David, and I learned to cook; by the time I was in tenth grade, I knew how to grill a fish and bake a crunchy baguette. We all soaked up experience: sex, travel, drugs, food, hard physical work—anything that would take us further into the sensual, immediate world that my parents insisted was the opposite of religion.

Chapter 2

Pilgrimage

When I was eighteen, never thinking once about my missionary heritage, I wrapped a toothbrush in my favorite cotton skirt, stuck it in a shoulder bag, and took a train from a dusty Texas border town to Mexico City, sitting upright on a wooden bench for the three-day journey. I was embarking on a pilgrimage of sorts, though I never would have thought of it that way at the time: I'd enrolled in a tiny radical college founded by internationalist Quakers and communists. All I knew about Quakers was that they were mostly old and had bravely opposed the Vietnam War; I thought basically the same about communists. Like most of my friends, my passionate left-wing sentiments about civil rights or the women's movement or Third World poverty or colonialism were felt, not studied, and our grasp of history was shaky. But the great worldwide upheavals of 1968 had riled us up, inspired us, stamped the phrase "power to the people" into our consciousness, and we were eager to plunge into activism. I didn't know, then, of the changes similarly sweeping through the Catholic Church that would turn so many of my Latin American Christian contemporaries into revolutionaries. I didn't understand how my own general beliefs—that the poor should be lifted up, prisoners freed, wars ended, and justice done—echoed biblical imperatives. I was just excited to begin.

Even in an era of experimentation, Friends World College was a radical experiment. It consisted of fewer than ninety kids, from all over the world, who moved among centers in Mexico, Kenya, India, England, and Japan with the goal of learning through experience, so that they might become "agents of social change." The school had no courses, no classrooms, no teachers, no campus, no dorms, no books. Instead, we made our own ways to places we knew nothing about, apprenticed ourselves to people we hadn't heard of, found places to live, got work, kept journals. It wasn't exactly an education, in the classical sense. It was, in the classical sense, nuts.

But it was 1971, and I got to live in a little house out by the jail in Cuernavaca. There was a banana tree in the backyard, which plunged precipitously to a garbage-choked ravine. At work, in a human rights organization that I'd realize later was an informal center for exiles from the military dictatorships of South America, a woman who'd been jailed in Bolivia gave me a book by someone called Carlos Marx. Another took me to the cathedral, hung with mysterious pictures of a bleeding Jesus, where a fiery bishop preached liberation. I didn't understand any of it. Cuernavaca was bright with heat and noise: I was dazzled indiscriminately by the ancient, lumbering buses; the Indian women with braids and shawls; the dogs and pigs and horses in the streets. Everything smelled like burning corn and dead meat and tuberose. The markets were overflowing with food I'd never seen before: iguanas, squash blossoms, corn fungus, bright pink sweets speckled with flies. I cooked tamales and big pots of pumpkin-seed mole and shared them with the boys and girls I fell in love with. Some afternoons I'd get a ride back to my house from a hippie kid who had an old van, and we'd bounce along listening to the Rolling Stones sing "Wild Horses" as far-off thunder-clouds swirled around the volcanoes. I was completely, utterly happy.

On weekends, I'd take a bus up to Mexico City and stay with a group of young activists I'd met through my work. They were Mexican students who'd been involved in the movement of 1968, and they had a worldliness I couldn't fathom. I was excited by their revolutionary ardor but didn't really understand their analysis; and I couldn't see why they took politics so seriously, as if politics were something that kids like us were actually responsible for. We'd sit around somebody's cruddy second-floor apartment and cook food and smoke a million cigarettes, and listen to music and flirt, and they'd try to explain it all to me.

Then, one afternoon, there was a big march planned, a demonstration in support of students trying to open up the university system to the poor. My friends Amy and Ricardo went out to see what was happening and came running back shouting at us to get down on the floor. We all crouched away from the windows, listening to shots and screams. I can still remember how hot it was, and the adrenaline tightness in my throat, and how the noise of breaking glass and screeching brakes and people yelling seemed to go on forever. I wanted to throw up. I wanted to cry. I wanted to think this was happening to somebody else.

In the next few days, from word of mouth, we would learn pieces of what had happened. Squads of plainclothes thugs, nick-named the *halcones*, had been provided with guns and clubs and chains by the Mexican police to attack marchers: They beat at least twenty-five students to death and wounded dozens more. The events of that day, a church holiday known as Corpus Christi in Mexico, would come to be known as the "Corpus

Christi massacre": as I would understand it much later, the murder of the body of Christ.

But there was no official report. Nothing in the news. Not a word from the authorities. It would take more than thirty years for the story to be told: Mexico's dirty war remained a secret, guarded not only by Mexican police, state security, and the ruling-party apparatus but by the United States, which covered up the massacre with official denial. Those of us who were there had experienced it, as the phrase says in Spanish, "in our own meat"—*en su propia carne*, incarnate.

I went on living in Cuernavaca for the rest of that year and hanging out with my friends in the city on weekends. But after the Corpus Christi massacre, politics stopped being abstract for me: It turned out that gunfire had a way of focusing my attention. And that I cared, passionately, about knowing the difference between the official story and physical reality. I had always loved to write, and now I was pulled into reporting, though I was unprepared professionally, inexperienced politically, and still an unworldly teenager. I just wanted to look at things more, to feel them in my own meat, and to try to figure them out.

Chapter 3

Standing the Heat

My unconventional college gave me a set of core values, along with some practices, to guide me. These would turn out to have a lot in common with the values of my religion and the way I'd understand the faith I adopted decades later. But first, these values shaped my politics and work as a writer.

To begin with, my education had been not formal but rooted in physical experience and questioning: This made me distrustful of dogma of all kinds. I couldn't swallow the official party line of the left any more than I could automatically trust a government spokesman. To figure out what was really happening behind the clichés, I'd learned, meant a practice of looking not at the center but at the edges of things—at the unlikeliest and weakest people, not the most apparently powerful. It meant asking lots of stupid questions, making room for inconvenient facts that didn't fit a schema, and trying to remain honest about what I didn't know.

Because my education had taken place among all kinds of people, on several continents, I was skeptical about the natural superiority of one culture over another. I'd learned how quirkily particular people could be, each with an amazing and separate story, and yet how much they had in common at the core. Through my travels, dependent on strangers for everything, I'd absorbed a deep trust in ordinary human generosity and goodness.

I'd also absorbed a confidence that was pretty overblown: I thought I could go anywhere, do anything, approach whatever work was at hand and take it on. Because I'd been encouraged to claim responsibility and to act, I didn't have a lot of respect for conventional credentials or the rigors of a discipline: I assumed I could learn whatever was necessary as I went along. I came back to the United States and, over the next few years, organized a "free school" in Baltimore modeled on the ones my Mexican student friends ran; I taught illiterate adults to read. I worked at the New Left magazine *Liberation* in New York and hung around with a bunch of socialist Puerto Rican poets who wanted to found a newspaper. I did some writing and research for a nonprofit law center that did civil rights and international human rights work; I wrote position papers for Third World activists; I organized demonstrations, edited an anthology of women's poetry, and sold occasional articles. All of this was great: I wanted to write; I intended to keep doing political work. But I was pulling in an income of around eight thousand dollars a year. I needed a job.

Like millions of other young or immigrant or aspiring New Yorkers, I entered the world of restaurants. I had no idea then that feeding people would not just be a way to earn a paycheck but would become a central part of my life, informing the way I experienced friendship and community, political organizing, and eventually belief. It would train me in physical suffering, sustain me with the most basic satisfaction of making a meal for someone, and, in midlife, bring me full circle to a strange church kitchen where I'd bang pots around on a six-burner range.

The trendy Village bistro where I landed in 1977 had a kitchen about the size of a hotel bathroom; a cramped, wedge-shaped dining room; and a nasty basement prep area. Serious restaurants didn't usually hire women to cook then; the fancy new downtown ones would—at $3.50 an hour—but they expected you to have ten years' experience at Lutèce before allowing you to wash their lettuce. Later I'd learn that turnover in the kitchen had been so rapid the manager was desperate to plug in any two-armed body. But that day I felt cocky; led downstairs to a steamy, crowded basement, I changed into whites, tied back my hair, and congratulated myself on passing as a real cook.

My résumé wasn't entirely invention: I did know, thanks to my parents, the basics of cooking. And I actually had worked at the joint in Baltimore I grandly described as a restaurant, waiting tables and tending bar before I fled to the kitchen and learned to dunk frozen hot dogs in a deep fryer. That job had helped me figure out that I enjoyed restaurant work but never again wanted to deal with "the public." I'd liked the cranky Irish grandmother who ran the kitchen, liked the privacy and the shoptalk by the stove, and liked, especially, the bad reputation that cooks enjoyed among the floor staff. "Don't *ever* talk back to the kitchen," they'd warn a new waitress. "Are you *crazy?*"

I came up the stairs to my new job, feeling ready for anything.

"Well now, well well well," a voice boomed at me. Robert filled the kitchen. Hair slicked back in a Little Richard pompadour, kitchen rag knotted jauntily at his throat, "to keep off the drafts, doll," black shoes gleaming, and jacket stretched over a monumental stomach, Robert, the head chef, beckoned to me.

Robert was in his late fifties, a black man who'd grown up

cooking with his aunt and worked for twenty years on the railroad, maintaining a militant pride as a cook alongside an exhaustive mastery of every sleazy trick in the business. He'd show me how to "blanch" the hamburgers before a rush, slipping them into the Friolator for later reheating on the grill; he'd time the roasts by track—"Put it in at Wilmington, doll, check it at Trenton"; he'd thin the soup with water from the steam table. Robert could spot a fake from thirty feet away and could poke a piece of beef with one forefinger and describe—accurately—exactly where on the cow it came from. He had no reason to be kind to me—this man who always said, "I don't know much, but I know a fool"—yet Robert welcomed me into his kitchen and decided to make me a cook. "My girl," he'd sing when I came in, humming the Temptations song as he took the knife out of my hand, spun it in the air, and showed me, one more time, the right way to hold it.

"You can't make an omelet without breaking eggs," Robert would intone, as if it were still funny, each day. Each morning, at the beginning of my shift, the dishwasher and I would break twelve flats of eggs. Every flat had seventy-two eggs, and we'd whisk them together in the white plastic bucket with a half-handful of salt, a quart of water, and a slug of Tabasco sauce, chatting as we prepped. The omelets at our restaurant had fanciful names—"Gold and Green," for example, to describe a blend of industrial cheddar and frozen spinach—and the variety of fillings got a little out of hand. We served ratatouille omelets, mushroom and sour cream omelets, jelly omelets, bacon omelets, powdered sugar omelets, and a repulsive mussel omelet. On weekends, when it was time for brunch, Robert could do upwards of 150 omelets in an hour.

"Robert's Rules of Order," I teased him, a few weeks into my apprenticeship. But his rules worked: Gradually the insane chaos of the kitchen began to take on a shape for me, and the wild flailing of four arms in a space six feet by five revealed an order, a logic, a dance. Bit by bit, the rules rearranged arbitrary, unconnected commandments into a plan for action. Talking in code—with grunts and gestures; with cryptic references; with song titles, puns, and rhymes—Robert laid out the how-to of standing the heat.

The basics—safety and attitude—came first. Self-preservation meant never picking anything up—"not even out the freezer, doll"—without a rag; meant keeping all knives sharp on a vicious two-foot steel; meant instant, Pavlovian response to a barked-out "Behind you" or a "*Hot* soup, hot soup, watch your back." It included Robert's tips on health, a crank assortment ranging from dire warnings about the consequences of drinking cold liquids in a kitchen to muttered suggestions that pork could give you hemorrhoids. "No no no," Robert would say gloomily, waving away the ham sandwich I offered him. "That bad boy will tear my insides up." At 225 pounds with a heart condition, he'd soothe his delicate constitution by drinking half-and-half from a quart container, then have a cup of coffee, black, to wash it down.

And self-preservation meant attitude: That aura I'd glimpsed around cooks in Baltimore was refined and glorified by Robert. "The public," Robert announced, "is a motherfucker."

That principle explained why he never did special orders for customers ("You don't want them to think you're in love with them, now"), why he refused to accept tips, and why he felt compelled to retaliate against any diner foolish enough to send an order back. "Must be their dentures acting up," he'd console me if someone returned food as too cold; "they can't tell the temperature right"—and put the plate in a five hundred–degree oven until it sizzled, then sail the same cold food out for another try.

Still, there were customers who adored Robert, who'd only bother to come when he was cooking, who'd poke their heads over the transom to make obeisance. The waiters were another matter: None of them loved him, but all of them kept a careful and extremely polite distance.

"R-e-s-p-e-c-t," sang Robert to me, winking, launching into the lesson on Waiter Control. To the waiters, he narrowed his eyes, spinning around to pin one he suspected of wanting to hurry us up. "You," he'd boom, pointing with the eight-inch chef's knife, "are a waiter." A moment of silence for emphasis, and he'd lunge forward: "That means, goddamnit, *you wait!*"

Robert disapproved of my familiarity with the waiters, who called me by my first name and were bold enough to try to sit at my table for the staff meal, but forgave it as youthful folly. I paid attention to their conversations, too, though, studying the complex ranking of restaurant hierarchy. It would be years before a maître d', through his graceful hosting of hungry street people, would teach me the importance of serving.

But it was the ongoing work in the kitchen that taught me the real basis for Robert's Theory of Divine Right with cooks as kings: "We don't mess around," he'd crow. "No, never mess around on a Monday [Tuesday, Wednesday, Thursday . . .]," running the waiters ragged during a rush, keeping the food coming when an overflow line filled the sidewalk outside, doing a day's work in an hour and a half, and earning our sovereignty by accepting responsibility for whatever went wrong. "Take the weight," Robert taught me, and I obeyed: Honor meant never shifting the blame when someone beneath us messed up, meant claiming the mistake—"Say it *loud,*" he'd sing, James Brown behind the grill—making it right and carrying on.

It was a gritty New York afternoon in August, the day after our restaurant won a rave review in the *Times* for "the best burgers in town." Exhausted waiters were trying to appease the customers who'd been waiting forty minutes for a table; the manager was doing double duty busing dishes and handing out menus; the house had run out of hamburger buns, and we'd sent a kid to the corner supermarket twice for emergency supplies. Inside the kitchen, we were rolling up crushed ice in rags to tie around our foreheads; the screen above the grill caught fire twice from an overload of grease, and the dishwasher was threatening to quit. I was staring at a line of dupes three deep and backed up to tomorrow night, grabbing meat off the grill with my hands and whirling around to save the French fries from burning. "Hello," said Robert, and I didn't even look up, slapping another order on. "Hello dolly, hello?" and I turned to catch his eye. He kicked a milk crate over and gestured me to sit down, then eased himself onto another, taking a cigar out of his breast pocket. Robert has lost his mind, I thought, but crouched on the crate anyway, panting. "How's the ice tea?" he asked. "With sugar, please, doll." I started to stand up to fetch it for him. Gently, Robert took my arm. "Got to slow down to speed up," he said. "Remember, doll: Slow down. When it's busy, slow down." We set our record that afternoon: 210 lunches in a forty-seat restaurant, and every one on time.

If I'd known more about food, I would have been appalled by most of Robert's techniques, scandalized by his mangling of culinary terms. But I learned how to make Robert's "mock béarnaise"—Hellmann's mayonnaise with dry tarragon stirred in—before anyone told me what the real thing was; accepted that the person at the cold station was a "gabagier"; and thought that "hit it with the hot sauce" was an apt corrective for almost any dish. Robert's palate was continually at war with the directives of the manager, who begged him to simply heat up what the prep cook had made.

They argued, and I learned: technique from Robert, theory from Patrick, the alcoholic prep cook in the basement who knew most of Escoffier until noon each day, when OTB opened, and, fortified by long slugs of the cooking brandy, he'd head out to place his bets.

Patrick left me eccentric handwritten notes when I worked the late shift. "Dear friend," I'd read, switching on the lights and bending over the prep counter, "Do you remember those golden days in Provence? The afternoons we swore to never forget? Looking out over the sea as we picnicked on *Savory Fish Stew:* thyme, a little bit of saffron, leeks, and fresh tomatoes—you may want to check the seasoning. Reheat to just below a boil, and don't let Robert add any more Tabasco. It's $6.75 with a salad; I made about ten portions; and now I must depart." I'd get the special out and find Patrick's postscript on the cooling racks: "*Helpful hint:* Most food keeps better if refrigerated!"

Putting away the tubs of poached chicken, the stocks and soup bases, the sauces and quiches for tomorrow, in the walk-in refrigerator, I'd gather the rest of my ingredients for the night's *mis en place* and head upstairs to learn.

Robert admitted grudgingly that Patrick could do the prep cooking, but "Doll, he ain't got that swing." It was the swing I needed to learn from Robert, the speed and grace behind a stove that no book can teach. Robert specialized in omelet making that was "all in the wrist": Never using an implement, often working two skillets at once, he'd shake a shapeless mass of egg into a smooth, perfectly folded, symmetrical form I despaired of ever achieving. To keep the eggs from sticking, burning, browning, or remaining indigestibly liquid; to turn the omelet out on a plate with its corners neat as a hospital bed; to master my motions so I could flip the whole thing in the air without looking seemed a dream. Robert laughed. With one hand, he'd crack a flat of eggs, whisk them quickly, then steer me over to the stove. "Practice," he'd say. "You can't make an omelet without breaking eggs."

Working with Robert made it clear to me that food, as I thought of it in private life—preparing and eating meals—had little to do with restaurants. My skills as a person who could make dinner for friends had nothing in common with what was demanded of us in a situation where lists that began "15 50# bags chix breast bone-out" made me feel I'd stumbled into a land of giants. Scale ruled sense; it meant that fussing and fine-tuning came definitely later, if at all. Robert rolled his eyes the first time he saw me measuring salt with a spoon: "No no no, doll," he said patiently, taking the container from my hand. "That's all right for the *home*, now," pouring the salt casually and steadily into the soup simmering on the stove, "but we don't play that here." I learned not to waste time washing six heads of lettuce when I should have done a crate; learned to cook four yard-long pans of bacon instead of dashing down to the basement an hour into the shift when we ran out because I'd figured two pounds was a lot. And I learned the right time and place for delicacy: After purée-ing gallon cans of tomatoes, filling industrial skillets with onions and whole cups of garlic and the grease that dripped into the pans; after simmering the mess and skimming the fat with wads of paper towels, dumping salt and pepper and arbitrary handfuls of herbs into the soup, I learned about the final touch before the resulting product reached a customer. "Wait," said Robert, pulling the dirty rag out of his waistband and wiping off the rim of the bowl. He picked up a handful of chopped parsley and meticulously dusted the surface; stepped back, squinting; and placed one leaf of garnish directly in the center. "There," he said. "Now we're talking. That's what I call some *nice* food."

Other, deeper lessons of restaurant work stayed with me, in-forming not just my kitchen technique but the way I moved in the world. I learned what it felt like to become invisible: When I pulled on my slightly starch-stiff whites, the uniform changed me from an individual, with my own tedious history, to a ritual figure, one of millions of restaurant workers, with a time-honored and predictable role. I'd learn the same thing again as a reporter: In the middle of a riot or a battle or a government press conference, a woman with a notebook and pen and a determined look can go anywhere. I'd even remember it years later in church, when I'd slip on a cassock and lose my identity as a civilian: Wearing robes and a purposeful attitude, I could stride through a hushed congregation without attracting the slightest attention.

But the pleasure of hiding in plain sight was just one of the benefits I picked up from working as a cook. I learned solidarity, the kind that only comes through shared bodily experience, sweating and lifting and hauling side by side with others. I learned from watching customers that the rituals of even the plainest or most cynically prepared dinner could carry unconscious messages of love and comfort. And at the end of a rush, when I sat down with the kitchen staff and waiters, I learned how central food is to creating human community, what eating together around a table can do. As a wise bishop would tell me, years and years later, in words I couldn't possibly have grasped back then, "There's a hunger beyond food that's expressed in food, and that's why feeding is always a kind of miracle."

Chapter 4

Cooking with My Brother

—

I wasn't thinking about miracles. I was, though, thinking more about family. Our grandparents had died, our parents were living upstate, and my sister and brother and I were closer than ever, talking constantly and hanging out in the bustle of New York.

My brother, David, was living in a dilapidated former Bowery flophouse across from the Roberto Clemente Social Club. A tall, long-haired twenty-two-year-old, David had toiled as a kitchen helper with occasional gigs as a house painter; I thought I'd get him to come work with me.

David was meticulous and slightly old-fashioned in his habits: His desk was always neat, and he was the only guy I knew who pressed his shirts. More than anything else, David liked doing things the right way. I figured he could fill in on the salad station, where it mattered that the croutons be arranged tastefully around the centered egg yolk on the Caesar and the presentation of the antipasto plate be symmetrical.

His carefulness was a trait I thought might be somewhat at odds with Robert's less than classical approach to cooking. But David, with his respectful manners, was the kind of kid adults liked. And he was willing to work hard. When I brought him into the restaurant the first time, David shook Robert's hand and called him "sir."

It was predictable, but still impressive, how quickly David surpassed me in the kitchen, leaving me only formally the older sister. David loved the language and technique of restaurant work. With a long boning blade in hand, he'd turn a rack of lamb inside out; with a heavy chef's knife, he'd chop carrots into a flurry of eighth-inch dice; with a paring knife, he'd sculpt a perfectly turned potato for practice, then chuck it in the stew. "That's a *nice* potato, now," he'd say, imitating Robert.

David didn't mind working rushes, which he treated as minor athletic events, and he was eager for study: He pored over *Larousse Gastronomique*, memorizing its arcane catalog of sauces. Within a year, he was taking classes in hotel and restaurant management at New York City Community College, riding the F train after work to Jay Street to learn restaurant management, cooking basics, the chemistry of food. My brother, it turned out, was not just a dogged but an inspired apprentice, mastering Robert's entire greasy-spoon trick-bag, and at school obediently beating mountains of meringue for a fabled pastry chef. He chopped thousands of onions until he could do it perfectly. He memorized the proportions for *pâte à choux, pâte sucrée, pâte brisée*, and puff paste and rattled them off at the drop of a hat. He made gallons of crème anglaise. He talked to purveyors. He tasted everything, carefully, and thought about it, and tried again.

We were having lunch together one afternoon in the empty dining room of the Village restaurant before the evening shift; our whites were still clean, and we were still hungry. I was happy enough with my quiche—some "Provençal" number that Patrick had worked up as a special. "That guy is a shoemaker," David said in disgust, picking an olive pit out of his portion. "I

mean, come on, take the pits out. What's so hard about that?"
He made a face. "And it's supposed to be a custard, not a piece of
rubber. For cryin' out loud."

"It's just a piece of quiche, David," I said.

"So why not do it right?" he said.

Within a couple of months, David and I were working at La
Fleur, a new restaurant on the Upper East Side, hired away by
Joe, an owner who'd been scouting young and cheap talent
downtown. Joe had flattered us, offered us cash money—fifty
bucks a shift, off the books—and asked David to design the
menu. "Classy food," Joe suggested. He meant steak and bone-
less chicken breast and eggs Benedict for brunch and maybe, for
the ladies, "something French." By the time David caught on to
how much work we were really facing, it was too late to go back
to the Village restaurant, and we both figured we could learn
something about running a place.

Joe was an old-fashioned guy: huge, Irish, with a .45 in the
drawer next to the cash register and a baseball bat under the bar.
He'd run saloons of one kind or another on the East Side since
the 1960s and knew every bartender within a forty-block radius;
he considered himself a well-read street fighter. His friends were
also big men, who dropped by to drink; his girlfriend, Francine,
was a tiny, tough hostess with frosted hair and an apartment a
block away. When things got too busy, I'd sometimes be dis-
patched to Francine's to collect Joe, who'd escaped the restaurant to do a little cocaine or take a nap in her living room.

Joe knew great stories, and he knew how things really
worked in the restaurant business. He was unfailingly polite to
the man we called Jimmy Linen, the octogenarian Mob linen-
supply guy who stopped by every week in his porkpie hat and

brown suit jacket to pick up an envelope. "Get Mr. Jimmy a Scotch, sweetheart," he'd tell me, as we were setting up for the evening service. "Mr. Jimmy, would you like the kitchen to pre-pare you anything?" I never saw Jimmy Linen eat, but he always thanked me for the drink, which he swallowed neat before swiveling off his stool and nodding at Joe. "See you next week," he'd say. It was rumored that Jimmy Linen, who also managed the cigarette-machine concession for bars and restaurants in the neighborhood, had socked away a few million in small, un-marked bills in the basement of his duplex in Queens.

Joe was also on respectful terms with Kwan, the godfather of dishwashers on the Upper East Side, who supplied us all with Fujinese near-slave labor. La Fleur's dishwashing slave was a small, chain-smoking man we knew only as "Koff-koff," for the hacking, tubercular cough he constantly emitted. Koff-koff was unclean, unfriendly, and almost entirely unable to speak English, except for *fuck*. He'd scream the word when a line cook threw a hot pan toward him: "FOCK!" He'd mutter it when a waitress dared to enter the kitchen: "Fock, fock, fock." And he'd snarl at David when it was finally two in the morning and we'd wearily finished scraping the grill clean. "Go home now, fock?" he'd ask, leering. Kwan stopped by every payday and took something from Koff-koff, until one week the cougher vanished and a new slave materialized. "Kwan sent me," this one said. We never caught his name either, but the new dishwasher taught us how to cook with "special spice," by which he meant a mixture of sugar and MSG sprinkled over impossibly thin shavings of beef. It was delicious, as were the shrimps he made us, pilfered from the freezer when Joe wasn't watching and roasted on a sizzle plate under the salamander grill.

David and I liked Joe, who was a gentleman as well as a big lunk. Joe paid us on time, mostly overlooked our thefts of food, and praised David's cooking. "That goddamn fish is goddamn great, David," he'd say. "I don't know how you do it." Once a month, after we were closed for the night, Joe would open the door, let in a middle-aged Indian woman in a raincoat, and ask us to cook for her. David would make an omelet or sauté a dainty piece of veal, and she'd take her plate at the bar. For the rest of the night, she and Joe would sit together going over the books, while she ran up an entire parallel set of cash-register receipts to report to the IRS.

La Fleur's food was only terrible to the degree it was pretentious, and David tried hard to avoid Joe's more outlandish suggestions about classiness. Basically, we cooked bar food: fat, protein, and salt, designed to accompany alcohol. We served rib-eye steaks, hamburgers, scallops or shrimps, chicken breasts, veal. We made pasta once in a while for a special. We melted and clarified a full sleeve—about six pounds—of butter a night and sautéed our sides of carrots and cauliflower in it. We bought our desserts from an East Side wholesaler—heavy, grayish cheese-cake; heavy, muddy chocolate cake; heavy chunks of canned brioche soaked in rum—and covered them all in whipped cream.

Food for us was sort of primitive; sort of industrial by virtue of its quantity; sort of magical and unreal at the same time. The smell of beef fat when we had the salamander going just right and the steaks were rolling off the grill perfectly charred could still make me hungry, but as stacks of bluish flesh in the refrigerator waiting for the fire, they made me sick. We cooked for the staff—"family meal" at a big table for the waiters and bartenders, a black and blue chop for Michael Wild, the aptly named, hyperactive porter who opened up each day. David and I and the cooks ate mostly for fuel: a plate of potatoes and eggs before the shift began; a handful of bacon, a slab of cheese, a couple of shrimps as the evening rush wore on. It was hard to eat at the end of the night: our feet hurt too much. And it was hard to taste when everything smelled of sweat and chlorine and raw garlic. We drank endless sodas from the bar or thin, tannic ice tea. We smoked cigarettes or chewed gum. We waited for break-fast.

Once or twice a week, we'd feed people who came to the kitchen door. We stole food for ourselves fairly constantly, and we slipped extra food to the kitchen staff, so we saw nothing wrong with spreading around some of the excess. There were a couple of street guys who'd stop by, and I'd fix them a plate: the day's special, some cut-up potatoes or a bowl of chili, a couple of pieces of leftover cheesecake. I liked watching them eat, balanc-ing the plate on their knees on our back stoop, wiping their mouths politely on the paper towel I gave them. It made more sense to me than the waste did, the huge barrels of soft vegeta-bles, half-eaten chickens, meat trimmings, stale bread, spoiled milk. "Thanks, hon," one of them, an older man, a neighbor-hood wino, would always say. "God bless you." I'd take back the heavy china plate, wiped clean. "You, too," I'd say. "See you soon."

The men at the door reminded me that there were worlds parallel to the world of restaurants. There was also the city full of believers, whose lives I only glimpsed once or twice—as through a glass, darkly. One night Artie, the Greek waiter, a lifer with a lugubrious face and a hopeless determination to make it as an actor, had pulled me aside and brought me to the kitchen door. It was late spring, but cool, and we stood with the urgency and brightness of the kitchen behind us looking out on an ordi-nary side street, where a ragged procession of people carrying candles was slowly moving in the darkness toward the East

River. "Orthodox Easter," said Artie conspiratorially. "From Holy Trinity. We walk around the church for the vigil. Then everyone has communion." I had no idea what he was talking about, but Artie was clearly moved, and I watched him watching the line of pilgrims in overcoats for a while before I turned back to the stove. "Sara," Artie called to me, "I'm working lunch tomorrow. Come in before my shift's done and I'll bring you some of my aunt's Easter bread."

And there were other worlds. There was my life in Brooklyn fighting with my girlfriend, Millie, a brilliant and angry black poet who starved herself and gorged at night on fistfuls of nuts. I'd cook supper for her teenage son, Jay, but she wouldn't let me cook for her. There was my life talking with friends, mostly writers and activists, who had neither the time nor the money to eat out and who thought fancy food was something only yuppies cared about. There was my research work for a Latin American human rights organization, which I mostly did alone, when I came home late at night, rinsed the smell of old cooking oil out of my hair, made a pot of coffee, and sat down to write.

Michael Wild flipped out one night, stole all the cash out of La Fleur's register, and took a plane to New Orleans. David got a collect call from him right before he got arrested for shooting a cop. Joe and Francine got married, and Joe sold his interest in the restaurant. Millie and I broke up. My best friend, Douglas, took me in, lent me sweaters, let me lie weeping on his ratty couch, and made me buttered toast. "You have to eat *something*," he pointed out.

"My heart's breaking," I said. I was crying so hard my head throbbed.

"You still have to eat," said Douglas, putting the chipped Fiestaware plate on the floor by my head. "Come on, take it."

The last time I worked with my brother was at a ludicrously pretentious Park Slope place done up in shades of pale green and pink, with an overwrought owner and a very early-eighties menu. We cooked shrimp with leeks and Pernod, cream of mussel soup with saffron, mousse of bay scallops with pale pink and green layers, salad with walnut oil. It was the beginning of a new era, as we started to see restaurant groupies—foodies—move in on what we'd considered just an honorable trade. Our dishwashers were Haitian, not Chinese, and for the first time, we had a sous-chef who'd been to culinary school.

The sous-chef, a big white guy who enjoyed listening to *Cowboy Joe's Radio Ranch* as he stirred the béchamel, even offered his own theories of food. "Cooking's just physics," he'd say. "It's scientific, like socialism." His interest in dialectical materialism, though, didn't prevent him from terrorizing the garde-manger, who always slunk in late. "A kitchen is not a democracy!" the sous-chef would shout at the cowering boy. "Move your ass! I want you to whale on those carrots!"

And he didn't like the foodies either. There was a difference, we'd bitch self-righteously, between thinking you worked in a kitchen and thinking you were contributing to the Cultural Life of the City. We all knew how to read: Each of us could say *chaud-froid* or put together a classical demi-glace, thick enough to use as a hockey puck. We had our own knives. But we were impatient with groupies who wanted to prattle on about balsamic vinegar and Richard Olney's private life, hoping the glamour would rub off and they'd be discovered by *New York* magazine. We'd tell them to shut up, stick around, and work like dogs: "If you can stand the heat," David would say sternly.

As with everything else I'd learned—as with the religion I would come to practice—I absorbed cooking through my body. Mostly the magic—the perfect hollandaise, flicked together over an open flame; the omelet flipped and folded as a free hand slammed a freezer door shut—mostly the stunt stuff came from the wrist. But the rest of it was arms and back and busted ass, varicose veins and brains. Like any other manual labor, like the finest jazz, cooking was all, finally, not about anything but working together in tight teamwork past the dogged repetition until time cut loose and we were effortless, floating, home on the range. "Sister," the sous-chef would say to me, gesturing toward that range, the red-hot Garland encrusted with grime, "this is where I learned about praxis."

But if I treasured cooking as honest work, it was becoming more work than I was able to handle. Once, the steel doors in the sidewalk that had been propped open slammed down on my head as I walked up from the basement carrying a tray of smoked trout. I fell backward, my scalp split open, into David's arms. Both of us were still in our dirty whites at the hospital hours later, when a smirking intern came out waving a set of X rays. "No fracture," he said cheerfully. "Come back in a week and I'll take the stitches out. Boy, I'd hate to see what you did to that door."

Having a piece of metal fall out of the sky and strike me on the head was a drag, but it didn't arouse any particular sense of message for me: I didn't believe in signs or omens. The next incident, a few months later, got more of my attention.

I'd come in early that morning to bake for the weekend brunch service; laid out the *palmiers* and the pies, the flaky tarts and meat-filled pastries. I was starting on vegetables for the salads: niçoise, a dilled chicken with corn, pasta primavera. Some sleazy restaurants used food coloring to keep the green vegetables green; others, a pinch of baking soda in the pot. But we cared about taste, so we blanched vegetables in brine, cooking them quickly and plunging them into a sink of freezing water.

By eight, I'd worked through my first pot of coffee and had switched to cold juice: The small kitchen was hot on that July morning as I hoisted a stockpot full of green beans from the stove.

Accidents always happen in slow motion. I went down slowly, slipping on the grease-slick floor. I watched the handles drop slowly from my hands, saw the beans pour slowly out and three gallons of boiling brine drench my legs.

It took only a second to scream. Then a morning waiter was there, ripping off my apron and whites, grabbing me from the floor, and thrusting me into the ice bucket. Even as I tore off my shoes, the blisters were forming; by the time the heavy cotton socks were peeled off, the flesh of my right foot had been burned away, and I stood half-naked, sobbing, in cold water, as the owner walked in to open up for breakfast.

At the Workers' Compensation Board, a seen-it-all middle-aged lady looked at me and shook her head. "We had more than five hundred cases last year from kitchen employees," she said. "You name it. I'd rather handle explosives than be a cook."

Soon after my accident, I got a chance to explore a safer line of work, when the Center for Constitutional Rights, a human rights organization, offered to hire me to go to Nicaragua and help its lawyers research and write about some cases there. The 1979 overthrow of Nicaragua's brutal Somoza dictatorship by the guerrillas of the Sandinista front, and the rising up of a popular revolution, had captured the world's imagination—even as it sparked a counterrevolution, funded by the United States and carried out by contra forces. Next door, in El Salvador, the United States was supporting a military government—and unofficial paramilitaries—trying to stop a revolution led by the leftist FMLN. The conflicts were growing, and the region was convulsed with violence: Contra attacks, death squads, the mining of harbors and massacre of refugees filled the news. Yet there was a sense of possibility in the air, too: Maybe a poor people's revolution could succeed; maybe an unjust war could be stopped. I had a yearning to find out more, to connect with these new political movements, to be back in Latin America on the ground. I remembered how it had felt, in Mexico, to have history in my flesh, and my body connected to others. I quit the restaurant.

Food remained something central for me, but I couldn't quite articulate why. I could see how, for David, the important thing was honoring tradition, getting the details right, then infusing each meal he cooked with a craftsman's pride. But for me, it wasn't about technique. Like David, I could taste well, and specific flavors were full of meaning; unlike him, I wasn't driven to make sense of the world through creating and interpreting those meanings. I was messier than my brother, and lazier, and I wanted something more direct, spoken less in the specialized language of gastronomy than in the ancient language of welcome. I had no idea then that what I was hungry for was communion.

Chapter 5

War Years

—

My work in Nicaragua as a researcher would take me to cover other revolutionary wars over the course of the 1980s—in El Salvador, in the Philippines, and later in South Africa. It would also drag me more deeply into activism. In both roles, as journalist and as organizer, I'd learn that it's possible to fall in love with a revolution—then doubt it, fight with it, lose faith in it, and return with a sense of humor and a harder, lasting love. I would have to learn the same thing about church when I was much older, and it would be no easier.

But the romance came first. In the heady early days of Nicaragua's revolution, the new foreign minister spouted poetry, the army (briefly) abolished rank, and a radical land reform gave starving peasants their first property. The country was tiny and destitute: Nicaragua had no paved road connecting its two coasts, and the population of just three million was largely illiterate. Yet the green, humid mountains and filthy slums of the capital shone with the intensity of an Old Testament prophecy—one where, after great tribulations, the evil rulers are overthrown, the slaves freed, and "peace and justice kiss." Idealistic twenty-year-olds were running the Ministry of Agriculture, oppressed peasants and beaten-down women were learning to read, and former jailers were pardoned in a spirit of collective generosity. More than fifty thousand "heroes and martyrs" had died to overthrow the dictatorship, and their presence, too, was palpable. Their names were shouted aloud at rallies and painted on cracked adobe walls: They were, a young soldier told me seriously, "resurrected in the new life of the people." Sergio Ramírez, a novelist and revolutionary leader, wrote that such sacrifices "made it possible to open the doors of paradise . . . a paradise for others, on earth."

I'd been told how much Christianity informed the Central American revolutionary movements: Many of the Sandinistas and their peasant supporters had been inspired by liberation theology and what Vatican II called "the preferential option for the poor." Other Nicaraguan Christians, mostly members of the new Pentecostal sects, adopted a strong anticommunist stance, challenging the social gospel of the liberal believers with strict fundamentalism, in a pattern that would persist for generations among warring factions of the faith.

But as an outsider to religious tradition, back then, I couldn't read the depth of the connection between religion and politics. What caught my attention in Nicaragua was the sense of forward motion in the society, of collective aspiration. It was seeing ordinary people—flawed, compromised, often weak—stand up and make history by hand, reaching for something larger than themselves.

But by 1983, when I made my second trip, the romantic, prophetic revolutionary "paradise" was already starting to fall apart. President Reagan's undeclared proxy war against Nicaragua raged in the countryside, terrorizing peasants and destroying infrastructure. The Sandinistas' promises of land reform and education and health care were crumbling under attack by contra forces; war was ruining the economy, food was rationed, and hope was giving way to fear. Citizens were sullen and despairing; many of the young idealists were bitter and burning out.

A group of friends and I began working with Sandinista farm cooperatives whose harvests were threatened by contra raids: Shuttling back and forth between New York and Nicaragua, I helped organize thousands of Americans to come and help pick coffee and cotton. The memory of the Corpus Christi massacre in Mexico guided me: I knew how much my own subsequent politics had been shaped by that unmediated, whole-body experience of violence and solidarity. I also knew how much it had changed me simply to be immersed in regular life with people who weren't like me, to share food and conversation and crowded buses. Similarly, we'd bring Americans to Nicaragua to share, at least for a few weeks, the dangers faced by peasants. They'd hang out with real people, not idealized heroes, eating and talking and doing sweaty, dirty, necessary work together. The volunteer brigades would be political education for participants, helping to make a covert war real. Their presence on the farms, we hoped, might also help protect the peasants from attacks: Dead Americans were going to be more of a problem for Washington than dead Nicaraguans.

Working with the brigades was like working in a restaurant again, with higher stakes. I loved the guy from Oregon who did seat-of-the-pants tractor repair with duct tape on a slippery hillside in Matagalpa and the sweetheart of a nurse from Texas who made all the farmhands pancakes. But there were also the drama queens and nutcases: the public, as Chef Robert would have said. Alice, a starry-eyed true believer in the revolution, lost it entirely, after two weeks of ten-hour days picking coffee with nothing to eat but rice and beans. "Come outside," she whispered to her bunkmates, who were trying to sleep in a grubby barn. "I see . . . I see . . . a flaming cross in the sky. We have to get out of here. It's the final judgment."

Apocalyptic visions and fevered political conspiracy theories flourished in those years, and not just among the borderline individuals who wound up, despite our attempts to screen them, on our Nicaraguan brigades. Yet, as a writer, I knew there was much more to the story. The wars in Central America weren't simple: They couldn't be explained by grandly invoking "imperialism" or "communism," or by knee-jerk references to Vietnam. Most liberals knew next to nothing about military affairs; pacifists acted as if singing "Give Peace a Chance" were enough to end all war forever. What mattered to me, increasingly, were the details: the how and the why behind the land mines and psychological operations manuals, the Salvadoran death squads and the Nicaraguan contras. What intrigued me was the way that political-military strategy played out on the ground, in the unexpected and completely unofficial places where conflicts were actually lost and won. I began to study war.

Over the next six years, I would travel widely, immersing myself in military doctrine, strategy, and tactics. In Nicaragua, I interviewed teenage girls who knew how to dismantle a rifle blindfolded; in El Salvador, I talked with guerrillas who operated a clandestine radio station out of their backpacks. At Fort Bragg, North Carolina, I met U.S. Special Forces officers who wore mirrored shades and specialized in covert operations. I read Clausewitz and Sandino and Sun-tzu and the *Strategic Air Review,* studying post-Vietnam counterinsurgency doctrine and following the interesting changes in U.S. military thinking as the "small wars" of the Reagan era blossomed around the world. I met other researchers and reporters, interviewed diplomats and spies, pored over military documents. And I kept coming back to the little towns and subsistence farms of Central America, to feel what these supposedly small wars were like for people who lived them incarnate.

When my long article explaining the concept of "low-intensity conflict" came out in 1983, sparking a bitter argument among activists who were still waiting for a conventional United States invasion of Central America, I was collaborating with a team of researchers based at the Jesuit-run university in Nicaragua. Along with colleagues in El Salvador, the Philippines, and southern Africa, they were analyzing the emerging new face of warfare as we'd come to understand it: irregular, political, and ruthless; or, as one U.S. strategist had explained it to me, "total war at the grassroots level."

Writing about and living in such wars absorbed me totally. I used to feel ashamed and confused that I found so much joy in the midst of the violence and dirt and ugliness. Some of it, I think, was about the simple adrenaline thrill of danger and a guilty but real happiness about coming out alive. Plenty of it was romance. But another piece was the intensity of connection that collective experience, even terrible collective experience, provided: the powerful intimacy of sharing life and death together.

What I learned in those moments of danger and grief informs what I now call my Christianity. It was a feeling of total community with others, whether or not I was like them, through the common fact of our mortal bodies. We all had bodies that could suffer and be killed; we all had hearts that could stop beating in an instant. In war, I looked at other, different people and saw them, face-to-face—and, seeing them, felt a *we*.

Never was that feeling stronger than when people fed me, which they did constantly. In El Salvador, a priest gave me cookies; in the Philippines, a peasant woman gave me fish. Over and over, despite the poverty of the places I visited, despite the danger my presence often meant, strangers fed me, freely. Food took on new meaning for me in the war years, as I searched to make meaning amid suffering.

Central America may have been the testing ground for U.S. low-intensity conflict strategy, but similar wars were under way around the world in the Reagan years. I traveled to the Philippines from Nicaragua, with a Nicaraguan colleague, to study the dynamics of the war between the new Aquino government and the NPA, the Maoist New People's Army. We held some meetings, attended a conference, and then she flew back. I stayed on to make a clandestine reporting pilgrimage to the jungle stronghold of the guerrillas—the place Filipinos reverently called "the mountain."

All over the Third World, "the mountain" was how a generation of rebels referred to their strongholds, their hiding places, what they called their "zones of liberation." In Spanish-speaking countries, people even said that a new convert to the revolution *"se montañó"*—he mountained himself. The mountain was the place rebel supporters—scared peasant girls, persecuted students from the city, underground labor leaders—would flee to, where they would take up arms and new names and prepare themselves to lay down their lives for their people. Unlike me, most of the people in the countries where I worked were Christians, and they were intimately familiar with the resonances of biblical narrative. When Ed de la Torre, a left-wing Filipino priest and theologian, once read Psalm 121 at an anti-Marcos rally, telling the crowd of demonstrators to "look up to the hills," he drew laughter and cheers.

My contacts in Manila steered me to a safe house, an inconspicuous one-story building with a little room behind the kitchen where, for more than a week, I waited to hear from the guerrillas, reading, listening to the radio, and visiting with messengers who'd come through to tell me "Not today." My caretakers were kind and went out on their motorbikes to fetch meals: greasy Chinese noodles, steamed rice in banana leaves, Coca-Cola, and lumpia. One night, three of them came in with fresh mussels wrapped up in newspaper and cooked them with chopped raw onions and a decorative squirt of bright yellow cheese from a can. I slipped out myself once, to the International House of Pancakes, where I held a secret interview with an underground officer from the general staff of the New People's Army. He had gray hair, rubber sandals, and a plastic shopping bag full of military documents, which he kept on his lap as we ate waffles with grape jelly and talked about counterinsurgency.

Finally my trip was arranged. Two young women in lacy blouses and blue jeans picked me up early one morning at a crowded city bus station and flanked me as we climbed onto a rickety bus. I was half a foot taller than almost everyone aboard, and blond, but the girls told me to pull a scarf over my head and look down. We rode for hours through clouds of dust, on dirt roads fringed by coconut palms. At one stop, I reached out the window where vendors were thrusting up wares and grabbed a plastic bag full of some kind of fried root. We chewed on the oily pieces for a while as we bounced along.

In the middle of a stretch of jungle punctuated by a roadside stand, the bus pulled over. The three of us got out and began to walk. I was wearing sneakers, and my feet were already swollen in the heat. My companions were wearing flip-flops. After about three hours, a group of armed teenagers appeared in a clearing. We stopped. They waved. They beckoned us over: Their group was just another four or five miles away.

I didn't much mind walking, though I got thirstier and

thirstier, and the damp brush was thick around us, hard to push our way through. But by the time we got to the NPA camp, I was covered in insect bites, and it was almost dusk: It was hard to see my way without stumbling.

The clearing was small, with maybe forty people, young men and women, gathered around a couple of banked fires. I was so hungry. A girl who was serving as sentry grinned at me. "Hi," she said. My companions pushed me forward. An older man with a pistol at his belt greeted me. "Come on," he said, and we started walking again.

The night fell quickly, a greeny black curtain, and the stars and the sounds of insects came up fast. It was close to midnight by the time the commander, his patrol, and I arrived at a bamboo hut deep in the forest. The place was built on stilts, with a pig grunting underneath in the dark. A barefoot woman came out and peered at us, then passed down a wooden ladder, and hands reached out to pull us up.

I sat down in the single cool room on a smooth bamboo floor, smoking and talking quietly with the commander, a candle in a tin can between us. A shy boy came over and pantomimed drinking; when I smiled at him, he brought me a tin cup of tepid water, which I drank all at once. I waited. The guerrillas with me were smoking cigarettes, one lying down and the other with his rifle draped lazily across his lap. "Are you hungry?" he asked me.

We didn't eat that night, but the boy brought us all more water, and a peasant man, naked except for shorts, gave me a piece of cloth and showed me a spot to make a bed. I lay down between two fighters—one already fast asleep, her mouth open like a child's—and looked up at the rafters, where the man had hung some beautiful homemade kites. He blew out the candle, and I listened for a while to the pig rooting under the house and the sentries changing position, and thought about his kites, and slept.

I woke right before dawn to the smell of smoke and the woman whose home it was touching my shoulder. She guided me out to the back of the hut, where children watched as a pot of something steamed over a fire, and ladled me out some porridge into a yellow plastic bowl. It was mostly grayish soupy rice, with cracked corn—animal feed—mixed in, and little bits of salty, stiff dried fish. She smiled at me. I took the bent spoon she offered and then a bite of grain and bones.

When I got back to Central America, it was the summer of the "final offensive" by the FMLN guerrillas in El Salvador—one of many offensives that turned out not to be final at all. Up a long path that wound through the grounds of the University of Central America were the offices of Ignacio Martín-Baró, a Jesuit from Spain. I'd get a taxi to drop me at the gates of the UCA and start walking up past sweet-smelling acacia trees to interview him. I was always thirsty; there were usually vendors at the gates selling sodas and violently colored ices and some of the dry Salvadoran pastries that looked as if they were made from pineapple jam and dust. The country was too poor for lots of packaging: glass bottles were scarce, so drinks were decanted into little plastic bags tied around cheap paper straws. I'd buy an "Esquirt," watch as the sweating pushcart guy poured the grapefruit soda into a plastic bag, and drink it all before I got to Martín-Baró.

His offices were dark and cool, crammed with books and papers. Like everywhere else in San Salvador during the offensive, they were frequently without electricity, though a light breeze sometimes blew through the second-story slatted windows.

We'd sit in uncomfortable wooden chairs and talk about war, about the political machinations of the previous week, about the possibilities and dangers of peace. I didn't get to interview him much, but there weren't a lot of people whose judgment I trusted more. I knew a few among the underground—a labor organizer, an FMLN subcomandante, a woman who worked in the clandestine radio—who I thought were maybe as smart, but they tended to be also a little crazy. Martín-Baró was not crazy. Nor was he shy, and some xenophobic intellectuals in the capital accused him of arrogance, but the man was essentially and deeply calm. He had big glasses and a real smile. Before I sat down, he'd make the first ritual offering of a coffee—"You don't want a little coffee?"—and smile.

I suppose there must have been a crucifix somewhere on Martín-Baró's wall, but I wasn't looking for it then and don't remember one. In any case, I wouldn't have seen it as a sign of hope, back then, just as a rather gory art object. The power of the cross—the idea that suffering for others can lead to new life—was for me then, as it was for the unbelievers Saint Paul wrote about, and remains for rationalists today, "folly."

I do remember trying to talk with the priest about fear. The UCA, traditionally the finishing school for the country's elite, had become a center for analysis of the war and was seen by the paramilitary squads and the right-wing politicians of the ARENA party as a hotbed of communism. Its rector, Ignacio Ellacuría, another Spaniard, was always getting death threats. Nonetheless, the Jesuits, to the great annoyance of the left, insisted on inviting politicians from all parties to speak at the UCA. Given that some of those politicians, notably the men from ARENA, served as legal fronts for historically fascist gangs who had murdered tens of thousands, I couldn't grasp how Martín-Baró could be so unworried. But it didn't seem to penetrate. He wasn't trying to be brave; he wasn't reckless: He simply wasn't scared.

Martín-Baró never answered my questions about fear directly, brushing them off. In that cool office, he talked not about blood but about democracy, which sometimes he'd call "fellowship." He recounted how, at a Jesuit retreat put on by the UCA, the fathers had been talking politics and discussing the issues of democracy in Latin America. Apparently they were sitting around castigating the FMLN for its authoritarianism. Then someone pointed out that in a real democracy, not just the priests but the women who were serving them lunch were going to have something to say about the way things were run, and one of the men blurted out, "You can't do that. They'd make horrible mistakes." Well, said Martín-Baró, that's right: Democracy definitely means that people will make mistakes. "And," he added, "we should welcome them."

We weren't friends. We weren't even colleagues. I knew nothing about his private life. Once in a while, he'd ask how I was feeling, which is as close as he ever got to a personal conversation. But I felt at home with Martín-Baró. Somewhere in the course of an interview, the man would feed me. I'd be pushing him to explain more about which industrialists were secretly backing which general, or to tell me what he expected when the currency was devalued next month, and he'd pause before answering, then stand up and go out to his secretary's desk. He'd come back with a tin of imported biscuits—dreadfully dry, just like the fly-ridden homemade Salvadoran ones in the stalls outside the gate, but prettily shaped and nestled in little paper cups—and offer it to me.

"Here," he'd say. "Take some."

It was hard for me to remember the days when I'd thought about food as cuisine, since where I worked now, the main characteristic of food was its scarcity; the only story it told was one of lack. In Nicaragua, in the poverty-stricken northern mountains, the workers we stayed with on coffee farms lived in barns and ate *gallopinto*, broken rice and black beans, cooked over a wood fire, as their meal of the day. If they were doing well, they ate two meals of *gallopinto*. They drank dirty water. When the war came to them, they shared the food they had with whatever soldiers— Sandinistas or contras—marched through their area, and sometimes were killed for it.

I saw how basic and unadorned food was to the very poor when I traveled from one of those farms to Cuba to interview a Marxist counterinsurgency expert. Cuba at the time was held up as a beacon of modernity and wealth to the peasants of Nicaragua: Cuban soldiers, doctors, engineers, and teachers had come as "fraternal advisers" to the Sandinista government, and they regaled Nicaraguans with stories about heroic revolutionary Cuba, where there were paved roads, schools, electricity, and doctors.

I flew out of Managua on a battered Russian-made plane. My seatmate, a Nicaraguan peasant boy, was perhaps sixteen years old, with beautiful dark eyes. He had a horrible burn running down his neck, below the collar of his ill-fitting army uniform. He was being sent to Cuba for medical treatment, he told me, and, as if it weren't obvious, that he'd never been on a plane before. He looked like one of the feral, starving kids I'd seen on the coffee farms. Clearly he'd joined the Sandinista army with no chance to acquire worldliness before the phosphorus, or whatever it had been, melted the flesh off his neck. Now he was trying to be a good soldier and sit still. He didn't seem anxious when we took off, but when the Air Cubana attendant brought around trays of lunch, the boy was shocked. He ate everything, quickly and thoroughly, and then held up a paper packet and asked me what it was. "Sugar," I said. He looked blank, then tore two packets open, poured them into his hand, and ate them.

Nicaragua grew sugarcane in its humid coastal lowlands, but there was only one refinery, and everything it produced was for export. Peasants, if they had sweeteners at all, only ate *piloncillo*, the crude, molasses-flavored brown scrapings from the sugar mill, hardened into cones, wrapped in scrap newspaper, and sold for pennies. This boy had never seen white sugar before, and as soon as he finished it, he asked the attendant, urgently, for more.

Of course there was a lot of suffering in Central America, and predictably that suffering made lots of people ugly: crazy, dishonest, desperate, cruel. I knew why. I'd pretended not to understand Spanish so I wouldn't have to listen to a distraught taxi driver tell me about his son's death; I'd lied to a human rights lawyer so I could stay at home eating ice cream and reading a book instead of taking him to visit his clients; I'd told poor people I was broke. In big ways and small, I knew exactly how selfish a war could make me, and I saw all around me how fear and need drove other people to terrible betrayals. Yet over and over, I also saw how war created a community, a people, and how that community was nourished by gestures of sharing. It was sharing that didn't depend on personal intimacy, and a community that didn't depend on everyone's being friends; it foreshadowed what I would come to understand as church, at its best.

Toward the end of the war in El Salvador, I was staying with a group of guerrilla collaborators and underground organizers and their neighbors, in a run-down barrio on the edge of the city.

The houses were cinder block and tiny; the yards were bone-dry, littered with ashes from cooking fires. The union organizer I stayed with was illegal, and wanted by the army, but he walked around openly and laughed too loudly and asked his neighbors over to the house so he could show off to them, on a jerry-rigged VCR, the videotape of a battle shot by the clandestine film unit of the guerrilla Radio Venceremos.

Thirty people crowded into his windowless one-room house and shared six lukewarm orange sodas, and the kids ran in and out, and we watched the movie. All the neighbors were bored and kept chatting about other things, and then, one by one, they drifted away until at last it was just the union man and me and his family, and very late. There were a lot of fleas, and dogs outside tearing up garbage in the ditch. We lay down together on the floor in the stifling heat, and one of the boys kept making gun sounds like the ones in the movie, giggling, and his older sister shushed him, and the organizer bragged that soon, right after the offensive, they were going to have water pipes in their neighborhood. He was insufferable, and all I wanted was for him to shut up so I could sleep.

When I woke up, the man was dressed and waiting for me. "Come on," he said, and took me outside, and we started walking down a dirt path through the barrio. He knocked on the door of a shack that backed up on a weedy lot and said something to the old woman who came out. She disappeared for five long minutes, and we waited there, the smell of smoldering charcoal sharp in my nose. When the woman came back out, she had a jar filled with milk and handed it to me. The union organizer watched carefully as I drank it all: Still warm from the cow, the milk was rich and slightly sweet. It smelled like animals. "There," he said. "That's good for you."

It wasn't, of course, what I ate that mattered, though the details of what I was fed have stayed with me, vivid as dreams. The mineral taste of poor people's tortillas, their thick dough prepared with lime and scorched on an iron griddle. The slippery sweetness of mangoes. The chemical bite of bright red sodas; the funkiness of goat. Handfuls of gluey rice, spoonfuls of milky sherbet, cupfuls of spicy broth.

I remember the food of peasants, which always tasted of dirt. I remember the food of the urban poor, which always tasted of cheap grease. People gave food to me, and I ate it all: roots, leaves, animal hearts; raw, canned, cooked, or spoiled.

The impulse to share food is basic and ancient, and it's no wonder the old stories teach that what you give to a stranger, you give to God. When I first read about the Prophet Elijah—who was fed in the desert by ravens and in the village of Zarephath by a starving widow—I suddenly got a picture of that story, repeated over and over, tumbling down through thousands of years, repeating at every turn: *That's like the time we found fruit in the forest. That's like the woman who made me tea in the town.* The fact is, people feed one another constantly from their own bodies, their own plates, their own inadequate stores of insufficient food. Food is what people have in common, and it is, precisely, common.

And whether it was a fake fast-food frozen chicken nugget or an unadorned chunk of carrot with the dark earth still clinging to it, what mattered to me was not what I ate. What mattered to me in those years, when everywhere I was wasn't home, was that I could launch myself into a morning, an unknown town, a war zone, and be fed—usually by strangers and sometimes by comrades, occasionally by enemies, but always by someone who was as hungry as I was or hungrier. We had hunger in common, and we had food.

Caught up in the moment, every moment, I didn't know that those war years would be formative Christian experiences. They would introduce me not only to big Christian themes—love, death, fear, and sacrifice among them—but to hard lessons about what it means to be a Christian. Long before I went to church or ran a food pantry, wars would reveal my weaknesses and mistakes—*sins*, to use a word that never occurred to me then—and make me find a way to continue working, past shame. They showed me how helpless I was to save anyone, or to fix suffering, and how it mattered anyway for me to be there with people. I'd have to learn to receive when I was proud and give when I was burned-out and poke around in strange places without knowing what I was going to uncover.

Watching priests and nuns and lay catechists struggle for justice in Central America, I came to respect Christians more than I ever could have imagined growing up. But in the war years, I still thought of believers the way I thought of revolutionary party militants and communists—as a different order of beings, who belonged to something I'd never belong to. My communist friends lived underground, "in the catacombs," as they said, and had given their entire lives faithfully to their movements: fighting, bleeding, and starving in jail. They'd lied and been lied to uncomplainingly; they'd been tortured; they'd seen their best friends blown apart and had killed other human beings in the name of their cause. Both Christians and communists had leaders who'd betrayed them, and institutions that had endured scandals and strife. Both groups had an opaque faith that I could only guess at.

"I think a lot these days about the people who gave their lives for our movements," I wrote, "and I think as well about all those who died by mistake, by accident, who didn't want to be martyrs or heroes. I'm not always able to think about so much loss without bitterness and anger. I don't know if I'll ever be capable of loving my enemies; I'm not always capable of forgiving myself."

And yet, during the last urban guerrilla offensive in El Salvador, something was stirring inside me. I had fallen in love with another journalist, Bob, and spent half a dozen reckless months with him covering the craziest of the fighting. It was more than romance: Every day felt as if it could be our last. We bonded intensely, as we did with the other reporters who followed the escalating offensive. Two of our Salvadoran colleagues, on their way to cover an election rally, were shot in the back by soldiers at a roadblock; a Dutch reporter was killed in crossfire. The radio correspondent whose house we were staying at left the country. The end of the old order was coming: A whole society was collapsing, spectacularly, around us. Bob and I went to exhumations, to funerals, to the aftermaths of bombings; we drove around with killers and spies and huddled together in a borrowed house, terrified and listening to the shortwave radio.

It was hard for me not to be afraid. The night I got pregnant, someone was tortured and murdered. The road past our house ended, miles away, in an overgrown ravine outside town. I can't be exactly sure which night it happened, but I know that pretty much every morning during that fall of 1988, we'd turn on the radio and learn that a body had been dumped in the ravine. Getting pregnant in the middle of a war wasn't exactly an accident, but it wasn't a rational choice. There was death everywhere; there was unspeakable cruelty and loss. There was a wrecked country and my own shaky, overwhelmed self. But I wanted new life so much. I longed for more life.

Then there were the romantic daydreams. Sometimes having a baby seemed like the single great gesture that was going to save me, redeem the mistakes I'd made, create enough joy to dim all the suffering around me. I imagined that Bob and I were making a noble promise to the future, a vow that would transform everything.

All around me, though, other real people were living with that promise, and as their children grew and the sweetness of their love increased, so did their heartbreak. I saw hungry kids; maimed kids; lost kids; scared, sick, shot kids. I saw a mother holding a dead child with the plastic barrettes still in her hair. I saw the relatives of soldiers, sitting outside the gates of the military hospital with their legless boys. Night after night, I knew that mothers and fathers were still awake, waiting for their children to come home alive. I had moved through the world without having to fear for a child. Now Bob and I were opening ourselves to that suffering, as well as to love.

But I could feel life moving inside me. As a foreigner, a reporter, I'd been able to at least pretend to have a certain distance from ordinary humanity. Now I was just another pregnant lady, my body marked as sharing it. I kept being drawn closer to people I didn't know. Women patted my belly familiarly. A fighter from the guerrillas stopped our interview, made me take his chair, then went out to find me something to eat. And at a political rally held by the leaders of the death squads, a furious young man spat at me. "Whose bastard is that?" he said.

By the time I was six months pregnant, the fighting had reached the capital. We went to cover a battle on the edge of town. It was a crummy little barrio, with unpaved streets and families jammed on top of one another. The guerrillas were trying to shoot their way out of a cul-de-sac, and army troops were firing blindly at them. I got pinned behind a yellowish wall, along with a group of people from the neighborhood. Every once in a while, as the afternoon wore on, someone would try to dash across the street to safety but be driven back by the cross-fire. I remember that the woman next to me cried a little bit, quietly; there was a guy with a gold tooth who was holding his kid tightly by the shoulder. I tried to decide if it would be better to keep my belly toward the wall, to protect the baby, or better to face out so I could see what was happening and maybe make a run for it.

We got home okay that night, but I was badly scared. Bob and I talked, trying to balance our politics, our work, and the danger they meant to this unborn child. It was impossible to know what was right, but we decided to get out for a while. Bob and I went back to the United States, thinking we'd probably return after I had the baby.

Chapter 6

First Communion

—

We settled in San Francisco—"the northernmost city in Latin America," as a Salvadoran friend had explained to me. We knew only a few people there, and there wasn't a whole lot of demand for writers on counterinsurgency. But I got a temporary staff job at a left-wing magazine, and Bob and I rented an apartment from an older woman I'd met through the Nicaragua brigades.

Katie was born. In the common fact of her, I was plunged into mystery. A nursing child is elementally flesh and blood, linked to the mother through eating in the most literal way. But something beyond my own mother's relentlessly secular rationality flickered when I contemplated Katie at the breast, eyes open, swallowing and growing.

Six months after Katie's birth, in 1989, I would hear from a stranger that Ignacio Martín-Baró had been dragged out of his house by Salvadoran soldiers, along with five other Jesuit priests and two Christian women who kept house for them, and shot in the head.

The next few years would unfold in a dizzying blend of joy and anguish, as Katie grew, the Central American wars lurched to their desperate ends, communism itself cracked and dissolved around the world, my relationship with Bob ended, and I stayed in America.

My entire personal and political landscape was breaking apart. I had no idea whom or how to organize: Years of living among continents had left me feeling like a stranger everywhere. My family lived on the other side of the country; my comrades from Central America had scattered. Around the world, all the revolutionary fervor of the last decade was dissipating in a haze of Realpolitik and sorrow, with dingy deals and patched-together fixes replacing the outrageous and unrealistic dreams of freedom and justice. There was no more communist utopia on the horizon, and certainly no capitalist utopia: just the inevitable wreckage of war and the scrambling for postwar power.

Even as the wars ended, death was coming closer to me. My best friend, Douglas, called to ask if I would come to New York and help him end his life: In the last excruciating stages of AIDS, his lungs were filling up with Kaposi's sarcoma, and he couldn't breathe. He died in my arms, as I was whispering to him. I stumbled out of the hospital, walking forty blocks in the raw spring air to Douglas's apartment, where his boyfriend and I cooked a ham, ten pounds of salt potatoes, green beans, and two pies for the wake. "The last time I cried this much," I told his boyfriend, "Douglas said I had to eat something."

Two months later, I watched my friend Bo die in San Francisco: He couldn't breathe either, and by the end, there was nothing I could cook that he could swallow.

Then my father, who had never spent a day of his life in a hospital, was diagnosed with lymphoma and died, out of the blue, four days later.

None of this drove me to thoughts about God or heaven. I was anchored by Katie, beautiful and alive, and by the repetitive physical demands of motherhood: food, bathing, picking up, sleep, food, picking up, food.

It was once the acute grief abated that I could start to see new things. We'd bought a big, cheap wooden house among Latino neighbors in the Mission District, from a Guatemalan couple I'd encountered in the old days when they'd done logistics for the guerrilla army. Bob, who had come out as a gay man, had moved just two blocks away, and Katie—a luminously happy, talkative child—tromped back and forth between us, wearing pink sneakers. There was an apricot tree in my backyard, and lilies, and wisteria and jasmine twining over the deck. Katie entered kindergarten in the school across the street, where she was the only Anglo kid in the class, and brought home arithmetic work sheets in Spanish. I began taking long walks, up over the greening hills, by myself. I bought oranges and melons from the Mexican guys who sold fruit from the back of their pickup trucks, discovered the market where I could get three bunches of anything for a dollar from Hmong farmers. I found freelance work again, writing about domestic politics. I covered and participated in the passionate movements that sprang up in response to AIDS, as formerly marginalized gay people discovered their voices and became a community. I made new friends. And at a party in the rainy season, I met Martha, an editor, and we fell in love. She was brilliant, funny, and unafraid of pain, having been through a great deal of it herself. Once, as I lay in her arms weeping over the loss of Douglas, Martha offered me a Kleenex and some excellent advice. "Honey, just cry," she said. "There are way worse things. Not crying, for example."

Over the next five years, I cooked dinner every night for Martha and Katie at home. And every day, Katie kept talking and laughing and reaching for more. As my life got happier, ease and love began to enter me, side by side with the memories I carried.

While the classic conversion story involves desperation, hitting bottom, and a plea for help, I think now that it was gratitude, as well as the suffering I'd seen, that made room for me to open my heart to something new.

Early one winter morning, when Katie was sleeping at her father's house, I walked into St. Gregory's Episcopal Church in San Francisco. I had no earthly reason to be there. I'd never heard a Gospel reading, never said the Lord's Prayer. I was certainly not interested in becoming a Christian—or, as I thought of it rather less politely, a religious nut. But on other long walks, I'd passed the beautiful wooden building, with its shingled steeples and plain windows, and this time I went in, on an impulse, with no more than a reporter's habitual curiosity.

The rotunda was flooded with slanted morning light. A table in the center of the open, empty space was ringed high above by a huge neo-Byzantine mural of unlikely saint figures with gold halos, dancing; outside, in the back, water trickled from a huge slab of rock set against the hillside. Past the rotunda, and a forest of standing silver crosses, there was a spare, spacious area with chairs instead of pews, where about twenty people were sitting.

Later I'd learn much about the mission of St. Gregory's, founded by two priests determined to reform the ossified Episcopal liturgy by reclaiming the ancient Middle Eastern roots of Christian worship. I'd learn about their struggles with the hierarchy, their theology of open communion and baptism, their radical ideas about architecture and music. And I'd learn, also, about the blindness inside the vision, the contradictions inside the prophecy, the struggles inside the community. I couldn't foresee then how I'd be changed and moved by the people I was meeting, or how much I'd come to love the very beams of the building. But that morning, I didn't even know what *Episcopal* meant: I had no idea Episcopalians were part of the worldwide Anglican Communion, a "catholic and apostolic" church, or how they worshipped or what they stood for. I didn't realize St. Gregory's was unusual. I assumed that everything I saw was just plain "church" and that I was there as a spectator.

I walked in, took a chair, and tried not to catch anyone's eye. There were windows looking out on a hillside covered in geraniums, and I could hear birds squabbling outside. Then a man and a woman in long tie-dyed robes stood and began chanting in harmony. There was no organ, no choir, no pulpit: just the unadorned voices of the people, and long silences framed by the ringing of deep Tibetan bowls. I sang, too. It crossed my mind that this was ridiculous.

We sat down and stood up, sang and sat down, waited and listened and stood up and sang, and it was all pretty peaceful and sort of interesting. "Jesus invites everyone to his table," the woman announced, and we started moving up in a stately dance to the table in the rotunda. It had some dishes on it, and a pottery goblet.

And then we gathered around that table. And there was more singing and standing, and someone was putting a piece of fresh, crumbly bread in my hands, saying "the body of Christ," and handing me the goblet of sweet wine, saying "the blood of Christ," and then something outrageous and terrifying happened. Jesus happened to me.

I still can't explain my first communion. It made no sense. I was in tears and physically unbalanced: I felt as if I had just stepped off a curb or been knocked over, painlessly, from behind. The disconnect between what I thought was happening—I was eating a piece of bread; what I heard someone else say was happening—the piece of bread was the "body" of "Christ," a patently untrue or at best metaphorical statement; and what I *knew* was happening—God, named "Christ" or "Jesus," was real, and in my mouth—utterly short-circuited my ability to do anything but cry.

All the way home, shocked, I scrambled for explanations. Maybe I was hypersuggestible, and being surrounded by believers had been enough to push me, momentarily, into accepting their superstitions: What I'd felt was a sort of contact high. Probably my tears were just pent-up sadness, accumulated over a long, hard decade, and spilling out, unsurprisingly, because I was in a place where I could cry anonymously. Really, the whole thing, in fact, must have been about emotion: the music, the movement, and the light in the room had evoked feelings, much as if I'd been uplifted by a particularly glorious concert or seen a natural wonder.

Yet that impossible word, *Jesus,* lodged in me like a crumb. I said it over and over to myself, as if repetition would help me understand. I had no idea what it meant; I didn't know what to do with it. But it was realer than any thought of mine, or even any subjective emotion: It was as real as the actual taste of the bread and the wine. And the word was indisputably in my body now, as if I'd swallowed a radioactive pellet that would outlive my own flesh.

Much later on, I'd read what Jesus's disciples said about the idea of eating a body and drinking blood. "This is intolerable," they declared. Many of them, shocked, "could not accept it and went away and followed him no more." Well, it *was* intolerable.

The gory physicality of the language wasn't what bothered me, the way it must have bothered the disciples, who lived surrounded by religious rules about blood, animal slaughter, and eating. I didn't share those taboos: I'd understood the world first, and best, by putting it in my mouth. In restaurants, I'd been fascinated to cut open the side of a pig or the heart of a cow, revealing the chambers and fat, the muscles and shimmering lines of tendon. In war, I'd not shied from bloodshed, had touched the dying and the dead. I'd dared myself into sex with strangers and kept opening my mouth to strange foods; I'd turned my own body into food for my child.

But eating the body of Christ, and drinking his blood, was too much. My own prejudices rose in me. Ignorant about the whole historical sweep of Christianity, I had no particular affection for this figure named "Jesus," no echo of childhood friendly feeling for the guy with the beard and the robes. If I had ever suspected that there was such a force as "God"—mysterious, invisible, "silent as light," in the words of an old hymn—I hadn't bothered to name it, much less eat it, for crying out loud. I certainly had never considered that this force could be identical with a particular Palestinian Jew from Nazareth. So why did communion move me? Why did I feel as if I were being entered and taken over, completely stirred up by someone whose name I'd only spoken before as a casual expletive?

I couldn't reconcile the experience with anything I knew or had been told. But neither could I go away: For some inexplicable reason, I wanted that bread again. I wanted it all the next day after my first communion, and the next week, and the next. It was a sensation as urgent as physical hunger, pulling me back to the table at St. Gregory's through my fear and confusion.

The bread, I learned over following Sundays, was baked by the people I took communion with. Caroline made the crumbly, slightly sour loaf I'd tasted first; someone called Tom made a dense whole wheat bread; Jake baked a sublime brioche. Each of the loaves was slashed with a cross, and when the people at the table broke the bread, if I was standing close enough, I could smell the yeast. The wine was sticky and sweet: pale gold, not at all red, but it warmed my throat as I swallowed and then passed the cup to the person next to me. "The blood of Christ," I'd repeat, in turn.

Yet obviously it *wasn't* blood: It was Angelica fortified wine, alcohol 18 percent, from a green screw-top bottle, as I saw once when I peeked in the church kitchen. It was no different in its basic chemical makeup from the zinfandel I'd drink with my brother in between bites of a nice hanger steak. So, then, was it a symbol? Did the actual wine symbolically represent the imagined blood? No, because when I opened my mouth and swallowed, everything changed. It was real.

I went around and around like this, humiliated by my inability to articulate, even to myself, the nature of what was happening. It seemed as crazy as saying I had eaten a magic potion that could make me fly. Much later, a friend would tell me that I'd looked like a "deer in the headlights" during that time. "You didn't know what direction to go in; you simply stopped. You were mystified, confused. . . . What you were experiencing in your body didn't jibe with what you knew in your head." He laughed gently. "You thought you had lost your mind."

I thought I probably had. I went through my days excited beyond words, frequently on the verge of tears, then confused and scared. My throat was tight as if facing danger or intense sexual excitement; I'd be ravenously hungry, then unable to eat, as you are when you're heartbroken or newly in love.

This went on for a while—me going to St. Gregory's, taking the bread and bursting into tears, drinking the wine and crying some more. It was inexplicable. I knew I couldn't say a word about it to my mother: The very idea of her scorn filled me with dread. Communion? Jesus? What was I thinking? Luckily, I could talk with Martha.

To my surprise, she said she could see that I had been yearning for, or even missing, certain things, and she wasn't horrified that I was reconsidering God. "I always knew you were basically a religious person," she said. "I didn't know what form it would take, but I could sense you needed to have a faith."

Martha's own experience of discovering faith, ten years ago, had been a conversion of sorts, if not an explicitly religious one. Brought up in a completely secular Jewish family where God was dismissed as irrelevant, Martha had nothing to help her through a childhood of trauma and tragedy. In her twenties, wrecked and desperate, she'd stopped a suicidal addiction to Scotch by going to AA meetings, where, she said, she'd learned how to pray. "It's about giving up," she told me. "You get to a point where you just have to give up. And then you learn to be honest." Martha didn't feel the need now to belong to a congregation or profess a creed, but she deeply understood the "relief" of finding yourself to be small in the face of mystery.

So she understood what was happening; more, she wanted it for me. She didn't think that I was crazy to believe in God or that my new interest automatically meant I was going to become the worst kind of dogmatic Christian fanatic. But it wasn't easy. When Martha came with me to church, she couldn't get past the Jesus part. "He's so skinny and scraggly," she said, with distaste. "And I don't like that eating him thing." Martha, who had never attended synagogue or learned a word of Hebrew, nonetheless held completely reasonable historical anxieties about being in a room full of people crossing themselves. I could see why my sudden interest in Christianity might make her feel more like a Jew.

Moreover, she had an immediate and visceral dislike of St. Gregory's. I was finding the services beautiful, with their a cappella chants, long silences, and sung prayers; church didn't feel as if I were watching a performance but like a whole group making something together. When "the Peace of the Lord" was proclaimed, there was fervent hugging and kissing. The people sang, danced, shared bread; even the sermons at St. Gregory's were participatory. Instead of proclaiming from a pulpit, preachers sat in a wooden chair, spoke from their own experience, and invited the congregation to respond with quasi-Quaker "sharings" after a period of contemplative silence. The silences filled me with an openhearted calm, a deep willingness to listen to whatever came next. But Martha wasn't impressed. "All they talk about is themselves," she complained. "Enough about God, let me tell you more about *me*." She couldn't stand the slow liturgical dance congregants did around the altar after communion either—"the goy hora," she called it. Martha was fine with God if it meant hanging out with a bunch of drunks in a basement testifying to a higher power, but she couldn't imagine spending her Sundays at St. Gregory's.

"If you're going to go to church," she urged me, "why don't you look around?" So we visited a very elegant Episcopal church full of middle-aged Anglophile gay men, and a brick, steepled Lutheran church where pictures of the king and queen of Sweden hung in the parish hall. Both places were pleasant enough, but I couldn't handle the organ music, the rows of pews, and the whispered formality. When it came time to take communion, I was unmoved by the dead white disks of wafers and the fussy little shot glasses full of grape juice, dispensed decorously to parishioners who knelt in line at an altar rail. These were the kinds of churches my parents must have grown up in, I realized: where good manners ruled, the traditional authority of the clergy went unquestioned, and the body of God was draped decorously in an ironed white napkin.

But my background had made me responsive to a different set of cues. There was the immediacy of communion at St. Gregory's, unmediated by altar rails, the raw physicality of that mystical meal. There was an invitation to jump in rather than official entrance requirements. There was the suggestion that God could be located in experience, sensed through bodies, tasted in food; that my body was connected literally and mysteriously to other bodies and loved without reason.

And there was, as well, my intuition that I wasn't going to find a better place to work out what I believed in. Martha's criticisms of St. Gregory's were quite likely right, but even at the beginning, I was able to see, somehow, that any church was going to be disappointing. Wherever I went, I'd have problems as well as glorious epiphanies. Wherever I went, I'd have to meet myself, and other people, if I wanted to get closer to God.

"I don't really understand it," I said. "But I think I'm going to keep going to church at St. Gregory's for a little while and see what happens."

Katie had grown into a fantastically curious girl, but she manifested no interest in religion either, except for admiring Yemaja, the Santería goddess, whose image, draped in a fabulous blue gown, adorned a nearby storefront. We launched a new routine on Sundays: Martha and Katie stayed home, contentedly secular, and read the paper together. I went to church, heart pounding, and tried to figure out why.

Chapter 7

Crossing

—

My first year at St. Gregory's would begin, and end, with questions. Now I understand that questions are at the heart of faith, and that certainties about God can flicker on and off, no matter what you think you know. But back then, I thought "believers" were people who knew exactly what they believed and had nailed all the answers.

My first set of questions was very basic. I covertly studied the faces of people at St. Gregory's when they took the bread, trying to guess what they were feeling, but I was too proud and too timid to ask either priests or congregants the beginner's queries: Why do you cross yourselves? What are the candles for? How do you pray? And, more seriously: Do you really believe this stuff?

My next question was not about God or church; it was nakedly about me, and my fears. What would my friends think?

In America, I knew exactly one person who was a Christian. It turned out that my friend Mark Pritchard, an introverted writer with a tongue piercing, attended a Lutheran church with wooden pews where he sang old-fashioned hymns every Sunday. So I took some walks with Mark, trying to draw him out, but despite his orange Mohawk and wild sexual politics, he was a fairly Lutheran guy, not much given to discussing his emotions or spiritual life. "Sure, well, I believe in first principles," Mark said to me, cautiously, when I probed him about his beliefs. He might as well have been speaking Greek. "Oh," I said. I didn't know anyone else who went to church.

Poor people certainly believed in God. San Francisco might be the least churchgoing city in the nation, but there were still plenty of churches within the run-down blocks around my house—the left-wing Chicano Catholic parish with its gorgeous altar to the Virgin of Guadalupe; the "Temple of the Lyre of the Valley," an evangelical Salvadoran storefront; the black Pentecostal dive, the Santería chapel, the cruddy white-trash Assembly of God building with its dirty curtains. Poor people said "God bless you" and crossed themselves and stood on street corners singing loud, bad hymns; they bought their little girls frothy first communion dresses; they buried their dead gang-banger brothers with incense and Scripture.

Nationally, middle-class Christians—even though many seemed to enjoy portraying themselves as a picked-on, oppressed minority, ceaselessly battling secular humanist regimes—weren't exactly an endangered species either. People who called themselves Christians comprised 85 percent of the population. Christian rock music alone was a billion-dollar-a-year enterprise; there were more than 150 million Christian websites, and there had never been a non-Christian United States president.

But my own friends weren't poor urban believers or smug God-talking suburbanites. My friends, at the most, read about Buddhism or practiced yoga. They tended to be cynical, hilarious, and overeducated, with years of therapy and contemporary literature behind them, and I was afraid to mention that I was slipping off to church and singing about Jesus on Sundays instead of sleeping late, cooking brunch, and reading the *New York Times Book Review* as I'd been raised to do. I couldn't tell them about communion, or that I had started to read the Bible I'd bought, furtively, at a used-book store. It would be years before I'd meet Paul Fromberg—a funny, profane priest who would become my closest friend. He believed that "the craziest thing about Jesus is that church life never gets in the way of feeling close to him" and would teach me about the ironies of religion. At the time, though, I had no idea that I could be pals with anyone who described himself, unabashedly, as both "a big fag" and "Jesus's man."

My social circle was shocked when I first shyly broached the subject of church. An activist lawyer I knew sputtered. "Are you kidding?" he said. He launched a litany of complaints about the church that I'd come to hear over and over: It was the most reactionary force in the world, anti-Semitic, misogynist, homophobic . . . the Vatican . . . the Crusades . . . Jerry Falwell . . . child-molesting priests . . . Ralph Reed. . . . I'd hated, during the 1980s, being expected to defend left movements or revolutionary parties, even when they were screwed up. I had no interest in defending another more fabulously corrupt institution. "It's not about the church," I said. "It's about—"

"Good deeds?" the lawyer asked incredulously. My desire for religion just didn't make sense to him. He worked harder than anyone I'd ever met, spending fourteen hours a day defending Haitian refugees and Muslim political detainees and the victims of war and empire. He'd listened to prisoners at Guantánamo sob as they described Christian jailers destroying the Koran; he had represented a Nicaraguan woman raped by evangelical soldiers who sang hymns as they took turns with her on a dirt floor. Whatever faith drove him forward in his vocation, it had nothing to do with the Almighty God so readily invoked at prayer breakfasts in Washington.

But the Christianity that called to me, through the stories I read in the Bible, scattered the proud and rebuked the powerful. It was a religion in which divinity was revealed by scars on flesh. It was an upside-down world in which treasure, as the prophet said, was found in darkness; in which the hungry were filled with good things, and the rich sent out empty; in which new life was manifested through a humiliated, hungry woman and an empty, tortured man.

It was a picture that my friend Jose Suarez, who'd left his Cuban Baptist family in Texas to become a psychiatrist, had also glimpsed—but only briefly. Devout as a child, saved as a teenager at a Billy Graham rally, Jose made it through a year at a conservative Christian college before he began to feel "betrayed" by the inauthenticity of religion. "I'd go to services," he said, "and it was all very social, unexamined, class-bound. I mean, didn't they read the words of Jesus?"

But the hypocrisy and insincerity of church, what had driven my own parents away, was only part of it. "I was actively listening," Jose said. "I really wanted to hear God. Ping—nothing. Ping—nothing. I couldn't find it. I'd drive out this highway into the country at night, lie back on the hood of my car and look at the stars, and have these arguments with God. It was like: Say something, show me, give me a sign, some sort of experience. I'd watch the stars move across the sky, but I couldn't find it inside. The container didn't contain anymore."

And so Jose had been wary, though curious, when I told him I was going to church: I was the first friend he'd had since high school who was anything close to a believer. It was in talking with him that I was able to articulate, for the first time, something about what prayer meant to me: what I was searching for, beyond the psychological, with all my questions about faith.

Jose and I met for lunch at a small café with outdoor tables one afternoon, when he was in the middle of an excruciating breakup. We sat on the patio and talked, picking at some complicated California sourdough-and-vegetable sandwiches while the fog came in.

Jose was in analysis then, and seeing a dozen patients, and serving as the medical director at a community mental health clinic, and writing scholarly papers on Freud, and doing energetic yoga for hours every morning, and generally overachieving, but he couldn't fill every minute, and whenever he paused, the heartbreak would pour in. "Maybe I should go sit at the Zen center again," Jose said. He was a small, handsome man with wiry hair and little glasses and perfect posture. His eyes were wet. "I'm not sleeping so well anyway; I might as well get up at five, what the hell."

We finished lunch, and I took Jose's hand. "Jose," I said, "you should pray."

As soon as I said it, I felt like an idiot—worse, like a proselytizing busybody who knows, without ambiguity, what's right for everyone else. Jose looked genuinely surprised. Then he put on his analyst face. "Hmm," he said. "What do you mean?"

What did I mean by prayer? I didn't mean asking an omnipotent being to do favors; the idea of "answered prayers" was untenable for me, since millions of people prayed fervently for things they never received. I didn't mean reciting a formula: I loved the language of some of the old prayers that were chanted at St. Gregory's, but I didn't think the words had magical power to change things. I didn't mean kneeling and looking pious, or trying to make a deal with God, or even praying "for" something. What was I telling him?

"Um, well," I said. I was embarrassed. Then I looked at Jose again, and the word *tender* filled my mind—tender as in sore to the touch and compassionate, at the same time. After my father had died, Jose had listened to me cry with the deepest empathy and patience, not trying to "comfort" me but just being present. As tenderly as I could, I said to him, "I really don't know. I don't know what I believe or who I'm talking to. Sometimes I just try to stay open, sort of. Especially when it hurts. And I try to—I know this is corny—but I try to summon up thankfulness."

"When you told me to pray," Jose would remember later, "it was incredibly earnest. You said prayer was like having this intense, profound longing that you just had to be with. That you put the longing in the hands of God, in a certain way. That it was important to be receptive to the unfulfilled, and not fill it or deny it."

I *had* to be receptive or go crazy—because even as I kept going to church, the questions raised by the experience only multiplied. Conversion was turning out to be quite far from the greeting-card moment promised by televangelists, when Jesus steps into your life, personally saves you, and becomes your lucky charm forever. Instead, it was socially and politically awkward, as well as profoundly confusing. I wasn't struck with any sudden conviction that I now understood the "truth." If anything, I was just crabbier, lonelier, and more destabilized.

All that grounded me were those pieces of bread. I was feeling my way toward a theology, beginning with what I had taken in my mouth and working out from there. I couldn't start by conceptualizing God as an abstract "Trinity" or trying to "prove" a divine existence philosophically. It was the materiality of Christianity that fascinated me, the compelling story of incarnation in its grungiest details, the promise that words and flesh were deeply, deeply connected. I reflected, for example, about Katie, and about what it was like to be both a mother and a mother's child. The entire process of human reproduction was, if I considered it for a minute, about as "intolerable" as the apostles said communion was. It sounded just as weird as the claim that God was in a piece of bread you could eat. And yet it was true.

I grew inside my mother, the way Katie grew inside me. I came out of her and ate her, just as Katie ate my body, literally, to live. I became my mother in ways that still felt, sometimes, as elemental and violent as the moment when I'd been pushed out from between her legs in a great rush of blood. And it was the same with my father: He had helped make me, in ways that were wildly mysterious and absolutely powerful. Like Jesus, he had gone inside somebody else's body and then become a part of me. The shape of my hands, the way I cleared my throat, the color of my eyes: My parents lived in me—body and soul, DNA and spirit. That was like the bread becoming God becoming me, in ways seen and unseen.

I tried to remember my own passionate spiritual feelings as a child, when I had no religion and no language to understand them. There had been one early spring afternoon, raw and chilly, when I lay by myself in the muddy backyard in my snowsuit examining a fallen log, looking and looking and looking. There were patches of snow on the wet wood and, around it, spears of onion grass just beginning to poke up, and I sat up after half an hour contemplating the log. The cloudy sky above me was so huge, and I was so small. The phrase "the whole universe" occurred to me. I must have been in third grade, and no amount of papier-mâché solar system models had prepared me for the vast, heart-beating calm I felt, or for the inarticulate desire to just stay there, suspended, looking and breathing my tiny puffs of the whole universe's air, until I had to pee and went inside, shedding my wet mittens.

I remembered how I used to pray—there really was no other word for it—when I was six or seven. I'd been reaching for something solemn, obligatory, ritual: wanting God and not even knowing what that was. In an upstairs bedroom in my parents' home, I'd once been taught, by a girl who went to Catholic school, the vaguely sexual language of the Hail Mary. It remained a mysterious, private poem to recite, the way I recited, as I walked home from school, lines from other poems: "The breaking waves dashed high / On a stern and rock-bound coast." But I had no framework to understand it as prayer, linked to the same longing I'd feel alone, at night, when I looked at the ceiling and made up words.

What would religious instruction have done for me then? What would have sustained me more as a child than my own atheist parents' love, my father's soft voice at bedtime as he invented stories for me, my mother's hand on my back? What would have fed me more than cooking and eating with them, or given me more courage?

Food was a lot of what had grounded me before, shaping my family, my work, my relationships. It had meant a five-gallon plastic bucket full of broken eggs. It had meant a generously offered bowl of rice porridge in the jungle. It had meant the thin blue milk leaking from my own breasts. Now food, in the form of communion, was collecting all of those experiences in one place and adding a new layer of meaning—not on my time but on God's.

The child I was, protected from religion by her parents, at some point had become the woman crying at the communion table. Those tears weren't a conclusion, or a happy ending, just part of a motion toward something. It was still continuing. God didn't work in people according to a convenient schedule, by explaining everything or tying up the loose plot lines of every story. Sometimes nothing was settled.

So I sat by myself a lot and mused about God, and my mother, and flesh and blood. I read the Bible. I prayed; I tried to stay open to the questions that flooded me. I didn't tell anyone I was becoming a religious nut.

Chapter 8

Histories

—

The year I started going to church was 1999, and in the long run-up to the election that would lead to George W. Bush's remaking of America and the world, religion was everywhere. The cultural jihad of right-wing Christianity, with its absolutist thunderings about school prayer and homosexuality, filled the news. Powerful coalitions of evangelicals infused the Republican Party with their apocalyptic worldview; fundamentalist preachers raised money for Bush; grassroots armies of believers stormed women's clinics. St. Gregory's congregation seemed to be generally liberal; it had a woman priest and a couple of gay ones. Of course that was a political stance, too: I knew perfectly well that all religion was political, and before too long, I would come to delve deeply into the issues that divided the church.

But whatever was happening *out there*, it wasn't going to tell me what I most urgently wanted to know. It was tempting to sidestep my disturbing spiritual questions through the familiar process of making a political analysis, but right now, politics, for once, wasn't the most interesting thing for me to figure out.

Instead, I burned to understand what felt to me like the heart of Christianity: communion.

I remembered and reconsidered conversations with radical liberation theologians I'd met in Mexico in 1972, in El Salvador in 1987. I went back and read the piece Ed de la Torre had written about developing a "Eucharist of rice" in the Philippines, using the rice cakes called *bibingka* and native palm wine as the offerings. Preaching about the breaking of the host to desperately hungry peasant farmers, de la Torre explained simply, "We break it because we are poor, and we don't have enough. We must share the little we have." Later, from jail, on a hunger strike, de la Torre wrote a poem and smuggled it out to his church. "To starve after justice," it began, "to ache for it, like food."

Someone at St. Gregory's had shown me the Book of Common Prayer used by Anglicans around the world, and I read the section on communion avidly, along with a Russian Orthodox mystic's book about the sacraments of bread and wine. I read a sermon by the archbishop of Canterbury, Rowan Williams, explaining that "it's the really hungry who can smell fresh bread a mile away. For those who know their need, God is immediate— not an idea, not a theory, but life, food, air for the stifled spirit and the beaten, despised, exploited body."

The writing on the subject by Rick Fabian, one of the founders of St. Gregory's, was extensive. From his essays, I learned that the meal at the Table had many names, each with a history: sacrifice, Lord's Supper, Eucharist, Mass, Divine Liturgy, great offering, communion. *Eucharist* meant Thanksgiving, and the celebration of the Eucharist collapsed a number of pagan and Jewish rituals into one meal in which God's very life was offered freely to believers. *Communion*—with God as well as with all other humans—was the great gift, and it gave life to everyone who shared it.

Early Christians, worshipping in houses, shared full feasts, following Jesus's promise that he would be among them when they ate together in his memory. They ate believing that God had given them Christ's life and that they could spread that life through the world by sharing food with others in his name. Later churches, reducing the feast to bread and wine, wrangled over the right way to understand Jesus's presence: Was God physically there in the meal or conjured up through the repetition of particular words? And they began to license and control the distribution of the elements central to the faith. Bread became stylized wafers; wine became grape juice, and church officials—much like the temple authorities Jesus had ignored—imposed rules about who could and could not receive communion. Different denominations made their own restrictions: No communion for Catholics or Orthodox in each other's churches; no communion for the unbaptized or children below a certain age; no communion, in the words of the Book of Common Prayer, for anyone living "a notoriously evil life . . . those who are a scandal to the other members of the congregation." Instead of being God's freely given gift of reconciliation for everyone—the central point of Jesus's barrier-breaking meals with sinners of all descriptions—communion belonged to the religious authorities.

The entire contradictory package of Christianity was present in the Eucharist. A sign of unconditional acceptance and forgiveness, it was doled out and rationed to insiders; a sign of unity, it divided people; a sign of the most common and ordinary human reality, it was rarefied and theorized nearly to death. And yet that meal remained, through all the centuries, more powerful than any attempts to manage it. It reconciled, if only for a minute, all of God's creation, revealing that, without exception, we were members of one body, God's body, in endless diversity. The feast showed us how to re-member what had been dis-membered by human attempts to separate and divide, judge and cast out, select or punish. At that Table, sharing food, we were brought into the ongoing work of making creation whole.

I read a commentary by Grant Gallup, a cranky liberation theologian and Episcopal priest who'd retired to Nicaragua. "The little loaf-sharing church," he wrote, "stole away from the neighborhood of Jerusalem Temple and the synagogues of the diaspora, hounded by a good imperial government to martyrdom for hundreds of years, and then, one day, found its bishops enthroned and basilicas built for it by emperors. It issued rescripts and itemized its metaphysics. It created a dogmatic mind of Christ to supplant the flesh of Nazareth. But there was always and remains still the opportunity to make Jesus your friend, and to invite him to share your supper."

Supper with God. This was what had grabbed me—and it wasn't an accident. My year of questioning drew me to lift my head and look around, more thoughtfully, at the place I'd wandered into: Saint Gregory of Nyssa, named after a fourth-century married bishop from Cappadocia, in what is now Turkey. A mystic, universalist, and humanist, Gregory had proclaimed that "the only thing worthwhile is being God's friend."

For more than twenty-five years, at the experimental fringes, then the conflicted center, then the respectable fringes of the Episcopal Church, St. Gregory's founding priests, Rick Fabian and Donald Schell, had pushed an articulate, challenging vision of reform centered on innovative liturgy and open communion.

Drawing on a long tradition of liturgical reformers, Rick and Donald saw themselves as messengers and prophets, with a call to save the church from its mindlessly rote worship, its autopilot traditions, and its deadening clericalism. Even politically liberal Episcopalians were almost all liturgically conservative: Their services seemed trapped in amber. The liturgy Donald and Rick had painstakingly developed was by turns solemn, joyful, contemplative, and communal, almost all sung, and led by a mixture of ordained and lay people who told the congregation what was happening at every step, so that newcomers wouldn't be lost. Lay men and women and children—some in robes, working as unordained "deacons," and some in jeans and T-shirts—served bread and wine; lay people led prayers, preached, and read the Gospel. Worship at St. Gregory's, drawing on Rick's astonishingly extensive and slightly eccentric scholarship, was deliberately physical and participatory, in the ancient Byzantine style; there was dancing, singing, smoke, candles, brightly colored cloths, bells, a great bustle of people sweeping through the sunlit church and encircling the altar. It was lively and not archaic, yet utterly without the cheesiness of "contemporary" Christianity; instead of soft rock, there were a capella Shaker hymns, Middle Eastern chants, and plainsong psalmody. The music director, Sanford Dole, used a tuning fork as his only instrument and insisted that everyone join in four-part harmony. I found, to my utter surprise, that I could sing with others, easily and fluently.

The building itself, newly constructed in 1995 after the church had spent nearly twenty years in a rented space, was in the Potrero Hill neighborhood, across the street from a brewery. The church was meant for dancing and unaccompanied voices; its collection of crosses, fabrics, and art from around the world was replete with Ethiopian Orthodox icons and liturgical umbrellas, nineteenth-century Russian menorahs, and Tibetan bells. And as the people danced around the altar, the saints danced high above them: Mark Dukes, a local African American iconographer, had painted the entire rotunda with a mural of ninety larger-than-life figures, ranging from Teresa of Ávila to Malcolm X and a naked King David, dancing in a circle led by a dark-skinned, risen Christ.

The rotunda icon made a monumental and surprising statement of faith. Its wildly different saints represented musicians, artists, martyrs, scholars, prophets, and sinners from all times, from many beliefs and backgrounds. Some were Christian; some, such as Anne Frank or Rumi, were not. Many, such as Ella Fitzgerald or Queen Elizabeth I, were chosen not because they had lived blamelessly but because they had moved through terrible moments of suffering or wrongdoing. Rather than piety or orthodoxy, the icon proclaimed a sweeping, universal vision of God shining through human life.

St. Gregory's very floor plan, designed by Donald with the architect John Goldman, spoke of a mission centered on inclusive communion. In most churches, I learned, the baptismal font is planted at the entrance, and the altar far away at the end of the church, behind a rail, making it clear to visitors that initiation is required before receiving bread and wine. The font serves as a gate to keep the wrong people from the feast, and the Table remains mysterious and distant, something only priests can approach. But at St. Gregory's, the front doors opened on an empty space under a soaring cupola, with a round table right in the middle, the first thing visitors saw upon entering. During services, the people gathered, singing, around that Table to share communion. Usually a priest chanted the narrative over a many-layered drone rising up from the people: the story of Jesus's dinner with his friends. Sometimes, though, the entire congregation would sing together in harmony, standing close around the altar. "Take, eat. This is my body given for you. Do this in remembrance of me."

Right before the bread was broken, priests and deacons lifted the bread and wine up: "Holy gifts for holy people," they sang, and then invited everyone, without exception, to share the meal. After passing the bread and wine to one another, the people danced around the altar, then set out coffee and more food on the same Table, to keep the feast going. Outside the doors, set into the hillside, stood the baptismal font: a huge chunk of rock with a basin hewn out, spilling forth water for anyone who wanted it, after dinner.

The theology embodied in the building and liturgy was physical, yet mysterious; beautiful and yet handmade. But I struggled with complicated feelings about the flesh-and-blood reality I was discovering at St. Gregory's.

The founders' personalities dominated the church, which had grown up around their particular gifts, tics, and weaknesses. Rick was sixty, gay, wealthy, wry, a Cambridge- and Yale-educated scholar and art collector who lived alone: He was the kind of genius who frequently misplaced his eyeglasses. Donald was a married father of four, an aikido black belt, and a theater aficionado who worked in bursts of creative, big-picture thinking and got impatient with follow-up. Neither one of them had ever held a lay job. Donald and Rick were visionaries, yoked together in a lifetime partnership built on envisioning a church unlike any other.

Together, starting in 1978, the two priests had collected a rather self-consciously "artistic" and close-knit congregation who were proud of everything that distinguished St. Gregory's from conventional, tradition-bound churches. The members were mostly highly educated, liberal, middle-aged San Francisco professionals, with a sprinkling of Republicans, older people, and younger families; nearly half were gay; almost all were white and quite well off. In the early days, when just eight, then twelve, then twenty people would meet in the rented basement of another church, members were all close friends, minding one another's kids and having dinner together each week. Once they moved to the new building, and the congregation multiplied in size, the effort to establish St. Gregory's special identity took on a new urgency. Now it was a congregation of 150 artists, scholars, theater designers, psychologists, and composers. Many of them had spent years away from religion and come to St. Gregory's because of the innovative liturgy; they were looking for a way out of the hack routine of mainstream churches. Others were refugees from fundamentalist congregations where they'd suffered for being gay, or Catholic churches where they'd felt shut out as women. At St. Gregory's, there wasn't an entrance exam for membership or a list of required beliefs.

I should have felt at home with these thoughtful, open-minded intellectuals. But probably because I felt so defensive about my lack of formal education, money, and official Christian formation, I tended to get irritated with the members of St. Gregory's community. I thought they were clubby and precious; I sneered at their early music concerts. As I ducked out the door at coffee hour, fleeing one more generous attempt at conversation, I would feel by turns superior, condescending, horribly inadequate.

Yet my own snobbery couldn't protect me from being drawn, more deeply, into the place. I had to admit that these people, with all their specific flaws intact, had opened the door to grace—not because they had good taste, not because they were rich, not because they were exceptionally intelligent or even always likable. Donald and Rick and the people of St. Gregory's had let God in, because they—no matter how imperfectly—were committed to letting in clueless and unprepared strangers like me: because they believed in the absolute religious value of welcoming people who didn't belong.

"Blessed be God the Word," Rick would chant before services, "who came to his own and his own received him not, for in this way God glorified the stranger. O God, show us your image in all who come here today, that we may welcome them, and you." His prayer expressed the fundamental theology of St. Gregory's, as did the church's practice of open communion. "Jesus welcomes everyone to his table," someone would announce during each service, "and so we offer communion to everyone, and to everyone by name." Hospitality to strangers—baptized or heathen, pious or unrepentant—was at the center of St. Gregory's mission; the church believed that because Jesus ate with sinners, breaking down the barriers between clean and unclean, offering communion to all without exception was the "one true sign of God."

As Rick argued in a paper, churches faithful to Jesus should offer communion to strangers first, before converting or baptizing them:

> Jesus abandoned baptizing and instead sought out, welcomed, and dined with unprepared, unreformed, unwashed sinners. His action was a prophetic sign suiting his own more radical message: here comes God now, ready or not! And seen against Jesus' contemporary religious background, the presence of obviously unqualified diners was essential to his sign. Perhaps Isaiah's vision of a banquet for all nations inspired his choice: there, the prophet says, the pure and impure will share one feast. Nevertheless such dinner company was politically scandalous for a teacher, and many scholars today . . . judge that above all Jesus' actions it led to his death.
>
> Our common life dare not hide Jesus' chosen sign, whatever the risk, or we will forfeit our apologetic for

Christian faith in a world where spiritual hunger and spiritual alternatives abound. How can we tell people today what we believe about Christ, and yet keep his table fellowship in the way he distinctly refused to keep it?

And so I kept taking communion, unprepared and unreformed. I figured communion would take me, too—wherever I was going.

Meanwhile, as that first year went on, I read more broadly about the religion I'd stumbled into. I looked, now, at the politics of the church, beginning with its history. I was hardly thorough; I studied the same way I'd studied military affairs as a reporter: unsystematically, with omnivorous, autodidactic enthusiasm. I read books about monks and icons and liturgy and saints. I read about Saint Paul, the midlife convert, knocked upside down by the conviction that Jesus, whom he had never met, was blazingly alive in him. "It was as though I was born when no one expected it," he told the church at Corinth, on his way to yet another arrest and incarceration. I read about Dorothy Day, the agitator and mystic who founded the *Catholic Worker* and was hounded by the FBI.

And I read, to my huge surprise, a cache of papers from my grandparents, whose interpretation of the Social Gospel turned out to be far more radical than I had ever suspected. While I had been studying low-intensity conflict in Nicaragua, I discovered, my grandmother Margaret had been keeping the faith in her small Massachusetts town, railing at her fellow parishioners to resist the war in Central America through civil disobedience. In a typewritten church bulletin, right next to the announcements from the music committee, she had explained, "Yes, it is true: I have been arrested as a 'disorderly person.' Jesus told his disciples to preach, teach, and heal, and likened them to light, salt and yeast, permeating the whole of society. To me this means challenging the racism, greed, and planned murder of our empire. You may as well get used to the idea of some of your fellow Christians spending time in jail." Dryly, she added, "There are many distinguished precedents for this situation."

But times had changed. Now the newspapers were full of stories about Christians who blockaded abortion clinics, shouted down science teachers at school board hearings, picketed the funerals of gay men. The airwaves were full of preachers ranting about Sodom and "family values" and baby-killing. It was no wonder that, to most of my nonbelieving friends, *Christian* was shorthand for fanatic fundamentalism, anti-intellectualism, and right-wing intolerance.

In America, the rising up of "Reagan Democrats" and the remaking of a Republican coalition around the white working and lower middle class was resonating through the world of religion as well. For generations, the mainstream Protestant denominations had been home to senators and captains of industry; local bankers and national power brokers sang from the same respectable hymnals. "The Episcopal Church was elegant, upwardly mobile, very above-the-fray, thank you," California's bishop William Swing would tell me later, rolling his eyes. "We ran things." The nondenominational revivalists and evangelists, self-taught and fanatic, congregated on the fringes of town.

But now, after decades of struggle, the scorned white-trash snake handlers and hallelujah singers were gaining power, and the Episcopalians and Presbyterians and Methodists were losing it. Just as old-money liberals were being edged out of politics by upstart right-wing populists, so mainstream churches and their members were losing influence while born-again evangelicals ascended. Aging congregations in proper Gothic stone buildings shrank from eighty to sixty to twenty members, while nondenominational suburban megachurches, radio ministries, and shopping-mall fellowships packed them in.

Part of it reflected the way Christians had struggled with changes set off in the 1960s, choosing sides in the great cultural battles over civil rights, the role of women, war, and abortion. Then, in the culture wars of the 1980s, feminism, gay liberation, and postmodernism blazed through Yale and Harvard and the elite seminaries run by mainstream churches, while conservative Christian colleges kept their students apart from the corrupting influences of the academy and taught them to mistrust relativism. A friend who'd gone to Moody Bible Institute remembered a New Testament seminar in which his professor resolutely steered students away from all metaphorical interpretations of the Gospel. "He had this furrowed brow," said my friend, "and he told us the way to do good exegesis was to stay literal. Of course there were a few renegade professors trying to open up the world for us, but the overall idea was, why be relative? There's right and wrong, there's truth and lies, that's it."

But along with the cultural, political, and class differences among believers were serious theological disagreements. A pleasant little guide called *Welcome to the Episcopal Church*, by Chris Webber—an introduction to the faith for newcomers, endorsed by the presiding bishop in the United States—revealed a lot about the differences. "The Bible is not a set of instructions that can give us simple answers," wrote Webber, "nor a text with which to prove points. . . . The guidance the Bible gives was provided for a society very different from ours . . . and any set of words is open to different interpretations."

Webber went on to talk about "inclusivity" and "diversity" and said, as if it were obvious, "The discovery of truth is a continuing journey guided by the Holy Spirit, and the answers we find are always provisional answers."

Such mild-mannered assertions were the kind of thing that enraged people who clung to fiercer, less flexible beliefs. The Christian pollster George Barna found, in 2005, that 40 percent of American adults believed that they had "made a personal commitment to Jesus Christ that is still important in my life today" and contended that, after death, they would "go to Heaven because I have confessed my sins and have accepted Jesus Christ as my savior." A much smaller subset of this group—remarkably, given their political influence, just about 7 percent of American adults—contended in addition that they had a personal responsibility to share their religious beliefs about Christ with non-Christians; that Satan exists; that eternal salvation is possible only through grace, not by being good or doing good deeds; that Jesus Christ lived a sinless life on earth; and that the Bible is totally accurate in all it teaches.

Webber's matter-of-fact liberalism about "different societies," his easy ecumenicism, and his reiteration of the principle that Anglican faith was centered on "reason, tradition, and Scripture" would be heresy, obviously, to this most fundamentalist group. "Reason," after all, could be a slippery slope.

Such liberalism would also enrage many fellow Anglicans, I learned. Because Anglicans govern themselves without a Rome— a central body that imposes universal authority—Anglican dioceses around the world can represent different styles of worship, different politics, and different approaches to social issues. The Book of Common Prayer set forth an order for the Eucharist, but it could be celebrated with singing and dancing—as at St. Gregory's—or with worshippers sitting rigid in pews; liturgical innovation didn't mean heresy. In social outlook as well, the Anglican Communion had long managed, however awkwardly, to straddle the divide between its liberals and conservatives and still sheltered believers as different as Barbara Bush and Desmond Tutu.

The balance of power had been shifting, though, from my grandparents' missionary days: There were seventy-five million Anglicans worldwide now, just two million of them U.S. Episcopalians. The Anglicans of the global South—in particular, the thirty-seven-million-member African church—tended to be unforgiving of the ecumenical gestures of the shrinking Western church and its "theological drift" away from "Christ-centered, Bible-based" values. As Henry Orombi, the archbishop of Uganda, said, "A hundred or so years ago, the fire was in the Western world. And many of their great people went over to the countries in the Southern Hemisphere, and reached out there, and planted seeds there. . . . It now looks like the Western world is tired and old. But, praise God, the Southern Hemisphere, which is a product of the missionary outreach, is young and vital and exuberant."

In the United States, even though class and tradition gave a gloss of similarity to most Episcopal churches, local bishops had always had authority to set the tone in their dioceses. A bishop could encourage female priests or shut them out; speak at peace rallies or chum around with generals; he could insist that parishes use only approved Sunday-school curricula or encourage experimentation. Conservative Episcopalians might rail against left-wing reformers in dioceses such as California—"a bastion of amorphous Christianity and aggressive revisionism," sniffed one conservative—and high Anglo-Catholics might scorn folk-singing liturgists, yet a tradition of respect for local governance kept the communion together.

But shortly after I started going to church, the Diocese of New Hampshire ordained an openly gay bishop—in fact, an old friend of Donald Schell's from seminary, Gene Robinson—and it set off shock waves in the American church and the worldwide Anglican Communion. Conservative African Anglicans joined with reactionary American Episcopalians—the same ones who had threatened to leave in the 1970s over the ordination of women—threatening to pull out of the communion entirely if the heresy were not stopped. Mainstream United States Episcopalianism might be culturally conservative, with its dull prayers and dreary sermons, its gray-haired parishioners in sensible shoes. But the denomination, under generally liberal leadership, had grown theologically flexible to a degree that made orthodox Africans and Americans anxious. "The battle is about the authority of Scripture," proclaimed conservative bishop Robert Duncan. "It's about the basics of Christian faith. . . . The issues have to do with sexuality and morality, but at the very heart of it is whether Scripture can be trusted."

It wasn't just about gayness, of course, but a more fundamental conflict between believers who craved certainty and those who embraced ambiguity; those who insisted Scripture was inerrant and unchanging, given once and for all time, and those who believed that the Bible was only part of God's continuing revelation. The struggle was also about how to define a Christian: as one who sought to keep religion "pure" or one who welcomed outcasts. It was hardly a conflict unique to Anglicanism or, for that matter, Christianity. As Andrew Linzey, an English priest who edited a book on Anglicans and homosexuality, wrote, "The agenda of conservatives is a rolling one: today it is gays, but biblical inerrancy, interfaith worship, women bishops, remarriage after divorce will surely follow. The logic of all purity movements is to exclude."

And so the denomination that had sheltered generations of diplomats and university presidents, that had raised up presidents in its elite boarding schools, whose bishops played golf with newspaper publishers and whose National Cathedral in Washington was as close as America came to a state church—this was the denomination cracking most publicly, as was the larger Christian church around the world. In a way, I felt lucky. I'd walked into St. Gregory's right at the moment when Episcopalianism was moving precipitously from the unquestioned center of Establishment power in the United States to the despised periphery. And there, on the edges—as I'd learned before, when I was a student and a cook and a reporter—was where the most interesting truths were to be found.

Before I knew anything about church, I'd assumed that most Christians spoke the same language, shared a sense of fellowship, and beyond minor differences had a faith in common that could transcend political boundaries. But if I had imagined that, initiated as a Christian, I was going to achieve some kind of easy bond with other believers, that fantasy was soon shot. Just a few months after I began going to St. Gregory's, I found myself at a restaurant counter in the Denver airport, waiting for a flight home from a reporting trip. A woman—perhaps noticing the silver crucifix I had recently and self-consciously started to wear around my neck—caught my eye and smiled as she took the stool next to me. She had short blond hair and a cross of her own, and was wearing some kind of sexless denim jumper that reeked of piety.

I smiled back, and we exchanged small talk about the weather and flight delays, and then she asked me what I was reading.

I showed her the little volume of psalms that I'd borrowed from Rick Fabian. "From my church," I said proudly.

"What church is that?" the woman asked. She leaned forward, in a friendly way.

"Saint Gregory of Nyssa Episcopal Church, in San Francisco," I said, as her face rearranged itself, froze, and closed. It may have been the "San Francisco," I realized later, but the city's name was a reasonable stand-in, by that point, for everything conservative Christians had come to hate about the Episcopal Church as a whole: homosexuality; wealth; feminism; and morally relativist, decadent, rudderless liberalism. The church I'd unknowingly landed in turned out to be a scandal, a dirty joke at airport restaurants, a sign—in fact, thank God, a sure bet—that I was going to eat with sinners.

Chapter 9

Crossing II

—

Bit by bit, I was getting a picture, one that might very well have been incomprehensible to fellow Christians in stern fundamentalist Nigeria or pro-life Colorado or even other Episcopal parishes in San Francisco. Of course, just like them, I was becoming more and more convinced that I was right and that what I had figured out about faith, on my own lovely little spiritual adventure, was going to uplift and sanctify and generally improve my life.

When I talked with my secular friends, I could make a thoughtful case for church as a site for social change, or earnestly analyze the denominational politics of Christianity, as if that were what I cared about. I tried to justify my interest in St. Gregory's by telling Martha that understanding contemporary politics required understanding religion. I acted as if I were an interested reporter, and not really that hungry.

The reality was different: deep, nonrational, desiring.

Poking around in the Bible, I found clues about my deepest questions. Salt, grain, wine, and water; figs, pigs, fishermen, and farmers. There were psalms about hunger and thirst, about harvests and feasting. There were stories about manna in the wilderness and prophets fed by birds. There was God appearing in radiance to Ezekiel and handing him a scroll: "Mortal," he said, "eat this scroll," and Ezekiel swallowed the words, "sweet as honey," and knew God.

And then in the New Testament appeared the central, astonishing fact of Jesus, proclaiming that he himself was the bread of heaven. "Eat my flesh and drink my blood," he said. I thought how outrageous Jesus was to the church of his time: He didn't wash before meals; he said the prayers incorrectly; he hung out with women, foreigners, the despised and unclean. Over and over, he told people not to be afraid. I liked all that, but mostly I liked that he said he was bread and told his friends to eat him.

As I interpreted it, Jesus invited notorious wrongdoers to his table, airily discarded all the religious rules of the day, and fed whoever showed up, by the thousands. In the end, he was murdered for eating with the wrong people.

And then—here's where the story got irrational. I didn't exactly "believe" it, the way I believed in the boiling point of water or photosynthesis, but it seemed true to me—wholly true, in ways that mere facts could never be. I believed this God rose from the dead to have breakfast with his friends.

I read about the crazy days after Jesus's arrest, death, and burial, when the terrified disciples were scattering, just as I'd seen peasants and revolutionaries run from the violence of soldiers in Latin America. A stranger hailed them on the road to Emmaus. They told him what had happened, and he explained it all by citing Scripture, recounting old prophecies in impressive detail. Then, according to the book, they came to a village and invited the stranger to eat with them, as the night was drawing near. He sat down at the table, took bread, and broke it. Suddenly "their eyes were opened," reported the book. "He made himself known in the breaking of bread, and they felt their hearts on fire." Then he vanished. In another story, he reappeared cooking food on the beach. In another, he showed up to tell his followers that he was hungry and wanted something to eat. They gave him a piece of fish.

All of it pointed to a force stronger than the anxious formulas of religion: a radically inclusive love that accompanied people in the most ordinary of actions—eating, drinking, walking—and stayed with them, through fear, even past death. That love meant giving yourself away, embracing outsiders as family, emptying yourself to feed and live for others. The stories illuminated the holiness located in mortal human bodies, and the promise that people could see God by cherishing all those different bodies the way God did. They spoke of a communion so much vaster than any church could contain: one I had sensed all my life could be expressed in the sharing of food, particularly with strangers.

I couldn't stop thinking about another story: Jesus instructing his beloved, fallible disciple Peter exactly how to love him: "Feed my sheep."

Jesus asked, "Do you love me?"

Peter fussed: "Of course I love you."

"Feed my sheep."

Peter fussed some more.

"Do you love me?" asked Jesus again. "Then feed my sheep."

It seemed pretty clear. If I wanted to see God, I could feed people.

But my hands still shook when I took the chalice. Then Donald Schell, who'd kindly ignored me for the better part of a year, sent me a note, asking if, "since you seem to be a regular now at the early service," I'd consider serving as a deacon—at St. Gregory's, the name given to the laypeople who helped run the services, leading the prayers, guiding the singing, cuing the priests, and serving the bread and wine.

St. Gregory's practice of encouraging laypeople to serve in this role was controversial among traditionalists: Most Episcopal churches required parishioners to take a formal course, complete with mimeographed worksheets and mandated study guides, to become licensed "lay Eucharistic ministers" who distributed communion. That seemed more like the Department of Motor Vehicles to me—and less like Galilee, where Jesus just grabbed random strangers and told them to feed the crowd.

Meanwhile, ordained Episcopal deacons—whose vows, in the Book of Common Prayer, required them to "serve all people, particularly the poor, the weak, the sick and the lonely"—were frequently treated as second-class clergy, low-ranking and generally unpaid assistants good mostly for handling the menial tasks that priests were too important for. As a result, many ordained deacons were defensive of their position and possessive of their tasks: St. Gregory's practice seemed to many of them to imply a lack of respect, at best.

But as a newcomer, I didn't have anything invested in tradition. Besides, I liked the idea of *deaconing* as a verb rather than *deacon* as a title or an identity. Basically it sounded a lot like the old days—restaurant work—to me. I'd come in early, set the table, light some fires, prepare the meal, serve it, and clean up afterward. I'd have special work clothes and help choreograph service for a room full of people, and my feet would probably be sore. I'd have colleagues—priests and cantors and other deacons—with whom I could stand around, share professional shoptalk, and bitch about the public. "A motherfucker," Chef Robert had described the public. "Brood of vipers," as the Bible said.

And since I still felt shy on Sundays, having a job seemed like a good idea. So I started to deacon. I put on the vestments, those stupid tie-dyed robes, and discovered, once again, the joys of invisibility conferred by a uniform. I listened to incredibly detailed instruction from Rick Fabian, who wanted everything done perfectly. "It can*not* be done that way," he scolded me early on, when I lit the wrong candle, and I almost cried. But I memorized the chants and speeches in the twenty-page deacon's script. I spoke prayers aloud. I sang. It felt somewhat like a performance, complete with postliturgy critiques and constant script revision by Rick and Donald, who wanted to make sure every word spoken during services would communicate the essence of St. Gregory's approach to hospitality.

In fact, they had just commissioned an expensive new altar that physicalized their philosophy of open communion. It stood alone, in the center of the rotunda: Hand-built of gorgeous, polished hardwood in the style of an early Palestinian altar, it was inscribed in gilt letters with two quotations. The first, in Greek, from the Gospel of Luke, recorded an insult to Jesus: "This guy welcomes sinners and eats with them." On the other side of the altar were the words of the seventh-century mystic Isaac of Nineveh: "Did not our Lord share his table with tax collectors and harlots? So do not distinguish between worthy and unworthy. All must be equal for you to love and serve."

I set the Table with a bright, heavy African cloth and put out the plates and chalices. I carried the loaves of bread and flagon of wine to the Table and stood there in my robes amid a crowd of singing worshippers as young kids played underneath it. I lifted up the vessels as the priest sang "Holy gifts for holy people." And then, one Sunday, I had to pass the body of Christ to the people around me—the body of Christ.

"Jesus welcomes everyone to his Table," I recited, "and so

we offer communion to everyone, and to everyone by name." I broke the bread, big chunks from Tom's round wheat loaf, and put a piece in the hand of the person standing in front of me, and looked at her. Something happened, again.

What happened once I started distributing communion was the truly disturbing, dreadful realization about Christianity: You can't be a Christian by yourself.

While I'd been lucky to discover a church where I liked the liturgy, and while I was beginning to feel comfortable among some of St. Gregory's less reverent members, I couldn't count on it. Sooner or later, if I kept participating in communion, I'd have to swallow the fact of my connection with all other people, without exception.

Just like the strangers who'd fed me in El Salvador or South Africa, I was going to have to see and understand the hunger of other, different men and women, and make a gesture of welcome, and eat with them. And just as I hadn't "deserved" any of what had been given to me—the fish, the biscuits, the tea so abundantly poured out back in those years—I didn't deserve communion myself now. I wasn't getting it because I was good. I wasn't getting it because I was special. I certainly didn't get to pick who else was good enough, holy enough, deserving enough, to receive it. It wasn't a private meal. The bread on that Table had to be shared with everyone in order for me to really taste it.

And sharing it meant I was going to be touching Christ's body at St. Gregory's, through Donald and Rick and the angry older deacon with the clenched jaw. Looking into Christ's eyes outside of church, through the cheery atheist yuppie with the sports car and the veiled Muslim clerk at Walgreens. Listening to Christ's voice in other churches, through the middle-aged woman with the annoying nasal whine, and the self-righteous homophobic radio evangelist, and the conservative African bishop. I was not going to get to sit by myself and think loftily about how much Jesus loved me in particular. I was not going to get to have dinner, eternally, with people just like me. I was going to get communion, whether I wanted it or not, with people I didn't necessarily like. People I didn't choose. People such as my parents or the strangers who fed me: the people God chose for me.

I ate the bread.

Conversion isn't, after all, a moment: It's a process, and it keeps happening, with cycles of acceptance and resistance, epiphany and doubt. As I struggled with bread and wine and belief over the following year at St. Gregory's, it stayed hard. I began to understand why so many people chose to be "born-again" and follow strict rules that would tell them what to do, once and for all. It was tempting to rely on a formula—"accepting Jesus Christ as your personal Lord and savior," for example—that became itself a form of idolatry and kept you from experiencing God in your flesh, in the complicated flesh of others. It was tempting to proclaim yourself "saved" and go back to sleep.

The faith I was finding was jagged and more difficult. It wasn't about abstract theological debates: Does God exist? Are sin and salvation predestined? Or even about political/ideological ones: Is capital punishment a sin? Is there a scriptural foundation for accepting homosexuality?

It was about action. *Taste and see,* the Bible said, and I did. I was tasting a connection between communion and food—between my burgeoning religion and my real life. My first, questioning year at church ended with a question whose urgency would propel me into work I'd never imagined: Now that you've taken the bread, what are you going to *do?*

Chapter 10

Seeing More

—

It sounds way too pretentious to say that I had a vision. But standing at the altar, week after week, flooded with hunger and gratitude, I began seeing a picture. It looked sort of like Sunday communion, when, as I wove in and out of the crowd with other deacons carrying the bread, with a hundred voices singing around me, I could sometimes glimpse what Saint Gregory of Nyssa had termed "the harmony of that motion . . . the whole of creation rejoicing." Everything was happening at once during communion. And yet, as one of the deacons told me haltingly, it could be astonishingly intimate despite the music and the kids underfoot and people saying "the blood of Christ" over and over as they passed the wine. "Like being the center of a wheel, feeling utterly still and grounded while they're whirling around me," the deacon said. "Like there being a little bubble around me and the person I'm serving."

As my church life went on, I felt as if I were leaning forward, trying to make out images from across a room. I'd seen a blurred photo taken at St. Gregory's of the congregation dancing around the altar with the circle of saints dancing above, the whole lit by candles. That was close. But at the edges of my vision was something even bigger, brighter, noisier. There were more kids and way fewer white people. And my picture was centered on food.

Of course, the whole city was centered on food: San Francisco was possibly the most food-obsessed place in America. My brother had left New York restaurant work to become executive chef at a culinary school in Vermont. His interns begged to work in San Francisco; his graduates settled gratefully among the oyster fanatics and organic strawberry farmers. San Francisco's fanciest restaurants had become glamorized as high culture, with chefs as local pundits and celebrities. Even neighborhood cafés offered baby mâche salad and grilled fennel, lavender crème brûlée and pedigreed beef. All over the city, gleaming boutique markets displayed the perfect organic peach, the rarest handmade goat cheese, twelve different kinds of artisanal bread. There were stores that sold only chocolate or only virgin olive oil or only rare coffees. It was foodie heaven.

Yet access to food varied drastically by neighborhood: Some poor areas were served only by corner liquor stores selling cigarettes, Slim Jims, and potato chips, and in the ghettos, it seemed easier to buy drugs than to find a fresh tomato.

I lived among Central American immigrants in the Mission, a gritty neighborhood full of bougainvillea, beauty shops, and gangs. I wouldn't at all have minded starting my days at any one of the elegant patisseries across town, enjoying café au lait and an ethereal *gougère*. However, my block was home not to chefs and wine snobs but to Salvadoran refugees and extended Nicaraguan families; they mingled in the Mission's streets with white Jehovah's Witnesses, Palestinian shopkeepers, black teenagers from the housing projects, Filipina mothers doing home health care, and Chicano security guards with tattoos and big gold crosses.

They ate poor people's food: *nacatamales* made in someone's kitchen, wrapped in banana leaves, and sold out of a Crock-Pot on the counter of a corner store; *pupusas* from the "Mexi-catessen," where women patted them out by hand over huge griddles; dollar burgers from McDonald's and greasy "Indian pizza" from the Punjabi pizza place. There were trucks selling cheap tacos full of beef or brains or stewed pork innards; pickups piled with bruised oranges and watermelons from the Central Valley; guys pulling little coolers stuffed with Baggies of nopal cactus or sliced-up mangoes. Food was everywhere in this part of San Francisco; yet I'd learn that hunger was also real.

Each morning when I took Katie to school across the street, I'd see drug dealers and day laborers, the guy selling *paletas* from a pushcart, the seamstress opening her shop: working people, I assumed, not destitute. Then, once, Katie's teacher pulled me aside. Because I worked at home, writing and editing, I was usually around during the day and sometimes stopped by to chat with her and the other teachers. "See that boy?" she said, indicating a short, neatly dressed kid putting away his knapsack in a cubby. "We went around the circle last week saying what we would do with three wishes, and he talked about food and how he wished they had more of it in his house."

Virtually all of Katie's classmates were eligible for free lunch. But that didn't give them enough to eat at home. And there was no lunch program for people such as the day laborers, small, dark Mixtec immigrants who thronged the nearby boulevard by the paint store, trying to flag down passing cars, hoping for someone to hire them for a few hours of painting or yard work. I'd drive by and see them, wearing jeans and windbreakers, shifting from foot to foot to stay warm in the fog as the day passed. They'd be there at noon, at two, at four, at six thirty when the paint store closed. Once I saw a group of laborers with homemade signs demanding *JUSTICIA* in large letters: The cops had been trying to sweep them away, and a local organizer had convinced the men to stand firm. Katie and I went to the supermarket and bought big bottles of soda and some packages of cookies, and dropped them off on the makeshift picket line, and everyone came running.

I could walk from the Mission to Potrero Hill, where St. Gregory's was, in about half an hour. The back way, past the county hospital and up a steep, narrow road, landed me smack in the middle of another hungry place, the city's second-worst housing projects. Potrero Terrace and Potrero Annex weren't as bad as it got in San Francisco, people told me, but they were made uglier and more shocking by contrast with the million-dollar homes just four blocks away, dotting the other, white side of Potrero Hill, where St. Gregory's wooden cupola rose.

The projects had been built in an amazing spot: Past an open field of waving wild grasses, you could see the great curve of the Bay, the soft hills of Oakland, and the fog rolling in across the light-splashed city. But they existed in an alternate universe, full of boarded-up windows and broken glass and smashed fences and garbage. Two-story barracks sprawling over more than thirty scraggly, hilly acres overlooking the port, the Potrero projects were built during the Second World War as temporary housing for military families and war workers, then abandoned for generations to the depredations of cynical white politicians, murderous black gangs, crack dealers, bad cops, and the elements. They were almost entirely African American, with a sprinkling of Samoans, Latino families, and a few white women. According to a report by the scandal-ridden San Francisco Housing Authority called "Souls on Board," only 2.3 people occupied each of 606 units. But there was nowhere in the increasingly expensive city for poor people to live, so extended families unofficially shared each apartment, five and six and nine at a time. I knew that thousands of desperate people were jammed in behind the steel doors of "the Hill."

Like many poor parts of town, the Hill had no grocery stores. A couple of Yemeni-owned liquor stores stocked cigarettes, beer, soda, porn magazines, and corn chips; one of them, the M&M market, also sold quarts of milk and did some trade in "fresh sandwiches" made of processed cheese and white bread, sealed in plastic. On the white side of Potrero Hill, there was one upscale organic grocery called The Good Life, which stocked olive bread, smoked salmon pâté, and nice tomatoes. But the nearest supermarket was miles away—too far to walk and a long bus ride for someone juggling toddlers and shopping bags. There was nowhere to buy regular food at decent prices, nowhere to get a dozen apples or a sack of potatoes. So many in the projects were fat and suffering from diabetes. Most of the kids lived on chips and ramen noodles from the corner store, and French fries when an older sibling with some cash made a run to McDonald's.

In San Francisco, astronomical housing costs contributed to hunger: I'd seen in the paper that a minimum-wage earner would have to work sixty-one hours a week just to pay the rent on a one-bedroom apartment, leaving nothing to buy food. Anyone who'd been unlucky enough to land here after the tech boom made housing costs soar had trouble: I knew parents who worked two jobs and still juggled constantly to cover meals and clothes for their kids. It wasn't the Nicaraguan countryside: By comparison, the Mission was overflowing with food and wealth. It wasn't the jungle in the Philippines: On the Hill, poor people were fat from getting by on sugar and cheap grease, not emaciated from simple lack of calories. Still, it bothered me to see the moms counting out pennies at the Cala supermarket checkout or trying to bargain for soft fruit at the corner store; it worried me the way Katie's friend Jessica would linger every evening at our house as supper approached.

I don't remember why I bothered to look at the junk mail: maybe because the word *food* caught my eye. One day, I dumped a pile of it on the kitchen table and opened a standard fundraising letter from the nonprofit San Francisco Food Bank. "A 1999 report on hunger in San Francisco," it began, "found that more than 90,000 people in the city—the majority of them children and women with families—live with the threat of hunger. Since then, the number of fixed- and low-income families forced to choose between rent, health care and groceries has been growing." The leaflet was pretty well written, which surprised me, and it continued on, describing the Food Bank's new program of neighborhood food pantries:

> The San Francisco Food Bank works with nearly 400 local churches, community groups and agencies to provide food resources for the poor. Most of these groups run soup kitchens or emergency shelters that serve meals. But women and working families tend to avoid soup kitchens, and often go hungry instead of taking their children to meal programs at shelters. To more effectively meet the needs of hungry families, the Food Bank is starting a city-wide network of neighborhood food pantries. Set up locally, food pantries provide groceries, not meals, enabling families to prepare food in their own homes. Food pantries can help keep families together, and give them a sense of normalcy and dignity as they work to escape poverty.

It was the abundance of American agriculture and the vast excess in the food system that made the work of food banks possible. U.S. agricultural policy allowed farmers to hold their product off the market to support price, meaning that when production increased, farmers could plow food under or feed it by the truckload to cattle instead of putting it on the market. This excess food—along with any fruits and vegetables that didn't meet the criteria for the perfect, unblemished, and standard-size produce retailers wanted—was gleaned by the food banks.

There was a national network of these nonprofit warehouses, I learned, called America's Second Harvest, and for more than twenty years, they'd been collecting donations of surplus food from growers and grocers and manufacturers. In the 1980s, after a recession combined with Reagan-era cuts in public welfare programs, food banks were a start-up, activist response to what was perceived as an emergency affecting the homeless. But hunger had persisted, becoming entrenched among the working poor—even as cheap fast-food proliferated and millions of pounds of fruits and vegetables kept being plowed into landfill each year. Now hundreds of established, professionalized food banks, such as the one in San Francisco, collected nonperishable goods and fresh produce, bought wholesale staples in bulk, and resold all the food for pennies a pound, delivering it to nonprofit agencies and churches that ran food programs.

That picture in the back of my head was getting clearer. It was communion, after all, but with free groceries instead of bread and wine. With the "everyone" of "Jesus invites everyone to his table" extended, so that more sinners and outcasts could share the feast. With the literal bread of life served from the same table as the bread of heaven. This is it, I thought, what I'm supposed to do: *Feed my sheep.* I phoned the Food Bank and, panicking slightly as the words left my mouth, introduced myself in a way I never had before. "I'm Sara Miles, from St. Gregory's Church," I said. "I'd like to talk with someone about starting a food pantry."

The director of the new food pantry project at the San Francisco Food Bank was not a patient woman; when I called to schedule a meeting with her, she said, "Tomorrow?" Thin, blond, and intense, Anne Quaintance had been working on issues of food and hunger for more than a decade in San Francisco; she had an utterly clear-eyed and unromantic analysis of the nonprofit and government agencies she worked with. I met with her a lot, and each time, we'd get swept up in conversation about politics; it had been years since I'd talked with an activist who could so sharply articulate both the big picture and the way things really worked on the ground. "The food world," Anne said to me once, briskly, "it's all evil. We're on the good side of evil, I guess, but we're right here in the middle of it."

As assistant director of programs, Anne was struggling with how to get more food out where it was needed. "Donors love pictures of cute little kids having snacks at school," she said. "And they support meal programs for seniors. But nobody's lining up to say, Gee, I want to put food in the cupboard for really poor black mothers who use drugs; I want to buy groceries for everyone living in the projects. Very few donors trust poor people enough to just give away food without conditions."

Anne held a dim view of charity kitchens that kept poor people waiting in line two or three times a day just to get a meal ladled out. "They're convenient for staff," she said, "but they take away people's dignity, and they reinforce dependency. They're

about control." In addition, she said, institutional meal programs, such as those in school lunchrooms, tended to provide
unhealthy food that was fast to make—bologna sandwiches on
white bread, instant mashed potatoes, canned fruit cocktail.

Anne helped explain the contradictions I'd noticed already in
our food-crazy city. Her analysis of food politics was one of the
few I'd heard that focused on the poor instead of on the purity of
ever more rarefied and expensive organic products. Surrounded
by abundance, poor people had trouble buying food that really
nourished them. Fat was cheap and filling, vegetables were complicated and scarce, so salt, grease, and sugar reigned. Obese
kids ate corn chips and soda for breakfast; ninety-nine-cent
hamburgers and soda for lunch; fries and soda for dinner—with
liberal helpings of candy, potato chips, and soda in between. Old
people crippled by diabetes sat in front of their televisions and
ate ramen noodles, four packs for a dollar. Teenage moms gave
their babies orange soda and their toddlers government cheese.
"You know," Anne told me, "well-fed people like to say, 'Oh, if
you're hungry enough, you'll eat anything.' That's probably
true, at some point. But it's not good for people. It's wrong."

So Anne had dreamed up the "Neighborhood Grocery Network" of food pantries and was trying to launch as many new
pantries as she could. Pantries, she argued, were cheaper than
meal programs, because they didn't require a lot of staff or big
kitchens; there was less waste and fresher food. What she called
"client choice" was at the heart of the thinking behind the food
pantry network. Provide a range of healthy groceries, let people
choose what they want, allow them to cook their own meals: It
was a simple and empowering idea.

Anne had driven me around, talking nonstop, to see a few of
her successes. In the Mission, the world's oldest hippie—a sweet

guy named Tree with a stringy gray ponytail—gave away groceries to a couple of hundred people each week on the sidewalk in front of a Lutheran church. In the Potrero Hill housing project, Anne had helped a group of women set up a pantry in an unused shell of an apartment. The rangy, gap-toothed woman in charge there looked at me carefully when we were introduced. "St. Gregory's?" she'd asked. "Right down the hill?" I wondered aloud if it might be too much to have two food pantries in the same neighborhood. "You could give away food every day of the week up here and it wouldn't be too much," she said, showing me the beat-up white refrigerator full of lettuce and onions in the corner of the room. "We always run out."

Anne said she thought St. Gregory's, located so near the projects, and not far from the Mission, would be a perfect spot for a new pantry. "Are you up for it?" she asked, grinning.

"Absolutely," I said, absolutely unsure.

Charity had always slightly creeped me out: There was nothing quite as condescending as the phrase "helping the less fortunate" rolling off the tongue of a white professional, as if poverty were a matter of luck instead of the result of a political system. As a left-wing activist, I'd shared the skepticism of my comrades about the "faith-based charities" that provided scanty cover for a conservative agenda.

And yet, I reflected, in a time when the new administration was embracing what could only be called "a preferential option for the rich," any direct action that actually helped poor people seemed not superfluously "charitable" but radically necessary. A food pantry might even turn out to be the kind of hands-on political work the Nicaragua brigades had been: a way not only to provide concrete help but to empower poor people, giving them the opportunity for direct action.

And there was that vision of a Table where everyone was welcome. Our neighbors, friends and strangers, were hungry. The very least a Christian church could do, for starters, was feed them.

Chapter 11

"Good Works"

—

But first, I'd have to talk with the church.

As a congregation, St. Gregory's members had largely focused their energies on music, liturgical reform, and art, leaving what one lay leader sneeringly called "good works" pretty much alone. It surprised me that a place so innovative liturgically, so liberal theologically, and so committed to welcoming strangers would be so lackluster when it came to activism.

Lee Thorn, a self-described "fucked–up–PTSD–alcohol–drug–Vietnam vet," had launched his own ambitious reconciliation and community development project with a Laotian village he'd bombed decades ago, but he was impatient and angry and had a hard time working with other St. Gregory's members. The church in general tended to support healing the sick and feeding the poor in places located far away, through Episcopal Charities, though, once a month, a few members actually drove to a nearby Catholic Worker house and made soup for the homeless. The tiny community outreach committee held a lot of meetings, at which its members argued with one another about politics, and talked about the need to write "mission statements," and complained that there were never enough volunteers, and then scheduled more meetings.

Dave Hurlbert, a shy writer who called himself "a failed Southern Baptist," explained it to me. He'd been a full-time gay rights and AIDS organizer in London before moving to San Francisco and joining St. Gregory's, then a tiny close-knit community of about fifty members, where he was scandalized by the lack of ordinary, regular activism. "I mean," he said, "the Catholics feed people, the Methodists feed people, the Holy Rollers feed people. At St. Gregory's, we have great community dinners—everyone brings, you know, pasta with truffle oil—but we don't feed people who aren't like us. We're all arty and overeducated and terrified of people who are different."

Dave told me about one early foray into community outreach, soon after the new church was built on Potrero Hill: A member suggested that St. Gregory's "adopt" a poor family from the nearby projects. "*So* patronizing," said Dave. "The mother would send the kids to Sunday school, and somebody would drive them back to the projects with a bag of groceries." He laughed, embarrassed. "The preciosity of it—our little black family. Thank God we stopped that."

So he'd begun volunteering at the Catholic Worker soup kitchen and soon was organizing his arty St. Gregory's friends to hand-decorate a thousand Easter eggs for the homeless men who ate there. St. Gregory's put the coffee urn right on the altar after Mass, and Dave started making sure people brought real food to share at coffee hour.

Dave heard that I was considering doing something with food and poor people, and he took me out to lunch at Zuni. It was a warm afternoon, and we sat in the gleaming, spacious room drinking white wine and eating the most sublime French fries I'd ever tasted, hot and salty and fragrant.

"Well, my dear," said Dave, after I'd described the idea for a food pantry and prodded him for a while about the possibilities for getting it going at St. Gregory's. He was unfailingly polite and didn't express his opinions directly unless pushed. "You don't want to go too fast and not have the support you need. It would be dreadful if this fails—bad for you and bad for the church." He offered me a bite of his Meyer lemon soufflé. "The desserts are exquisite here," he said.

"But really," Dave said, "I'll do whatever it takes to make this happen. You are filling in a word in God's crossword puzzle."

I called up Donald Schell. I still wasn't quite sure of the protocol surrounding priests, so I stood rather awkwardly in his office while he finished typing something furiously on his laptop. "Um, Donald," I finally said, "this sounds really strange, but I think I'm having a vision."

He glanced up, unperturbed. "Well, what does it look like?" he asked.

I spent months trying to organize the pantry. Later Donald would tell me that "for some reason, I trusted you and knew this was going to happen." But he was more aware than anyone of the resistance I might encounter, and he decided not to weigh in actively but watch what happened in the parish when I brought my proposal forward.

He smiled when I told him I'd been inspired by the new Table, with its inscriptions. "That altar was extravagant—six thousand dollars or something," he'd remember later. "And then you came and said, fine, now let's use the Table to do what it says." Donald sighed, recalling his anticipation of a fight. "I thought, wow, this will be interesting. We just spent all this money on an altar, and now we're gonna bring in people who will scuff it?"

At his suggestion, I wrote an open letter to the staff and the church's governing board, the vestry, setting forth my idea. With the annoying enthusiasm of the new convert, I informed them that, according to the Gospel, there was nothing to fear.

Then I explained what Anne Quaintance at the Food Bank had told me about her ambitious plan to open food pantries all around the city. I described the logistics of the pantry: how I imagined that it could work at St. Gregory's.

I told the vestry that first we'd distribute flyers in schools and clinics, advertising the pantry and letting people know that everyone was welcome. Once a week, we'd shop at the huge Food Bank warehouse: beans, rice, pasta, cereal, and snacks would cost us fourteen cents a pound; bread was two cents a pound, and all the fresh fruits and vegetables were free. Anne estimated that it would cost us about a dollar a week to provide several bags of groceries for each pantry visitor. That was just sixty bucks to feed sixty families: A few dollars a month from every member of our congregation would run the food pantry for a year. I said I'd raise it myself and wasn't asking for any money from the church budget or collection plate.

All the groceries we bought at the warehouse—several thousand pounds—would be loaded on pallets and delivered to St. Gregory's the next day by the Food Bank truck. Then, I said, we'd set up tables encircling the altar, unload and lay out the food right in the center of the church, and offer it to whoever came until it ran out. We'd set up a sign-in sheet on a table outside, so we could welcome everyone by name and keep count of how many we were serving. We'd invite them in, five or six at a time, to walk around and choose the groceries they wanted. As the first group finished, the next group could enter and shop. We'd have volunteers greeting visitors and helping at the tables and keeping things orderly as we went along. And yes, we'd make sure we cleaned up thoroughly at the end.

The main thing, I said, was that the food pantry, as I envisioned it, was another way of doing church—though one that didn't demand belief or expect people to pray. It wasn't a social service program but a service, modeled on the liturgy of the Eucharist. So we weren't going to spend time inventing "intake forms" or "means tests" to keep the wrong people out, because Jesus welcomes everyone to his Table. Because, as the inscription on our altar reminded us, he ate with whores. Because none of us "deserved" communion, and we still received it every week.

Similarly, I assured everyone breezily, we weren't going to have trouble finding help. I argued that St. Gregory's already organized dozens of lay deacons to feed bread and wine to all comers at Mass, three times a week, and a food pantry would be far easier to run than our complex liturgies. Volunteers would help out at the pantry for the same reason they became deacons or bread bakers or choir members: not because they wanted to go to meetings but because they wanted to *do* something, be part of something. And, I said, I wouldn't be surprised if some of the people who came to eat stayed to help out: After all, that's what had happened to me.

I even quoted Rick Fabian back to himself. "Do not shrink from the person beside you, the shoulder ahead of you in procession," he'd preached in a sermon that I'd read reprinted in the church newsletter. "Feel Christ's body there; feel the shoulders of humanity. . . . God has made these people into Christ's body for you to caress, to anoint, to comfort, to give and receive and share affection. These people and the human race outside our church doors."

Donald suggested a meeting with the church's community out-reach committee. The perennially overwhelmed woman who co-ordinated it was blunt. "Fund-raising is difficult," she said. "This whole committee basically consists of me and two others. That's all the time and energy that we have been able to muster. We're getting burned out. We will not be able to raise anything like sixty dollars a week."

I was secretly relieved: The last thing I wanted to do was go to more meetings or have the community outreach committee, which couldn't shake itself out of inertia, direct my work. My suspicion was that committees in churches served the same pur-pose as committees in other institutions: They were holding tanks for people who professed interest in an issue but didn't always want to act. I favored the jump-in, personalized, occa-sionally dictatorial method of organizing: Why spend months coaxing a perfectly worded position paper on hunger and service out of a committee when you could just grab some helpers, buy some food, and give it away? Why try to fix the frazzled, depres-sive committee members instead of just hustling the money myself?

So I met with the parish staff. One of them called me sympa-thetically after I presented the proposal. "Well," she said, "we discussed the food pantry idea after you left, and I'd say the re-actions basically ranged from 'Over my dead body' to 'When hell freezes over.' "

Donald sent me a summary of the objections, with a pream-ble saying that he was worried about "polarization" over the proposal for a food pantry. The staff had reasonable enough worries: What if we became a magnet for hundreds of poor, crazy, homeless, potentially dangerous street people? How were we going to decide whom to serve—what if people came who didn't really need the food? What if thieves started coming back after the pantry to steal from us? And how, by the way, would I possibly raise enough money to pay for feeding all comers? How would our nice neighbors react to crowds of hungry strangers from the projects on St. Gregory's steps? What would happen if I couldn't recruit enough volunteers? How were we going to deal with the mess, and damage to the sanctuary floor, and security, and garbage, and the risk of damaging our beautiful icons and art and the new altar?

But my new friend Steve Hassett—a hip young graphic artist who had quit his tech magazine job to become St. Gregory's parish secretary—had no patience with their anxiety. "Twenty more minutes of blather in staff meeting today," he reported, "about what if poor folks start coming around asking for food when the pantry isn't open." Steve had pale skin, a swoop of very black hair, and a high forehead; he and his girlfriend lived near me, in the Mission. "I wanted to ask them, What the fuck would Jesus do?"

I took the proposal to the congregation, asking members to write me with their concerns and thoughts about a food pantry, so that I could collect all the responses and hold a churchwide meeting to discuss them. "Has anyone spoken up to say this prospect is an insane waste?" one woman wrote angrily. "Why don't fifteen people haul their asses down to Episcopal Charities' already-in-place infrastructure or a half dozen other brilliant projects around this big, fat-hearted city?"

A deacon fired off a scolding note about housekeeping. "We can't keep the church picked up and the kitchen clean as it is," she said. "Nobody ever takes responsibility for putting things away. . . . and now you're talking about having food, garbage, boxes everywhere. Not to mention hundreds of people leaving their trash all over. It will be a total mess."

Really, said another, Sara was new to church and didn't understand the pattern of volunteer burnout. "At first, people are filled with holy fire," he said kindly, "but then they fall away, and one or two people are left. How are you going to keep this going for the long haul?"

I compiled everything, then sent a letter out to the whole congregation, staff, and vestry. "I wanted to send a personal note," I explained, "to let you know why I've been pursuing the food pantry.

"The first time I came to the Table at St. Gregory's, I was a hungry stranger. Each week since then, I've shown up—undeserving and needy—and each week, someone's hands have broken bread and brought me into communion.

"Because of how I've been welcomed and fed in the Eucharist, I see starting a food pantry at church not as an act of 'outreach' but one of gratitude. To feed others means acknowledging our own hunger and at the same time acknowledging the amazing abundance we're fed with by God. At St. Gregory's, we do it now on Sundays, standing in a circle with the saints dancing bright above us. I believe we can do it one more time each week—gathered around the Table under those same icons, handing plastic bags full of macaroni and peanut butter to strangers, in remembrance of him."

I was being disingenuous by making it sound so simple—and so holy. No matter how idealistic I might seem to others, I was almost always determined to get my way. "When I first met you," an old New York friend of mine admitted once, "I remember thinking, Damn, this is the bossiest white woman I've ever seen." In order to run our Nicaragua brigades, I'd negotiated around rigid Leninist parties, liberal lobbyists, and dysfunctional revolutionary support groups. I was familiar with how sneakily and screwily power could work in organizations, no matter how high-minded the ideals. And I thought I understood how hard organizing really was. I knew how exhausting it could be to convince just one person to join a movement, much less to stick with mentoring and training and encouragement when the first romantic excitement faded. Now I was taking what I'd learned to organize the pantry, and in the process, I was trying to push St. Gregory's around. Martha was appalled. "You're shameless," she said, after I came home one night bragging about neutralizing some opposition at a vestry meeting. "It's like LBJ just walked into that church. They don't even know what hit them." She looked at me carefully. "Isn't Christianity about being humble?"

Donald, who was used to being guilt-tripped by liberals, called me in for a meeting one day. He hemmed and hawed and finally blurted out, "Rick and I used to go to a whole lot of workshops and present our design for liturgy, and we'd always get, 'You people are irrelevant; you should be out doing good instead of worrying about liturgy.' "

He stiffened, remembering the slight. "It was like we were engaged in a children's tea party, and the real work was elsewhere."

I tried to reassure him. I wasn't going to tell people they *should* do this; I wasn't going to nag them: Instead, I was going to offer them something they really wanted, something they hungered for and couldn't resist. I told Donald that I was just continuing the work he and Rick had started: making a physically expressive, participatory experience of communion, open to all.

I went away feeling manipulative. I *was* manipulative. I felt as shrewd and self-important as any smooth-talking, right-wing evangelist with a political agenda. I knew it was going to be hard for any self-professed Christian to argue against feeding the poor—and especially hard for a church constructed around the theology of welcome to close its doors just because the wrong kind of stranger showed up.

But side by side with all the talk and scheming was this other, unworldly reality. It was like the musical drone that rose up when the congregation gathered around the Table for Eucharist, a complex harmonic humming behind the priest's chant. It wasn't any one person's singing, it wasn't directed, but it filled the room. Somewhere beyond my own cynicism, I believed that the experience of the pantry, like my own experience of eating Jesus, would truly change everything. That the picture I'd seen was real.

Chapter 12

A Different Everyone

—

The first year of the food pantry, my second year of church, would unleash, for me, another level of conversion—this time more powerful because it would happen embedded in relationships. *You can't be a Christian by yourself* was a lesson I thought I'd grasped when I first started serving communion at St. Gregory's, but the conceit of individual salvation remained a powerfully tempting one. Offering groceries to all comers around the altar, I would discover how painfully like church the food pantry really was: how it asked me to leave the certainties of the past behind, tangled me up with people I didn't particularly want to know, and frightened me with its demand for more than I was ready to give.

Looking back, it seems no accident that I launched the food pantry the same week that I was baptized. Now I can recognize that both decisions were part of the same process and involved surrendering my fantasies of individual control. Baptism and the pantry would both carry me through fear into richer, if untidier, life with a wider, more complicated community. They would teach me about hurt and healing and restore to me some of the joy I'd felt working with others in kitchens and on the brigades in Nicaragua. But at the time, I couldn't articulate why I felt so tugged to take these steps: I just knew I had to see what would happen next.

After all the arguments had quieted, St. Gregory's agreed to give the food pantry weekly use of the church: We'd open on the first Friday in November. I made leaflets, in Spanish and English, and passed hundreds out at schools and clinics, in the county hospital, in the projects. *"Do you need more food for your family?"* they said. *"No forms to fill out! No advance registration! No ID required.—St. Gregory's Food Pantry / La Bodega de San Gregorio."*

I gave pitches at Sunday services and wrote little notes in the church newsletter asking for donations; slowly, in tens and twenties, I raised money. A woman in the choir gave me fifty. "We were always hungry when we were kids," she said. A little girl from Sunday school gave me a handful of change. To my chagrin, Martha's best friend, an atheist, wrote me a big check, as did two of the church ladies I'd most scorned.

The Food Bank set up a delivery schedule for us. I ordered cases of rice and beans and cereal. "What if nobody comes?" I asked Anne Quaintance nervously.

She looked at me for a moment as if she were trying not to laugh. "Um, I don't think that's going to be your problem," Anne said.

I got promises from six church members that they'd work with me. They weren't altogether the ones I would have chosen, though mercifully the smarmiest help-the-less-fortunate couple didn't volunteer. Tom, the bread baker, who wore long earrings and a kilt with his shaggy gray beard, stepped forward. "Feeding people isn't complicated," he said dourly. "I've done it at the soup kitchen; I can do it here." Dave Hurlbert gave me money and offered to "twist arms" to get whatever support I needed. And a strong, silent butch with a high-femme girlfriend pulled me aside after the service one Sunday to volunteer. "You know," she said, "I'm so grateful to have something to give now. I remember how people I didn't know helped me when I was trying to get off drugs and alcohol." She smiled, embarrassed. "I don't care if we give food to folks who don't look needy," she said. "I didn't always look like I needed help either."

Thirty-five people showed up on the food pantry's opening Friday to get groceries, and I watched, proud and nervous, as they walked around the altar choosing their food. Steve Hassett and I had laid out the prettiest altar cloths on some folding tables and stacked them with celery and apples and potatoes. There was a table for Cheerios, one for ramen noodles, and one by the door piled with loaves of sandwich bread. "It smells good in here," Donald said, walking in and sniffing. "Like a grocery store."

The Sunday after the pantry opened, I was baptized.

I'd been thinking about baptism since I'd read Rick Fabian's article in which he argued that baptism should be a conscious choice made after receiving communion, not a prerequisite to sharing the meal. And I'd read Donald's thoughts on the theology of baptism expressed by St. Gregory's architecture, where the font was a huge boulder set "beyond the Table, out the far door of the church, literally outside the church walls. . . . For many of us, from our first welcome to Jesus' Table, we find ourselves drawn to follow him in his baptism, going beyond the church walls to wash away, as he did in his death, everything that separated him from any person, even the worst or most desolate."

That was it exactly: I felt myself being drawn. Yet choosing baptism seemed like a betrayal of my parents, who had tried so hard to protect their children from Christianity and its discontents. Of course they could have gone along with my grandparents' fervent wishes and had us sprinkled as babies: So many people did, even without particularly believing. At St. Gregory's, I'd already deaconed at a couple of baptisms for strangers who never came to church but seemed to feel they should baptize their infants, just as they should be married by a priest, as a ritual gesture, a protection amulet, to somehow make things official. But my parents had refused because they didn't want to pretend, and it had cost them. "Of course," my mother had told me once, sadly, "your grandmother would have loved it so, so much if we'd baptized you."

Now here I was, an adult, with an irrational yearning for it— almost a hunger. The idea seemed dangerous and seductive, and I'd tried to resist it. I'd stand there at the Table, looking out the doors at the rock font, and try not to see the water spilling forth.

I impetuously called Mark, my Lutheran friend, and asked if he'd be my godfather. I told Donald I wanted to be baptized. Then, full of dread and superstition, I backed out.

At Donald's suggestion, I phoned Lynn Baird, one of the priests at St. Gregory's, and told her I couldn't go through with it. Lynn wore sandals with brightly colored socks; had long, dangly earrings; and believed in healing prayer. She said things like "Thank you, Jesus!" By every outward appearance, Lynn should have been too much religion and way too much California for me, but when I called, weepy and tormented, she was reassuringly matter-of-fact.

I told Lynn nobody had properly "catechized," or prepared, me for baptism. I still didn't understand the Trinity or the Immaculate Conception or the Nicene Creed. I wasn't sure I could honestly sign up to be part of the official "one, holy, catholic, and apostolic" church. I wasn't ready to become a "real" Christian.

And I was scared.

The faith I'd found since coming to St. Gregory's, I confessed to Lynn, was centered on food and eating and bodies, and behind the immediate physical delight of communion was something scarier, something that couldn't be prettified or sentimentalized. I was signing up, after all, for a religion with a tortured man at its center.

In my explorations, I'd read a book called *Torture and Eucharist,* a long, scholarly examination of the church in Chile during the dictatorship, which opened up memories of the wars I'd covered. Intellectually, it gave me a new way to understand Eucharist, as the knitting-together of a broken community, the reconstruction of a collective body dispersed by violence. But the most evocative part of the book for me was simply the title. Those words, forced together like that, evoked both hurt flesh and shared bread—the murdered, disappeared Jesus and the living, incarnate God in our mouths.

I knew, in my heart, that baptism wasn't about purity or the washing away of sins. It wasn't going to protect me from anything. Like carrying a child, baptism would require going deeper into mystery and darkness, into eating and living, eating and suffering, eating and dying. It would mean being baptized into the crucifixion of the world, as Saint Paul wrote, "into Christ's death . . . into the tomb with him."

Of course I was scared.

"Honey," Lynn said. She was chuckling. "Just look at the

baptismal vows in the Book of Common Prayer. See the first
line? 'Do you desire to be baptized?' All you have to do is want
it."

I wanted it so much.

The prayer book called baptism the "sacrament of new
birth" and promised that those sealed by anointing at baptism
would be "marked as Christ's own forever."

I wanted new life, as fiercely as I'd wanted a child in the middle of a war. I also knew that I could slip into the same kind of
romantic daydreams about baptism that I'd had during preg-
nancy. Sometimes I'd felt so uplifted by the thought of becoming
special, "marked as Christ's own," that I'd forget I was just one
of millions of people making a promise to suffer and to love.

And I knew the water couldn't magically reconcile all the
pieces of my life. My baptismal day would have been my father's
seventy-third birthday: I'd never know what he would have
thought of it, and it broke my heart. I still couldn't bear to tell
my mother what I was planning, and that filled me with sadness.

But oh, I desired it.

"Okay," I told Lynn. I gave up.

So, that Sunday morning, Donald Schell poured water over
my head from a scallop shell, as I stood outside St. Gregory's
back door at the fountain, where sweet water gushed from a
huge, split-open slab of rock. He made the sign of the cross, motioned Mark and the people around us to pray, and asked me to
make some promises. "Will you continue in the breaking of
bread?" he read aloud.

"I will," I answered, "with God's help." We sang a hymn and
walked back into the church. My face was wet.

Nobody gets baptized alone. I walked out the doors to that
rock in St. Gregory's backyard because of the prophetic witness
of a dead man, because of a cup of milk on a hot morning in a

Salvadoran slum, because beloved friends and total strangers had carried faith for me in the war years when I was unable to feel it. I walked out because of my missionary grandparents and my atheist parents and Martha, who wasn't afraid to pray. I walked out because somebody had been tortured and murdered, and because Katie was alive and beautiful.

I'd mentioned my work in El Salvador to Donald earlier and talked with him about Martín-Baró and the wars, and he came up to me after the service. "Wow, I never baptized anyone who'd been catechized by a martyr before," he said. "You had a really long catechism."

Once the food pantry got going, I spent all day at church on Fridays.

Serving at the pantry evoked muscle memories for me of long-ago nights on the restaurant line: hard lifting, sore feet, companionship. I'd help lug and haul literally tons of food in an afternoon, heaving fifty-pound sacks of potatoes, pushing industrial garbage cans full of spoiled onions into the reeking basement, sweating like a horse. I'd bend and lift and drink too much coffee; curse with my coworkers when the rush hit, wipe my dirty hands on my apron, and go home to discover huge purple bruises up and down my legs.

But the work also reminded me of what I was doing at church on Sundays: not just serving a crowd of people at the altar without spilling wine on them but trying to look past the ritual into their eyes. "Yeah," said Steve, who deaconed with me and also helped out at the pantry. "Isn't that freaky? When you actually see inside them. Like this God stuff is real."

With those first half-dozen volunteers from St. Gregory's, I'd unlock the church gate in the late morning. By noon, a huge truck from the San Francisco Food Bank would arrive with shrink-wrapped pallets of food, as much as three tons of it. We unloaded the pallets, set up a ring of tables right around the altar, and turned the rotunda into a big, messy farmers' market, with piles of vegetables and stacks of bread spilling under the icons and next to the silver crosses. From two until five, we gave out groceries. Most weeks, each visitor could walk out with five pounds of potatoes, some onions, a bag of oranges, pears, grapes, squash, tofu, lettuce, rice, beans, a box of cereal, a box of cookies, two loaves of bread, and some pasta. Often there were extras: milk or cottage cheese; bagels still warm from a wholesaler; even, once, an eight-foot tower of boxed trumpet mushrooms, fragrant and wild-smelling.

We set up a table outside, to greet people and check them in, entering their names in a big book. "There's always this look," said Susan Kellerman, one of our volunteers, "when I tell newcomers they don't need ID, I just want to know their name." She'd hand each person a number, in random order, and a snack; another volunteer would call out numbers, and, ten at a time, people would come in to pick out their food. We lit candles and put an icon at the door, serving everyone who came without exception, just as we did during the Eucharist.

It was a different set of "everyone" than I saw at church on Sundays. The first week, we had thirty-five; the next, fifty; and within three months, we had close to two hundred people walk through our doors each time we held the pantry. I remembered Anne at the Food Bank telling me not to worry about a shortage of clients, but it was amazing how quickly news spread by word of mouth.

A long line would form on Fridays in front of the church, beginning hours before we opened. While other volunteers finished unpacking the groceries, I'd go outside and talk with people in the waiting crowd: At least half my conversations were in Spanish. Here was the city I lived in, at last. The pantry wasn't hushed and pious; it was loud and holy. As the whores and cripples, widows and foreigners and thieves and little children gathered outside, it took on an almost biblical atmosphere.

There were a lot of extended Latino families, with fussed-over chubby babies wrapped in pink acrylic blankets. There were black grandmothers from the projects nearby and a beautiful deaf woman with her three kids. There were homeless crackheads and street kids and a couple of schizophrenics; a bunch of old Moldavian ladies in head scarves; Russians with gold teeth; chain-smoking Chinese men in jackets. There was a hyper, skinny black man who danced compulsively to the music on his headphones, whirling around on the sidewalk, shouting out "Love ya! Love ya!" over and over. There was a very sick prostitute and her faithful friend, who'd sit on the steps sharing cigarettes. There was Phil, the speed freak; and Michael, the big scruffy British guy; and Nirmala, the radiantly calm Chilean woman—all three of whom would later become volunteers themselves. Nirmala chatted easily with me. She lived serenely in a single-room-occupancy hotel, over a bar, on disability. "I'm not happy," she told me, "but I'm content. Content is deep."

I knew a bit about Nirmala's past: Raised by her grandmother in Chile, she'd been brought to Texas as a troubled teenager, suffered terrible depression, had a child, and abandoned her. "I mostly remember feeling overwhelmed, unable to keep things together," she told me. "I had problems with men, I felt inadequate, I couldn't keep a job."

I sat down with Nirmala once and asked her to tell me about her conversion twenty years ago, when she met a Hindu guru and in a dream received a "call" to go to his ashram in the Catskills. Like me, she'd never expected to run into God; like me, the discovery had propelled her into physical work. "I learned so many things in the ashram," Nirmala said. "How to cook, how to run a hall with five hundred people, how to sing in Hindi. I discovered I could work sixteen hours a day, an opportunity very few people get."

She laughed. "I'd never been in the snow before, but they gave me a job driving a van in the winter. I'd be up at four in the morning, scrubbing the snow off the van in this strange place, in the cold. I loved it. I was taking care of lives that depended on me.

"It was an awakening. I found that I was perfect the way I was."

I imagined running into Nirmala back when I lived in New York. I would have seen her as a cult member, possibly crazy, at best a harmless fool. I wouldn't have had the patience to talk to a spaced-out flower girl from an ashram any more than I would have been able to listen to a Jesus freak hustling me with tracts on a street corner. I wouldn't have been ready to hear what Nirmala was teaching me now about religion: that it meant becoming more tolerant, less interested in the distinctions among believers, and ultimately more accepting of suffering.

"Then what?" I asked. Nirmala gave me a sad smile. We were about the same age, and there was a lot she didn't feel she had to explain. I knew that she'd left the ashram, fallen for another bad boyfriend, then into drugs for a while; that she still endured depression.

"I lived with complete acceptance in the ashram," Nirmala said finally. "When bad things happened after that, I understood things in a different way. You know how it is, honey. We're not going to sainthood here, we're just on a path."

Where had the people like Nirmala been, all the years that St.

Gregory's was holding services and trying to entice worshippers, one or two at a time, into its experimental liturgy?

The people who came to get food at the pantry had been, to regular middle-class churchgoers, basically like Jesus—that is, invisible. We knew they were there, but we couldn't see them, and their sufferings and loveliness were imagined, not incarnate in a specific body.

But as I got to know them, I started to see more clearly how the people who came to the pantry were like me: messed up, often prickly or difficult, yearning for friendship. I saw how they were hungry, the way I was. And then, I had a glimpse of them being like Jesus again: as God, made flesh and blood.

Chapter 13

Church of the One True Sack

—

My conversion was not stopping. I was being drawn more deeply into a community, finding another way to understand God through people I didn't know. An older Latina woman sat down with a sigh on a chair at the edge of the rotunda one day that first year of the food pantry. "I just like to come in here and get some peace," she explained to me. We sat together companionably, gazing at the mural of the Dancing Saints, as kids ran around and volunteers shouted to one another. I knew what she meant.

The atmosphere of St. Gregory's drew people in: They came looking for something to eat, but often, like the woman seeking peace, or like me, they really wanted far more. I'd be lifting a box, in the noise and bustle, and someone would come up to me—a grieving mom, a lonely immigrant, a sick man, or any of the many varieties of crazy people who hovered around the pantry. "Will you pray for me?" they'd ask.

This was what I'd told St. Gregory's, after all: that the pantry would be church and not a social service program. Such sudden intimate requests shouldn't have surprised me, if I genuinely believed that we were extending communion through groceries.

But I felt awkward nonetheless: It was more than I had bargained for to confront these demands in the flesh. It was still hard enough to pray on my own, to let my mind open, to wait. Praying for someone else raised all kinds of questions: What right did I have? What did people think they were getting? What if I said the wrong thing? "It's not mysterious," Lynn Baird told me. "You just have to be willing to be there, and listen."

So I took a deep breath and began praying with anyone who asked. I didn't know then that I was also praying for my own conversion, to reach the next level of conversation with God. I'd get people such as Ed, a filthy white guy with long hair who'd frequently flop down on the curb, begging for help. One of our most insane and drug-addicted visitors, he'd sob and rant, in no particular sequence, about the secret lessons of First Corinthians, his imaginary machine gun, his father and the imminence of the Day of Judgment, the evils of the VA hospital, and his pressing need for healing prayer. I'd sit down on the sidewalk with him and wipe his nose. "Oh God," he'd say, "I can't go on like this. Help me, help me." I was sort of fond of Ed, despite his hysteria, so I'd pat his stringy arm and murmur until he calmed down a bit, then fetch him a snack, make the sign of the cross on his dirty forehead, and send him on his way with a few bags of food.

Or I'd get Miss Pollen, a bosomy black eighty-year-old with powdery, soft skin and an amazing faith. She'd lost one daughter to the Jonestown mass suicide and another, quite recently, to cancer; she lived alone and visited pantries to get enough to eat, but when she asked to pray with me, what she wanted was to offer me strength. "Don't fear," she'd say, kissing me. She'd take my hand, earnestly. "Never fear, Sara. We got a rock in Jesus. Solid rock."

I had a woman grill me about God's purpose, as if I had inside information and could arrange a better deal for her; I had a man plunk his severely disabled child down next to me and start to weep uncontrollably; I had an acquaintance blurt out a confession of her affair and suicide attempt. I'd feel bored and try to look attentive; feel skeptical and try to sound confident. For fifteen minutes, I'd try to actually listen to another person, letting myself be whatever was needed: the bowl of soup, the forgiving mother, the magic minister, a warm body.

"It seems really hokey sometimes," I said to Lynn.

"I know," said Lynn. "But big deal. You just have to be there."

So I'd sit down next to people and let them talk or cry; I'd listen and put my hands on them; at some point, I'd pray aloud, without really knowing where the words were coming from. It felt homey, not mysterious. But it usually made me cry, too.

It was like the experience of being pregnant in El Salvador—or, for that matter, the experience of eating a piece of bread and finding myself to be just another rather hopeful and screwed-up adult hungry for meaning. If my carefully calibrated difference from others wasn't the vitally important thing about me, then my identity was going to be bound up with all kinds of other people at their most vulnerable and unattractive. If I wasn't busy scoffing at believers for their gullibility, and I wasn't afraid of being sentimental and pious; if I didn't mind looking stupid or being a sucker for a hard-luck story, then I was probably going to cry when someone else showed me, even for a few minutes, her own weakness. It was my own weakness, my own confusion and hunger; it was everything I couldn't be sophisticated and together about. Of course I was going to weep, and pray, with her.

"God," I said once, with my hands on a middle-aged couple who'd found sobriety a little too late for their daughter, a bitter and broken girl whose life had been made hell by her parents' drinking. They were fervent AA members now and were doing pretty well. But they were consumed with guilt about their child, much as I was about the years my daughter had been lonely and worried while I battled my own troubles. I could still remember, so clearly, the terrible month when my best friend, Douglas, was dying and Katie's father had moved out. I would drag myself out of bed, feed and dress Katie, drop her off at day care, get carefully back into the car, and howl. Did I think I'd hidden my eyes puffy from crying? How could I undo the terror a four-year-old must have felt, sensing her mother's fear? And yet Katie was thriving now, unafraid and sunny. I had to believe that the hurt places in her, and my inadequacies, were not defining who she could become. That our lives were not about avoiding pain at all costs but about going through it, together, and finding gratitude for the experience. "God," I said, after a long time of sitting there with my hands on the couple. "Thank you for healing. For new life, after all. And thank you especially for the dark years. Thank you for everything that works in the dark."

I could tell that my praying at the pantry made some other people nervous: A seminarian told me that to see me "laying on hands" was uncomfortable, since he associated the practice with "exotic" charismatics and evangelicals. Furthermore, he worried that nothing in the Episcopal Book of Common Prayer "authorized" what I was doing. "Have the priests formally extended responsibility for this procedure to laypeople?" he asked anxiously.

People made up the priests they needed, I told him: Some would insist on calling me a "minister," no matter what I said to correct them, and go away convinced they'd been blessed by an ordained priest. Others, who'd been burned by bad religion, only felt comfortable praying with a layperson, someone who looked like me, wearing jeans and a dirty T-shirt. But authorization to pray, touching people as a "procedure," looking to official rule books and clerics to tell you how to act—this was what was wrong with religious life, as I saw it. It was like requiring "authorization" to give someone a sandwich. Here was the food, here were my hands: As Steve had said, "What the fuck would Jesus do?"

We were making a church. "Church of the One True Sack of Groceries," Steve said. "The Jesus Christ Love Shack," I said, "and House of Prayer for All, alleluia."

I thought about the visiting minister who'd approached me one Friday with a compliment about "your wonderful food program."

"It's not a program," I'd said immediately and confidently, surprising myself. "It's a community of prayer."

Just as St. Gregory's encouraged laypeople to serve as deacons in its liturgies, at the pantry, the people I thought of as "pantry deacons"—our volunteers—weren't a select or professional group. And fewer and fewer of them were from St. Gregory's. They were unofficial: visitors who came to get groceries and then stuck around to help. They were more often than not misfits: jobless or homeless or a little crazy or just really poor. They'd stand in line for weeks, then one day ask if we needed a hand. The next week, they'd show up early, and the next, they'd be redesigning our systems, explaining to me how things could work better. Little by little, these new volunteers were beginning to run the pantry.

I saw myself in them: I'd stumbled into church a misfit, too, a lesbian mother with a patchwork of freelance jobs. I'd never gone through official channels—college classes or culinary school or journalism school or seminary—but stayed on the edges of things, moving among professions and countries, pretending I knew what I was doing. But I had yearned to be of use.

So I identified with the new volunteers. My favorites, unsurprisingly, were the ones who turned out to have backgrounds in restaurant work: cooks, waiters, expeditors. Even if they were down on their luck, or getting over drug habits, they knew how to work hard. They were funny, they were fast, they liked to eat, and they ignored the sanctimonious church people who hovered anxiously, afraid that things would get out of control. Lawrence Chyall, a tall, bookish guy with decades of work as a restaurant maître d', dropped by on his day off. Calm and unflappable, he organized our chaotic line outside, dealing with hungry poor people as graciously as he did with rich, cranky customers. "It's all about 'Your table is ready,' " he said.

Lawrence started coming to church on Sundays. It wasn't long before I asked him to think about serving as a deacon in St. Gregory's services. "Wow," I said one afternoon at the food pantry, when he gently talked down an offended black woman who was insisting at the top of her lungs that someone had stolen her place in line. "Have you ever thought of taking a chalice? You'd be a natural at deaconing."

Lawrence demurred. "I'm not a good enough person to stand up there in front of everyone," he said. "I'd have to be a whole lot more holy." I laughed. "The thing about serving," I told him, "is that it's not about you."

Dave, an unemployed cook, had just planned to pick up some groceries the day I recruited him. I was outside, trying to chat with Christa, the lady with the bright pink hair. I could hear one of our meanest drunks shouting and being nasty to people at the end of the line. I went over and asked if he wanted food. "Hell yeah," he snarled. I could tell he really wanted, badly, to hit me.

An enormous black guy started to come over, protectively.

"I'm Dave," he said. He had a walleye and a shaved head and a vast neck; his voice was amused and gentle. "You need help?" I told Dave no, it was okay, and walked the drunk away from the line, telling him I'd get him some food. When I came back out with the groceries, the drunk was sitting down on the curb, and he'd yanked up a handful of pansies from our garden and was holding them out to me, roots and all. "Here," he slurred, "for you. I like you. These are for you."

Dave was cracking up. I could imagine him, in a restaurant kitchen, laughing and shaking his head at the customers. Next to him was Christa, preening. "Christa," I said, "your hair looks nice. Did you do it yourself?"

"Me and Jesus," said Christa.

"Wow, Jesus is a pretty good hairdresser," I said.

"Yeah, and he's cheap, too," Christa told me earnestly.

Dave had shot me a huge smile. "The public is a trip," he said. "Sure you don't want help?"

But not all our volunteers had restaurant backgrounds. Homer, a West Indian retiree, was fastidious and courtly, had just ended a twenty-one-year marriage, and was trying, as he explained formally, "to maintain myself on a positive path." He appointed himself director of the bread table and soon had recruited two other older men from his AA group to help out.

"Sure, great," I told Homer, just as I told Phil, the speed freak who'd started coming early to help out. Phil was gaunt, with dirty blond hair and a filthy blue mechanic's jumpsuit; he hated to see me lift anything and would unload the entire truck himself. Usually I'd fry him a couple of eggs—he'd forget to eat when he was on a meth binge—and we'd talk. He reminded me of Michael Wild from my restaurant days: hardworking, self-destructive, bitterly funny. Phil had grown up in a family of cops; now he was in and out of jail a lot but didn't seem to think it was a big deal. "C'mon, I'm not doing so bad," he said. "I mean, I've been doing speed for twenty-six years, and I still got my front teeth." As an old-timer—he was probably forty—Phil liked to bitch about the modern world. "Back in the day," he explained, "when the Hell's Angels used to make the speed, it was clean. Now they put all these chemicals in it, no wonder people get sick."

Starlight Wanderer was another one who'd been following me around for a few weeks, pestering me with questions and asking to help. In name as in style, Starlight was a casualty of the 1960s: She had long dirty hair, a childlike affect, voluminous peasant skirts, and an inordinate amount of fake Native American jewelry. A classic hoarder, with severe OCD that qualified her for SSI disability checks, Starlight nurtured a stalkerlike fixation with the rock guitarist Jerry Garcia, whom she considered her mystical soul mate. One Friday at the pantry, she beckoned me over, then pulled her journal out of a ratty embroidered bag. It was filled with technically amazing and quite psychotic drawings, all done in a superdetailed quasi-psychedelic style and featuring some combination of Jerry Garcia, eagles, doves, sunrises, and beautiful young women.

"Nice," I said.

She turned a page. "Can I tell you something?" Starlight asked suddenly. We were sitting down, over where the pallets were piled up. "My dad used to hit me, so I hurt myself." I asked her what she did when things were hard now, and Starlight looked up at me. "Oh, every time I drink a glass of water," she said earnestly, "I thank God."

If the food pantry was like a cross between a church and a busy restaurant kitchen, it was also more political than I'd expected, reminding me of the brigades. There was the same kind of charged intensity, rising out of the most ordinary interactions of people working together. I felt as if anything could happen at the pantry: A homeless girl could walk in with an iguana on her shoulder, a guy could break into tears and make a confession, a woman could start speaking in tongues. All we had to do was open the door. Hundreds of hungry people would walk in. And in the presence of shared food and the immediacy of such visible, common need, visitors could blurt out anything, open themselves to people totally unlike themselves, act out of character.

Most important, they could envision becoming part of the handmade and activist project they'd walked into: The food pantry wasn't an official organization with a membership list and professional directors, but a compelling, vivid community. They saw all the different people working and suddenly could imagine themselves needed, with something to offer. "I've never done anything like this before," a junkie or a shy church lady or an angry street person could say. "But can I help?"

It was the kind of political practice Martín-Baró had hinted at when he talked about democracy: It meant mistakes, sure, but also the opening up of genuine participation to all kinds of people. We had homeless guys and women with missing teeth and a couple who only spoke Tagalog come join us; a transsexual with a thick Bronx accent, some teenagers, an ancient Greek woman from across the street, and a dapper man from St. Gregory's choir who came and played the accordion during the pantry. They were all people who, like me, had come to get fed and stayed to help out. Who, like me, took that bread and got changed. We were all converting: turning into new people as we rubbed up against one another.

The transformation amazed me. I'd think about it as I unpacked the food: blushing red potatoes and curly spinach and ripe peaches that grocers had discarded, and that instead of being trash were feeding people. Once I picked up a huge grapefruit and showed it to a volunteer from St. Gregory's. "That's the stone the builders rejected," I said, quoting Scripture aloud with only a twinge of embarrassment. I could see, now, how we were like that, too: the volunteers, and the families who came for groceries. Each of us, at some point, might have been rejected for being too young, too poor, too queer, too old, too crazy or difficult or sick; in one way or another, cracked, broken, not right. But gathered around the Table in this work, we were becoming right together, converted into the cornerstone of something God was building.

When church people referred to the pantry as a "ministry," I'd get antsy: The term still sounded cloyingly Christian to me. But Steve, who was considering going to seminary to become a priest, thought it was great. "Hey," said Steve, "look, it's the biggest service St. Gregory's has each week. It's a church. You figured out how the liturgy should go, and you lead it every week. You recruit and train all these volunteers. You do pastoral care, you do administration, you have to deal with the rest of the staff and the building and raising money and take crazy phone calls from your congregants at home. Then there's the spiritual shit on top of it all." He laughed. "You're basically half-time clergy."

"Unpaid," I pointed out.

"Unpaid," he agreed. "I think the term in the church for that is *nonstipendiary*. Sounds more official."

I didn't want to be official: I hadn't been in a classroom since high school, I was used to moving on the edges of institutions, and I was lousy at obedience. Just as with my "unauthorized" laying on of hands, I intended to keep doing the service of the food pantry unless someone forbade it: I couldn't see stopping just to get professionally licensed.

Steve was right, though: We were serving more people at the pantry on Fridays now than at all the Sunday services combined. We had more volunteers. We even had our own vestments: I'd bought some red aprons, printed with bright yellow letters. "St. Gregory's Food Pantry," they said. "Peace on Earth, and Food for All." Passing the leftover bread and wine around during coffee hour after church on Sundays—"More Jesus?" I'd ask politely—I'd mention that the Eucharist continued on Fridays. "Same Table," I'd say. "Come feed and be fed."

Donald Schell still looked slightly alarmed when he walked in on Fridays and saw the compost bin next to his altar, the unkempt strangers with keys to his building, and the messy piles of flattened cardboard boxes by the baptismal font. But he made the leap: The pantry was church. "Come here," he said, at the close of one day. He beckoned me into the sacristy, where the parish register, which recorded all services, was kept in a huge, old-fashioned book. "Write down the number of people who come each Friday," the priest instructed me. "And the names of all the servers."

But it was the unofficial nature of the pantry that I really loved, nothing that could be written down in a ledger: the giddy sense that we were being propelled forward, almost too fast to be afraid, by a force as irresistible as the one recounted in Matthew's Gospel. I read the story about the loaves and fishes and thought about Jesus gazing at the hungry crowd, saying to his anxious, doubting, screwed-up followers: "*You* give them something to eat."

So we did.

Chapter 14

Gleaners

—

The food pantry was suffering from growing pains, and I was suffering from spiritual jet lag. I'd discover that, sooner or later, every church in the world faces the tension we were beginning to feel, torn between offering a safe, personal-scale refuge and remaining small, or growing fast and losing our sense of community. "God glorifies the stranger" was at the center of the pantry's ethos, and St. Gregory's. But how many strangers could we really absorb? It was far more than a logistical problem, though I thought about logistics obsessively, revisiting each Friday in my mind, replaying conversations, problem-solving our systems. It was a spiritual question: Who were we for? And, at the heart of it: What was the meaning of feeding people?

The food pantry had climbed rapidly to serving more than two hundred a week. "Poor folks' radio," explained Homer. "See, you get one Russian, then next week there's ten of them. You get one of them guys who camps under the freeway, and he tells all his buddies."

I didn't mind the homeless people at all; most of them lived in

tents or broken-down vans underneath a nearby freeway over-
pass and liked to chat when they picked up groceries. "Cool,"
said a smelly young guy covered in homemade tattoos, when he
saw our icon mural. He pointed at the image of Saint Seraphim,
painted next to an upright, dancing bear. "That bear's all dancing," he said, shaking his head. "That bear's doing the *mambo*."

I didn't mind the kids. Sometimes they came smiling shyly,
wearing their parochial-school white blouses and black pants,
led by the hand. Sometimes they came leaping and pushing and
shouting, finally freed from the middle school across the street,
slinging off their backpacks and chasing one another around the
front steps.

But I hated the Russians. Bent, stubborn, shaped like mail-
boxes, with caved-in peasant faces and babushkas, they pushed
and argued and grabbed with the skill of people who'd spent
their lives in line waiting for inadequate food. Only two women
spoke any English at all, and the rest would simply shout more
loudly at me in Russian if I didn't understand their complaints.

"He is saying you no justice," explained a middle-aged
woman with dyed red hair. "You give more bread to black people, not to him."

"He already took three loaves," I said. We were standing in
the church doorway, and Homer was trying to explain the limits.
"Three," he said, holding up three fingers. "There's only three
loaves per family."

The old Russian man leaned into my face, breathing garlic
and tobacco at me, wagging his finger and yelling something.

"He very hungry," said the woman.

"Sorry," I said.

I wasn't. "Jesus didn't have to deal with the fucking Russians," I said bitterly to Steve.

"Yeah, they're always sneaking around trying to get over on me, too," he said agreeably. "What're you gonna do?"

Maybe we just needed to get more food. I went to the Food Bank, hoping to find some answers from people who'd been doing this work for a long time. A huge glass-and-concrete structure in the industrial district at the foot of Potrero Hill, the state-of-the-art warehouse soared more than seventy feet tall, stocked to the rafters with shelves bearing leftover, discarded, superfluous food donated by grocers and wholesalers. And none of it would keep forever. All this food was in transit: on its way either to pantries such as ours where it would turn into someone's supper or to the landfill where it would become just more trash. The excess in the system amazed me: so many thousands of cases of bread about to be wasted, so many tons of fruit waiting to spoil.

I felt at home in the warehouse. I was always happy to be thinking about food on a giant scale, to be poking around in walk-in freezers and joking with guys in aprons. And I was happy to know a place where nobody thought it was a big deal that I wanted to give away more food to hungry people. The people who worked at the Food Bank were not all Christians, but I saw them as people matter-of-factly living out the central Christian imperative to share food with strangers.

At the front desk, a small, neat black man in a blue smock was talking with his coworker. "Hey, Arthur, Eddie," I said.

Arthur was in his fifties, trim and alert, a black man with a salt-and-pepper beard and an eager, engaging smile. He worked the front desk at the warehouse, which meant that he knew the inventory of the entire warehouse inside out: exactly where the most recent pallet of Cheerios was, whether tortillas had come in during the morning, if there were 200 twelve-up cases of one-pound bags of rice left on shelf 27, aisle A. "Hey, Sara," Arthur said, smiling. "Make yourself at home." He pushed an opened bag of chocolate Kisses across the counter. "You hungry?"

I took one and an order form. Each week we ordered "purchased product," the staples that the Food Bank bought wholesale and sold to agencies at fourteen cents a pound. I checked off St. Gregory's list: 275 pounds of rice; 10 cases of dry pinto beans; 25 boxes of the strangely named "Smack Ramen" noodles, in chicken flavor. I added a pallet of cereal, telling Arthur we'd take whatever he had 250 of, and crumpled up my tinfoil before reaching for another chocolate.

"Breakfast, my dear?" said Eddie, offering me a Tootsie Roll. Eddie had recently been promoted from volunteer coordinator to warehouse manager. A short, ambitious Latino guy who'd worked as a driver when we first opened our pantry, Eddie had always paused to look at the icons, ask questions, and talk with me about his longings for spiritual sustenance when he delivered St. Gregory's pallets. He didn't really go to church anymore, he explained; his Guatemalan girlfriend was a Catholic but left as a teenager after she'd been humiliated by a priest for having a baby out of wedlock. Eddie was raising the boy and said he thought the important thing was "just to love people. I mean, just love people, isn't that the commandment?"

"Anything for health," I said now, taking the candy. "Hey, Eddie, what's new on the floor?"

On the floor of the Food Bank lived "donated product," also sold at fourteen cents a pound: aisles crowded with pallets full of the food that manufacturers couldn't sell or supermarkets had overstocked. Donating food was essentially a break-even proposition for manufacturers: They made as much in tax write-offs by giving it to the Food Bank as they would by selling it to a secondary discount marketer. The inventory, unlike that of the purchased product, changed constantly: A month after Easter, there were little neon yellow marshmallow chicks, and in January, cases of leftover holiday cranberry sauce.

I grabbed a flatbed metal cart loaded with a dozen empty cardboard boxes, and Eddie started walking with me. "Here's some crackers your folks might like," he said, pointing at a tower of Triscuits. "There's no more cookies left, but check around the corner for those granola bars you had last week." I picked up a narrow, foot-long box. "What's this?" I asked. "Italian importer," said Eddie. "Breadsticks. They gave us Italian candy and some of those panettones, too."

I knew the Food Bank rejected truckloads of soda and processed sweets each week, but there was still an amazing amount of junk on the floor. I thought about the Wahoos. For nearly four months, the Food Bank warehouse had been crammed full of thousands of cases of what looked and tasted like extruded Styrofoam pellets, in pale orange ("Seasoned Original") or bright orange ("Backyard BBQ") flavors. The Wahoos took so much floor space that there was little room for other snacks and were an example of the kind of food that seemed a waste from its very beginning: What could possibly be gained by giving away bags of this salty, greasy, puffy fakery? "Sometimes I think it's a plot," Anne Quaintance told me once, only partly kidding. "The manufacturers test-market these shitty snacks on us, to see if poor people will eat them, and then if it's a hit, they stock them in the ghetto stores." Wahoos, however, were not a hit: Even our middle-school kids, whose appetite for junk food was bottomless, wouldn't eat them a second time. By the end of the Wahoo era at the Food Bank, Arthur was pleading with us to take away extra boxes for free.

I made my rounds, pausing at the shelves of USDA canned goods. These, like food stamps, were part of the federal government's strategy for helping farmers, by subsidizing the production of food and distributing excess to the hungry. But St. Gregory's pantry didn't take USDA product, even though it was free. Arthur had tried to push me, but I was stubborn. To begin with, it seemed crazy to give people canned green beans when we could give them five or six different kinds of fresh produce instead, for free. And to give away a can of USDA beans, we'd have to ask for a signature and proof of identity. "So many of our people are immigrants," I'd explained to Arthur. "Anytime you put 'government' and 'sign your name' in the same sentence, they get nervous. Anytime you ask for ID, they disappear. It's not worth it." He'd shrugged. "Whatever," he said. "Long as you got enough food."

I moved on, stepping delicately around a pyramid of pasta boxes. I piled my bread and snack selections into boxes and then pushed the cart back to the front desk and the floor scales. After it had been weighed, it would be put on pallets along with our purchased product and produce, wrapped up tightly, and put on a truck for delivery to our pantry the next day.

"Nine hundred twenty pounds," called out Eddie, weighing it. "I pulled the rice and beans and ramen already, and I'll tag the cereal for you. Go do your produce, then I'll check you out."

I always had to search the aisles for Calvin, the produce guy who packed up our fruits and vegetables, sharing whatever came in each day from the farms among all the agencies and pantries. St. Gregory's received between two and three tons each week, depending on what was in season. Calvin was shorter than I was, and thin, and was always wrapped in a huge jacket and a wool hat against the cold of the walk-in. Unlike Eddie and Arthur, Calvin was a loner, terse and barely cordial. But he lived in the projects on Potrero Hill, and he made a point of telling me each week what he had saved for us. "I heard about St. Gregory's," he'd said to me once. "I know what you do."

Three times a week, huge refrigerated semis would drive up to California farms and load up with dozens of different kinds of produce. Paul Ash, the executive director, had studied agricultural economics before coming to the Food Bank nearly twenty years ago; a tall, elegant man with piercing blue eyes, he'd explained to me how the system worked. "Logistics, pricing, movement, production," Paul said. "Agribusiness operates like General Motors . . . except that, in a way, its job is to hold back. It can produce any amount it wants, but if it does, it'll destroy itself. So you get these huge distortions all through the system, from tariffs on the international side to price supports to big farmers so they won't grow too much to people throwing away food to keep the prices high.

"And us," said Paul, "we're sort of scavengers, looking for ways we can use the excess."

Even protected by price supports, California's growers were dependent on constantly shifting weather and supply for their living. A good year for peaches could mean a big drop in price, as the market flooded and tons of fruit rotted before it could be sold. Donating extra produce to the Food Bank gave farmers a tax write-off and protected them from having to sell it too cheaply or plow the food under.

"Crop by crop, it really differs," said Paul. "Our orange connection developed from a finance guy at one of the huge packers, this giant agribusiness in the Central Valley, who saw oranges being thrown away, and it drove him crazy. We said, hey, we'd love those in the Bay Area, and he saw an opportunity to reroute the food. We made it easy by providing the bins and being there on time with a refrigerated truck."

Similar deals with other growers meant an essentially endless supply of oranges, lemons, grapefruit, peaches, pears, nectarines, cherries, tomatoes, melons, corn, plums—all the bounty of California's vast Central Valley—and then the coastal cool-weather crops of lettuce, chard, spinach, broccoli, onions, strawberries, and artichokes. "I feel bad for food banks in, you know, New Hampshire," Arthur told me once. "We've got so much here, and all year long. People from other states, their eyes pop out seeing what we give away on an average day. Our only problem is getting it picked up, into the warehouse, sorted, and out the door to you guys fast enough."

Since 2000, Paul explained, the Food Bank had begun dealing with growers as far away as Idaho and Arizona. "We work through Second Harvest, the national network, to hook up with an association of potato growers in Idaho. We grease the skids a bit: We pay a couple of cents a pound—nowhere near wholesale, but what they'd get if they sold it for cattle feed." He smiled. "We're simply a part of the market."

I spied Calvin zipping around the packing room on his forklift, maneuvering gracefully around pallets of potatoes. "Cal!" I called out, and he drove over, nodding curtly at me. "Got lettuce, potatoes today, some loose onions," he said, leaning over and wiping his face with a gloved hand. "Cabbage, loose pears." He brightened. "I got some grapes, too," he told me, "if you can use four hundred pounds."

I followed Calvin into a cavernous room where volunteers were sorting oranges on a conveyor belt and boxing them up. The grapes were in the corner, in waxed boxes. "I got to get rid of these by the end of the week," said Calvin, "because we're starting to get more citrus in, and we won't have room. Can you take them?"

I looked at the grapes: They were dark purple and firm, without any mold. "You know we'll always take fruit," I said. "Even if people don't have kitchens, they can use fruit. Give us the grapes, and if you have extra oranges, we'll take those, too."

I tried to keep track of our order. We'd been running out of produce lately at the pantry, and I wanted to make sure there'd be fresh food left for latecomers.

"There's hot peppers in the walk-in," said Calvin.

"Five boxes," I said.

Calvin reached into the pocket of his stained jacket. "Here," he said, handing me a tiny tangerine. "These are really sweet." He didn't smile. He drove away, beeping the forklift's horn.

Once I'd asked Paul Ash if he thought American agriculture was ever going to change, stop overproducing, and put the Food Bank out of business. He'd sighed. "It's a cobbled-together system," he said, "with its roots in Americana—that whole idea of the land, the family farmer. But you know, family farmers get less than half of a percent of agricultural subsidies. Corporate agribusiness gets all the welfare—it's addicted to those subsidies. Agriculture's much more about finance now than it is about farming, and I don't see that changing anytime soon."

To feed the hungry with the excess of an unfair system: to make bread out of injustice. It was like the Bible verses that instructed people how to leave food for gleaners: "When you reap your harvest in your field and forget a sheaf in the field, you shall not go back to get it; it shall be left for the alien, the orphan, and the widow."

At the front desk, as I waited for our printout, I stood gossiping with Arthur about the rise in the numbers of people coming to St. Gregory's pantry. "Two hundred and sixty people last week," I said, partly to boast and partly to beg for help. "Where the hell are they all coming from? We only had two-ten the week before." Eddie shot me a look. "You know about double-dipping," he said. "Lots of folks go to more than one pantry. You don't check ID, right?"

"I know," I said wearily.

"Yeah?" said Eddie.

I gave him an embarrassed smile. "I mean," I said, "feed my sheep. You know what I'm saying?"

"I know," said Eddie in a different tone. Arthur, who had pretended not to be listening, said, "That's right" under his breath.

"Feed my sheep, feed my sheep," I repeated. "He didn't say, 'Feed my sheep after you check their ID.' "

Eddie and Arthur laughed. Arthur handed me my invoice. "Okay," Eddie said. "Don't worry, sister, we'll get you more food."

So there was plenty of food. We could, logistically, continue to grow. But the social changes implied by the growth in our food pantry hadn't gone unnoticed by the church. Now, whenever a homeless person strolled in during Sunday services, I heard about it. "Dear Sara," read one e-mail, "I arrived early this morning, and there was an intoxicated man sleeping on the church steps. Perhaps this was one of your pantry guests?"

Donald let me know that the wooden floor was getting scratched. Rick couldn't stop worrying about our valuable silver crosses. "Are you remembering to lock the vestry?" he'd ask anxiously. "Anybody could walk in." I'd duck and say something pious, but the neighbors were also getting restless. "You all are doing a noble service, I'm sure," said the guy who ran the warehouse next door. "But there are people urinating in my parking lot and dropping trash in my yard, and I can't keep an eye on everyone." The manager of the brewery was less kind.

"We can complain to the city, you know," he snarled at me. "We have visitors who come for tours, and your program is scaring them away."

Meanwhile, the lines at the pantry were getting not just longer but angrier. We opened at two in the afternoon, and by noon, there'd be more than a hundred poor people outside, arguing and complaining. We checked them all in, writing their names on a master list, which had grown to nearly a thousand. I still wanted to blame it all on the Russians, but in fact, the Russians were being overshadowed by a new influx of elderly Chinese immigrants, who were twice as pushy. The black Americans were disgusted by the Chinese ladies. "Those people don't even know this is a house of God, how they act," one woman snorted. The Latinos warned me about the black guys. "They're delinquents," a man whispered to me in Spanish. "They live on welfare and don't work." Everyone yelled at the crazies. The simple fact was that too many people were coming for food.

I came home one weekend afternoon to a series of panicky e-mails from my volunteers. "Friday was insane," one wrote to me. "I shouted at people for the first time. It's clear we have to do something soon."

Lawrence chimed in. "Friday was stressful for all of us," he said. "We found ourselves in a very uncomfortable situation at the start of the afternoon when our guests nearly came to blows over the order of the line. I collected myself as best as I could, saying a silent prayer. I looked into the eyes of each person I checked off the list, trying to remember that they were not names on the list but holy people in whom the Divinity was truly present. It wasn't easy."

I called the Food Bank. This time, I talked to Anne Quaintance, not to the warehouse guys.

"Well," said Anne, "you can do what the other pantries do

and just serve people from one or two zip codes, so you can maintain a reasonable size. The idea is to give people food in their own neighborhoods, not to feed the whole city."

I imagined myself standing at the altar as a deacon during the Eucharist, addressing the congregation. "Jesus invites everyone to his Table," I'd recite, "so we invite everyone from zip code 94107 to share in communion."

"That's not how we do things," I told Anne.

"Whatever," she said briskly. "I mean, if it's a religious thing for you or whatever."

"Isaiah in the Bible talks about a heavenly feast where there's room for everyone," I said to Martha. " 'Come all who are hungry,' " I quoted, " 'eat without money or price.' "

"The Bible says lots of stuff," Martha pointed out. We were in the kitchen. Martha, who'd suffered from anorexia when she was younger, had never learned how to cook. "I lived on Scotch and potato chips," she told me once. "I was basically afraid of food my whole life." Now we'd go to the farmers' market together, buy armloads of vegetables, and she'd hang out with me as I chopped and washed and sautéed. She wouldn't eat meat, but otherwise she ate everything with astonished delight, as if for the first time. There was nobody I'd rather cook for.

I gave Martha a forkful of Swiss chard that I'd melted down with garlic and black olives. "Taste and see," I said. Martha rolled her eyes. We'd been arguing about how much time I spent, these days, quoting Scripture, and I knew she was worried I was becoming a fanatic. "I mean, I'm glad you feed people; that's just being a decent human being. But do you really believe all the rest of it?" I set the chard on our table, along with a gratin of leeks. I knew she was right to be skeptical. I wished I could still be that skeptical, too.

I hated to think that there were limits to communion, but once we started serving more than 250 people, patience and attention ran out more quickly than anything else. It was like working in a restaurant: Past a certain number of diners, even if everyone ultimately got fed, nobody got a really good meal. A parishioner with experience in nonprofits e-mailed me some sensible-sounding advice. "One of the biggest challenges for advocates," she wrote, "is to not get overwhelmed by constant growing need. It seems that no matter what we do, there are more people who need help. As tragic as it is, even if we operated a pantry every day of the week, we still could not meet the demand in this city. Given this, it's very important to set a scope of each program at the most optimum level, an optimum level of operation that is strictly adhered to. Beyond that level, a new program (at another location) has to be started if more need is to be met."

In order to cap the pantry at the "optimum level" of 250, though, we'd have to decide which way we wanted to be unfair. We could serve by zip codes: That would mean checking ID. We could check names on the master list we kept and send away first-time visitors, referring them to other pantries. That would mean limiting ourselves to a "club" of people who had been visiting our pantry the longest: I couldn't imagine a practice that would more effectively refute the theology of welcoming newcomers. But the alternative was to just buy food for 250 and run out, which, though it initially appeared fairer, was just as exclusive. Serving the first 250 people would turn away anyone who worked and had to come late, the least aggressive, and the weakest. It would also encourage people to come even earlier and form a longer line.

I was miserable: The sensible nonprofit advice seemed hollow and hopeless. All the options seemed wrong, a perversion of communion and the spirit of the pantry. I'd wanted to do something unambiguously good, make an openhanded, easy gesture of welcome to the poor, and here I was getting pulled back into the muck and compromise of organizational wrangling and political decisions about who "deserved" more. "Maybe we should just cut off at 250 right now," I said. "It's arbitrary, but that's the way things are."

The volunteers refused. "I can't accept turning people away from the Table," said Lawrence. We were leaning on the altar, before the pantry opened, arguing. "Maybe it'll be a little smaller this week," he added hopefully. "It'll be right after the first of the month, and people on disability and welfare will have just gotten checks, so they won't need to come. I think we should pray about it."

"I'm going to see if we can find a Russian translator," said Susan, who worked checking people in. "And a Chinese one."

I had a brief, wacko thought flash through my mind: Maybe God would provide. Back when I wasn't a Christian, the sentiment had sounded delusional. It was insulting to tell the hungry and suffering that God would take care of them, and it was absurd to make plans based on wishful thinking about providence. I shook my head.

"It'll all work out," said Homer. "I'm going to get that guy Michael, the big one who gave us a hand last week. He's got his head on straight, and he can help us with the line."

I didn't imagine, then, how Michael and the other new volunteers would resolve the conflicts we were facing. I couldn't foretell that our prayers would be answered not by heavenly magic but by opening ourselves, insecure as we were, to even more strangers; how wading deeper with them into the dirty water of human relationships would allow us to transcend the logistically impossible. But I couldn't stand to argue anymore. "Okay," I said. "Let's see what happens." I started moving some bags of onions off a pallet, wearily. I hoped there'd be enough for everyone today.

Homer came over to me. "Excuse me, Sara, can you come outside for a moment?" he asked urgently.

"Is there a problem?" I asked worriedly, following him out front, expecting a fight, something broken, someone in trouble. We stood by the church doors, where a dauntingly long line of people was forming, squabbling kids and tired men and old ladies with their shopping carts halfway down the block. Homer waved over at a wall where great purple plumes of California lilac were drifting down over a stand of calla lilies. "I just wanted you to see this," Homer said. "You know, people used to say to me, 'Stop and smell the flowers,' and I never knew what they were talking about."

I walked over and touched the lavender blossoms of the vine, with their tiny green centers. "My grandmother's name was Lily," Homer told me. "I think of her when I see lilies." He smiled at me. "You never know how long any of us are going to be around," he said, "or how long the flowers are going to be blooming, so it's good to take a moment and look at them while we can."

I came back inside. Lawrence was sweeping up some spilled rice. "I'll find more volunteers," he said. "It'll work, you'll see."

It was November: a year since we'd launched the pantry, a year since my baptism. I'd asked Donald if he'd celebrate Eucharist at the pantry for our anniversary and welcome everyone in to worship before we gave out groceries. I'd written the liturgy myself, putting parts in Spanish and parts in English, recruiting deacons, figuring out how the crowd could sing and dance around the tables of food. I'd also planned a "blessing of hands," something St. Gregory's hadn't done before. I'd wanted to offer an anointing that would make explicit the connection between physical work and prayer, between God and what people did with their bodies for others.

I'd invited the Food Bank staff and drivers to come to church for the anniversary, but they all had to work. So the day before, I'd driven down to the warehouse, carrying a little vial of rosemary-scented olive oil in my jeans pocket, and asked, rather shyly, if anyone wanted a blessing. Arthur, standing by the scales, had thrust his hands out at me. "Yes!" he'd said. "Oh yes!" Cynthia, a woman I'd met who directed a food program at one of the Pentecostal churches, came over, too, turning up her palms to receive the anointing. And Eddie had pulled up to us on a forklift, tooting the horn excitedly. "Me, too," he called out. "I really need that." I looked at each of them in turn and took their hands—soft, calloused, warm, damp—in mine. "Arthur," I said, dipping my thumb in the oil and making the sign of the cross on his palms, "every time you touch someone with these hands, may you show them God's love. . . . Cynthia, in all the work you do with these hands, may God's mercy and justice shine forth. . . . Eddie, bless all the work of your hands, and may God keep you in his hands, safe and loved."

Eddie turned his hands over when I was done. "Thanks," he said. He turned his hands over again, examining them. "Thank you." He looked quizzical, flushed, touched. "Eddie," I said, "thank *you*. Thanks for all you do."

As I'd gone out into the city after the anointing, I noticed hands giving me a cup of coffee at the coffee shop. Hands holding hands on the street or stroking a baby's face. Hands putting bread in a bag and opening a door and holding a broom and pouring water and touching a neighbor. I noticed how marking a body as holy made holiness more visible.

But now it was time for the service, and I was in a foul mood.

I'd wanted everything to run perfectly. But the truck had been late with our food delivery, and the waiting crowd outside was getting impatient. Starlight Wanderer was driving me crazy, clinging to me and complaining about her backache. "Starlight, we *have* to get the rice bagged," I snapped, finally. "If you don't feel good enough to work, just stay out of the way." She slunk off, teary. I tripped over a pallet that someone had propped against the altar, banging my shin hard. "Goddamnit," I said. "We have to get the altar set up in fifteen minutes for the service. Why the fuck can't people just keep it clear?" Steve smirked at me. "Hmm, you sound just like a priest," he said.

Donald showed up, and I wanted to be annoyed with him, too, but he looked too good. He was wearing a white alb, the food pantry apron, a splendid onyx cross, and a black-and-gold "I ❤ Jesus" skullcap. Then Lawrence strolled in with a tray of cupcakes decorated with maraschino cherries, and it was pretty hard to be mad at him. I went to prepare the bread and wine. "Use one of the English muffins," Donald suggested, pointing to the bread table, where stacks of them were piled up.

Then Homer, who'd been in the hospital the week before, limped over and hugged me. Starlight came in from the baptismal font, where she'd been bagging rice. Martha appeared, radiant, and she was carrying flowers for us. Then came the Russian ladies with their carts, some Salvadoran families crossing themselves, two punked-out street kids, a confused-looking Chinese grandmother, and then somehow everyone was standing in a circle around the Table, singing the Eucharistic music with Steve leading the familiar, newly resonant prayer. There was a smell of incense and wet cardboard and slightly rotten bell peppers; and fifty voices, out of tune, filled the rotunda; and some little kid was lifted up on a volunteer's shoulders to see Donald break the English muffin. I understood why Christians imagined the kingdom of heaven as a feast: a banquet where nobody was excluded, where the weakest and most broken, the worst sinners and outcasts, were honored guests who welcomed one another in peace and shared their food.

"Let this broken bread and shared wine be a foretaste of your kingdom," we sang, "and bring us finally to your heavenly Table, where no one is left behind, and we will join with saints and angels at the feast you have prepared from the beginning."

Chapter 15

Faith and Politics

—

Even as I was cracking open the door to see the heavenly kingdom, my own country was sliding into what I could only think of as hell. The destruction of the World Trade Center, just a few months before that first food pantry Eucharist, had unleashed a new era in American politics, and I hardly knew what to think about the catastrophe that was developing—here and around the world.

I was sick, sad, frightened. Numbly, after finding Katie and Martha that September morning in 2001, I'd gone to St. Gregory's and propped the doors to the church open, assuming that others would need a place to go, too. They did, over the whole surreal day, and by dusk, a group of strangers had gathered in the rotunda, praying, walking slowly around the altar. This was what it meant to be a Christian for me: that in the midst of undeniable suffering, it was possible to summon up gratitude and praise. "All of us go down to the dust," we sang, "yet even at the grave, we make our song: Alleluia, alleluia, alleluia."

That had been a breathtaking moment, a brief space in which I could feel the violent reality of human life collide with a faith that, beyond the very worst we could do to one another, there was God. When I emerged from it, back into the world of newspapers and phone calls and urgent demonstrations, something had shifted. Becoming a believer seemed to be giving me *less* interest in maintaining a set of rigid beliefs—about God and also about politics.

I don't mean I became a right-winger. I don't mean I slipped into a we're-all-God's-children kind of mush, where I felt at one with John Ashcroft. I stayed furious about the politics of the administration and outraged by the way President Bush invoked God to justify his crusade, as if it were clear to the whole world that God was on America's side.

I couldn't stand the right-wing Christians with their conservative PACs who supported American military might without hesitation. I wasn't exactly surprised: These were the same people whose entire religion was about rules, who maintained a strict set of litmus tests for who would go to heaven. Of course they wanted to separate the world into good guys and bad guys: "Either you are with us," as Bush said, "or you are with the terrorists." But I also found myself impatient with progressive Christians who thought it was enough to proclaim sanctimoniously that they were committed to "peace and justice." Their sloganeering was like taking a perfectly good piece of bread, smashing it into a wafer, then slapping the wafer on your car bumper to prove you were a person with the "right" politics. "War is not good for children," the wafer read. "*We* are the good ones," it meant.

I'd gone to Central America because I didn't think politics was simply a matter of opinion. It wasn't about having the right "line," having an ideologically pure analysis. It had to be incarnate.

And now I was seeing the same thing with faith. It couldn't

be about wrangling over the Bible to find justification for your convictions. Like politics, faith had to be about action.

So much of Christianity seemed to be about claiming sides, about making distinctions, about finding a set of beliefs to cling to that excluded other people or made them scapegoats for all the evil in the world. I read Saint Paul—that misogynist, strict, patriarchal apostle beloved of fundamentalists—and he made me laugh. "For in Christ Jesus," he wrote, "neither circumcision nor uncircumcision means anything. The only thing that counts is faith working through love."

In that dark time, I was inching toward what religious traditions called "orthopraxy" (right practice) rather than orthodoxy (right belief). I was hearing that what counted wasn't fundamentalist theology, or liberation or traditional or postmodern theology. It wasn't denominations or creeds or rituals. It wasn't liberal or conservative ideology. It was faith, working through love.

I could see the limitations of orthopraxy: Certainly plenty of insane right-wingers did ostensibly good deeds, in between spewing vitriol at me and the people I loved and acting to limit our freedom. But whatever others did, I knew *I* needed to do something that wasn't purely theoretical, that at the end of the day made a difference to real people.

I didn't know how I could make that real in the political world of 2002, waiting for war to come crashing through Iraq and the Middle East. I did some writing for my old lawyer friend, who was working feverishly to protect immigrants and Muslims caught up in the post-9/11 sweeps. I wrote a story about the detainees at Guantánamo. None of my tiny gestures seemed to matter.

But faith working through love: That could mean plugging

away with other people, acting in small ways without the comfort of a big vision or even a lot of realistic hope. It could look more like prayer: opening yourself to uncertainty, accepting your lack of control. It meant taking on concrete tasks in the middle of confusion, without stopping to argue about who was the truest believer. Whatever else, I could at least keep working in the pantry, feeding as many people as I could.

I'd go talk this all over with Jeff Gaines, my spiritual director. I'd begun seeing Jeff, at Donald's suggestion, around the same time I started the food pantry. " 'Director' makes it sound like he tells you what to do spiritually," Donald had said. "But it's not like that." He paused. "You're going through a lot of changes, really fast. I think you'll really like having someone to talk to about it all—and someone who isn't a part of St. Gregory's."

So once a month or so, I'd drive over to Jeff's immaculately neat home and talk about God, war, politics, and pretty much anything else that bubbled up. Jeff wasn't a shrink; he wasn't a confessor; he wasn't like anyone else I knew.

Jeff was a Presbyterian minister who said things like "My goodness!" in a sweet voice; he was handsome and trim with a perfectly groomed little beard and had chintz pillows arranged in rows on his sofa. He had a New Age streak ("Woo-woo," he explained helpfully to me, the first time he "invited" me to "visualize" someone "wrapped in light") and was very gentle, in a kind of classical-music-loving, sweater-wearing, great-cathedrals-of-Europe way; he was profoundly devout, really smart, and utterly unflappable. Jeff would ask me what my "prayer life" was like; he'd "invite" me to "dialogue" with Jesus; he'd gently suggest, occasionally, that I read a particular passage of Scripture. "Isaiah, treasures found in darkness," Jeff had instructed once when I was stuck in some bleak hole of doubt. He called me "dear one." I couldn't believe how much I loved him. "He's kind of like your swami," Martha suggested once. "Swami Jeff."

The swami wasn't otherworldly, though. I'd tried, early on, to be pious and chanted for him the little prayer I'd written for the volunteers to sing at the food pantry:

> *O God of abundance, you feed us every day.*
> *Rise in us now, make us into your bread,*
> *That we may share your gifts with a hungry world,*
> *And join in love with all people, through*
>   *Jesus Christ our Lord.*

I'd started to talk about the religious imagery of being bread. "Like I could *be* Eucharist," I said excitedly, and Jeff interrupted. "Um, Sara, dear," he said, "what is this like for Martha and Katie when you talk like this? I mean . . . that's a lovely prayer, but what's going on at home?"

The swami walked me through every bottleneck, upset, and gripe I'd run across on what he insisted on calling my "faith journey." He encouraged me when I despaired of belonging to a faith that encompassed right-wing fundamentalists: "There have always been different ways of being a Christian," Jeff said. "Claim your own, keep going."

He listened as I tried to describe what God was like, what my family was like, what St. Gregory's vestry was like, what it was like to stand in the midst of the food pantry and see my nutty, beloved volunteers moving trash cans around the altar. His listening had something so spacious in it that it became prayer. I'd find myself perched among the throw pillows; lost to my prepared narratives, my big ideas, my plans; gazing at the framed prints over Jeff's shoulder and listening with him.

When the bombing of Baghdad started in 2003, I had to listen for what it was going to mean to be a Christian in a war. Almost immediately, churches around the country took sides, following predictable political lines. At St. Gregory's, though, which I had assumed would be reliably liberal in a nice, reasonable, Episcopalian kind of way, conflict erupted. Leftists such as Lee Thorn leaped up in the silence after sermons to thunder that the church must "take a stand for peace," while more conservative members argued that the United States was right to get rid of Saddam Hussein. Others in the congregation—probably the majority—felt that church wasn't the place for politics and that Christians should stay out of the fray.

I asked Donald about it. "Look," he said, "I could lead this church into becoming a peace activist congregation, but I'm not going to do it. We need to make room for everyone to be heard." I asked Rick about it, and he said something erudite and complicated about the Emperor Constantine that I couldn't follow and then looked at me kindly. "Pray for your enemies," he said. "It's about praying for your enemies."

I asked Jeff about it. "How can I be a part of a church that doesn't *do* anything when there's an evil this big?" It was a rhetorical question.

"Dear one," said Jeff, "you *are* part of the church. You're a part of the whole of humanity."

"Okay, but your buddy Jesus is asleep on the job," I told him. "Look at what's happening to us."

I hadn't physically been in a war for almost a decade, but it was easy for the images coming out of Iraq to take me back, much faster than I had control over, to that place of fear and adrenaline and heartbreak. It wasn't only about politics. I loathed

George Bush and his smirk; I loathed the neoconservatives who had mangled Central America, cynically lied about it, and were now launching new wars. I was horrified by the costs implied by the military's doctrine and the stupidity of its pretense that overwhelming air power could crush an insurgency. But mostly I'd look at the pictures of Baghdad, its skyline in flames, and think about bodies. I called my mother to ask what she remembered from her childhood in Iraq; she was in tears about the park where she'd gone to play one afternoon in 1931. "I remember the gardens," she said.

I kept remembering what a person, one person, looked like, shot. I remembered the sound of a mother screaming as if her heart had been literally ripped out and the shocked, dazed face of a boy who had just killed someone. I remembered standing by the side of a newly discovered mass grave in a field, as barefoot workers pulled up stinking shreds of flesh wrapped in plastic shrouds. Pray for my enemies?

As an activist, whenever I heard church people saying that you had to listen to both sides, I thought they were trying to be "balanced" or broad-minded, above the fray. It made me nuts. It reminded me of the kind of journalism I hated—an on-the-one-hand, on-the-other-hand fetishization of the middle road—and the kind of liberal politics I hated even more, a willfully myopic "fairness" that ignored the real and violent facts of power. How could you not choose sides?

I was tormented. In the context of war, I felt something else looming over my religious practice that wasn't a Lamby-Jesus story, that was as dark as the water of my baptism. I went through my days as if looking over my shoulder—or trying not to.

It was like a storm when God blew in. Once, for no reason, alone in my garden, I blurted out aloud, "Show me, Lord," and then squeezed my eyes shut. I read the part in the Gospel where Jesus told Simon Peter that discipleship would take him "where you do not want to go" and closed the book.

I stopped taking walks for a while, in fact, because every time I was outside, with nobody phoning me or talking, with no radio and nothing to read, the hugeness of the sky and the God behind it would break over my head and make me want to cry. I told Jeff that I was feeling slightly haunted. It was around this time that I dreamed a dark penumbra barely concealing a brilliant light, like an acetylene torch, that I had to look at and had to look away from. *Tremble* was the word I awoke with, and I did, lying there cold and exposed.

"Tremble," said one of my favorite psalms, "but do not despair. Attend to your heart." I told Donald, reluctantly, I'd help design and lead a St. Gregory's "town meeting" about the war. I had an agenda, to be sure: Despite my urge to choose sides, I knew it was important to keep talking across the political divides, if there was ever any broad antiwar organizing to be done. As the war went on, I expected things would become more polarized. The longer the space for conflicted dialogue stayed open, the more time we'd have to become real to one another and form alliances that could last through worse times.

But the town meeting wasn't to be a debate or a forum for political discussion: I felt what we needed was essentially a liturgy, a gathering of a divided community in, as Donald had put it, "a time of lamentation." And I needed to look God in the eye.

And so, on a cool evening, I sat in the church beneath a cross with thirty others, chanting psalms I'd chosen for their difficulty, with long silences in between. "I step on my enemies' necks to destroy them," we sang. "I grind them fine as windblown dust." We waited. "Trapped here with no escape, I cannot see beyond my pain." We waited. "Have mercy on us," we sang. "Have mercy."

In the silence that followed, Lee Thorn stood up. "I'm a vet," he said. He was crying. "My oldest son is draft-age. I can't stand this shit."

Dave Hurlbert stood up. "I can't stand it either," he said. He was trembling. "I used to be a pacifist. I believe to the best of my knowledge this war is the right thing. I think it's horrible, but we have to do it."

It was a long two hours. One after another, people heaved themselves to their feet and spoke: not speeches but testimony, naked and unplanned, until all of our nerves were completely unwrapped, and there was nothing left to say. "Have mercy," we sang.

I'd come away sobered. There were Republicans I really cared for; there were leftists who made my skin crawl. My analysis was familiar: I could see the political value in maintaining dialogue with all of them. But the harder thing for me was listening to unreconciled difference, without thinking about that as a political problem—truly opening myself to people I would prefer to write off.

Being a Christian in wartime, for me, was turning out to be the opposite of having "God on our side." It meant expanding not just a personal capacity to suffer but the personal and institutional capacity to dwell in ambiguity and unsettledness. It occurred to me that the church was a place, maybe the only place, where that could happen.

And it meant not rushing to answer the unanswerable questions about evil with platitudes or turning the awesome mystery of God into a fairy story where everything turns out nice in the end. It meant bearing the real, scary, and unknowable.

"You know," I told Jeff, the next time I saw him, "when I was looking at it from the outside, faith seemed to be about certainty. What a surprise."

Chapter 16

Words and Acts

—

Yet things were knitting together for me in a deeper way: Christian words and acts were beginning to cohere, Scripture and tradition to resonate with what I was actually doing.

There was the every-week rhythm of the pantry and Sunday services; there was my expanding familiarity with the liturgical cycle. It began in the darkness of Advent, as we called out to God to come live with us; through what I thought of as the food pantry's feast day in November, when we marked our anniversary and I remembered my baptism. Then a surprisingly modest Christmas, then the Epiphany, when Jesus plunged into his political life on earth among refugees hounded by Herod's troops.

And then, beginning with the grave, slow marking of foreheads on Ash Wednesday, the whole congregation began walking into Lent. Traditionally, Lent was a time of preparation for the death and rebirth of baptism—though, in many churches, it had become, instead, an opportunity for personal religiosity or penitential sacrifice through giving up video games. At St. Gregory's, and especially the food pantry, Lent was embodied in my experiences with others. I could feel it as more than a metaphor:

Together, at the pantry, we really were turning into a people. We *were* dying, sort of—Homer to his drug addiction, Steve to his idea of a successful career, me to my fantasies of independence and control.

We were dying to our individual selves and becoming a body. It had sore places and unhealed scars; it wasn't perfect, but it was beautiful. It was Christ's body or, as we said in church, a church.

And then, as a church, we entered Holy Week. It was one of the only times during the year that the food pantry volunteers tended to show up at services. Palm Sunday began it, with a dancing outdoor procession of waving palm branches and praise. Maundy Thursday we knelt and washed one another's feet at an evening supper, then gathered in the church on Good Friday night to heap flowers on an icon of Jesus in the tomb. Almost inevitably, Good Friday ended a year in which we would have buried our own: watched a beloved member weaken, fed and cleaned him, stayed in the room as she died, then washed the body, singing. One of St. Gregory's members, a tenor with a brilliant, slightly trashed voice, had grown up in the Middle East, and on Good Friday, in the darkened church, he would chant like a muezzin in a keening wail that echoed through all our experiences: "We bow down to your sufferings, O Lord."

The blowout, ecstatic Easter vigil was the central focus of St. Gregory's. For three hours, until nearly midnight, the congregation sang and danced and listened to the whole story of Christianity, from Genesis through the Resurrection. Like the Greek Orthodox worshippers I'd spotted outside my restaurant door so long ago, we processed through the night around the church carrying candles, then, shouting our hymns of joy, burst through the front doors into a blazingly lit rotunda, hung with thirty-foot swaths of translucent pink silk and fragrant with clouds of incense, for more dancing, followed by a huge feast.

"We have two seasons at St. Gregory's," Rick had said to me—
"Easter, and Easter's coming."

But the holidays and feasts were only part of the rhythm; daily
practice was helping me, even more, to connect Christian words
and deeds. Steve and I developed a half-hour morning prayer
service and started singing it together at eight every day. Sometimes it would be just the two of us and my godfather, Mark,
alone in the church with early light glancing off the icons; sometimes strangers or friends would wander in. Once in a while, Phil
from the pantry would come, hungover or crashing from a speed
run, and sit in his greasy overalls, chanting in a surprisingly
strong baritone.

I loved the sweet, plain singing as we sat side by side in the
quiet church, listening to the birds and the traffic outside as our
own breaths rose and fell and rose. I loved the regularity and the
way, as time went on, we cycled through all the Psalms and
the Gospels.

The Psalms were lodging in my mind, with their complaints
and reverence and ecstatic praise and viciousness: They were
such an accurate mirror of my own conflicted human emotions,
it could be startling. I'd chant, "Caught up in God's beauty"; "I
am tranquil as a child resting in its mother's arms." Then, a few
minutes later, "I groan all night long, must my enemies always
win?" or "Do you create people for nothing?" or "My God, dig
a pit for the wicked."

These clashing voices echoed the cacophony of all the different books and writers of the Bible. Which, I'd heard Donald
preach, wasn't the Word of God. "The Word of God," he said,
"is what's heard by the people of God when the Bible is read."
That meant the Word was living not because it was magical but

because over and over, down the centuries, believers wrestled with texts, adapted them, edited them, interpreted them, swallowed them whole, and spat them out. The stories in the Bible were records of human attempts to understand God—attempts that were hopelessly incomplete. But, through words and acts, we kept trying.

One morning, we went to jail instead of to morning prayer. Phil had been locked up again and sent me a letter announcing the news. "Well well well," he wrote on a grubby piece of lined paper, "my dad always told me boy your going to get in trouble with that temper of yours. Sure would appreciate if your not to busy, come and visit."

In the parking lot for the San Bruno jail, Steve and I stood in the security line with a middle-aged Latina woman, her husband, and three young black mothers in puffy jackets. I was dreading the stuffy waiting room full of restless children, the Plexiglas booths where we'd talk over phones to our prisoners, the sight of Phil in an orange jumpsuit. The pantry volunteers had given me twenty bucks to put on Phil's commissary account, but everyone was getting pretty tired of his chronic problems. I was sick of Phil's letters myself: In the most recent, he'd told me how he'd gotten kicked out of his job in the prison kitchen for stealing.

The woman came over. "It's so cold here early in the morning," she said chattily. "Are you visiting a friend? Your son?"

"Um, someone from our church," I said. "What about you?"

The woman beamed at me. "Us, too!" she cried. "Daly City, Assemblies of God. Do you want a piece of gum?"

And there it was. Not the clubbiness of discovering we were

both from churches. Not the assumption that we were good Christians who shared the same views. It was the offering of the gum. The act, the physical thing in her hand extended toward mine.

It was like the time when a driver from the Food Bank had paused with a pallet jack full of groceries to look at our baptismal font. "That's where I was baptized," I'd told him conversationally. He was silent for a minute. He was an evangelical Christian, someone who probably would be horrified by 90 percent of the liberal waffling that went on at St. Gregory's. "And the thing is," the driver had said finally, cupping his hands in front of him, "he brought water, *water,* out of the rock."

I looked at him. He knew I was gay. I knew he kept a King James Bible in the cab of his truck, because all other versions were heretical.

"Yes," I'd said. "And that rock is Christ."

Any words from tradition that we quoted back and forth to one another, though, weren't the point. Christians could agree or argue about God as much as we wanted, but it was all essentially chatter. What bound that driver and me together was the obvious thing, so plain and dumb between us we could almost ignore it: the rough wooden pallet of onions that organized our days. *Feed the hungry, heal the sick, visit prisoners.* We fed people.

The words I read and prayed, and the different acts of a liturgical year, continued to bounce off one another: walking, talking, carrying plates of food to a table, eating. Somehow the sanctified and ritual parts of church, as I told Jeff, were merging with the parts that reminded me of ordinary life: dinner parties, working in a restaurant kitchen, hanging out with my friends. "It's like there's not really a line between what's holy and what's not," I said in amazement. "Or not such a sharp one."

"That would be correct," said Jeff.

I told him about my first Easter season as a deacon, when I'd been in the kitchen collecting a bunch of stainless-steel bowls for the Maundy foot washing and heard a priest call out impatiently from the other room for towels and basins. The church rotunda was dimly lit by candles, with tables clustered around the altar. There were fifty congregants; we'd all shared a meal together, in the style of a Passover or early home Eucharist, and we were going to take turns washing one another's feet. As I came out from the kitchen carrying my bowl, the cantor began the tune, a slow gospel number, and a few women stood rocking and clapping. "Jesus took a towel and he knelt himself down . . . ," they sang, swaying.

The big bowls of warm water were passed around each table, and I saw Tom from the pantry taking off his socks with a grin to show his scarlet toenails. I turned to face Rick, who was sitting in a chair and singing with an irritated expression: I worried that I'd made a mistake with the words of the opening prayer or used the wrong tablecloths once again. I knelt down before him. "Rick," I said, "may I?" As I unlaced his shoe and slipped his sock off a delicate foot, everything I'd felt for the man rushed through me: admiration, fear, frustration, anger, respect, affection, pity. I cupped Rick's heel in my hand, and splashed the water over him, and then bent over and kissed his foot.

I remembered what a sad, drunken visitor to the pantry had told me once. "Thank God," he said earnestly. "Thank God for Jesus. Because, you know, he was here like us, so he knows how hard it is to be a person. He must have a sense of humor about us."

I couldn't shut up about the food pantry. I talked to strangers I met at parties. I talked to my friends. I even talked to my mother, though I remained paralyzed by the idea of telling her I was going to church. I knew that in other parts of the country, it would sound laughable that a sexual deviant living in San Francisco with a bastard child could be shy about her secret life as a Christian. But afraid as I was of opening up old wounds for her, I knew I could tell her about the food pantry, which she responded to with immediate enthusiasm. "That's terrific," she said warmly. "I'm so proud of you." It would be years before I learned that my grandmother had also had a food pantry at her church.

Then, with a newcomer's nerve, I asked to make an appointment with the bishop of California, Bill Swing, so I could talk with him, too. Bishop Swing was a neat, kindly man with old-fashioned diction and an iron will: He'd served for twenty-five years, pushing a vision of ecumenicalism and international solidarity that would have delighted my grandparents. We sat in his stuffy office above the great stone cathedral atop San Francisco's highest hill. It was hung with oil paintings of previous bishops and had a rich Persian carpet on the floor. I asked the bishop to tell me about bread.

"There's a hunger beyond food that's expressed in food," he said promptly, "and that's why feeding is always a kind of miracle. It speaks to a bigger desire." He crossed his legs and smiled at me.

"The feeding of the five thousand," he said, "the miracle wasn't that Jesus multiplied the loaves. It's that the disciples took the bread and did what they were told, got up and started feeding, and something happened."

He laughed gently. He was wearing a magenta shirt and a

cross tucked into his pocket. "I consider myself as one of those people who's got to do what Jesus said when he told the disciples, shut up, just go feed the people," said the bishop. "You know, it's a mystery. But sometimes you just have to trust and eat."

I ate. I trusted—more or less.

It was in a moment of not really trusting that I started to preach. My incessant talking about the pantry had finally driven Donald to challenge me to preach about it. I'd seen Lynn cry during a sermon, after blurting out intimate details about her multiple sclerosis; I'd watched Donald stop midway, abruptly, and wait in the quiet for what would emerge next. St. Gregory's sermons emphasized "critical scholarship and unfinished personal experience." There was a lot of teaching about Scripture, but the words of the Bible took on another dimension as they were bound up, by the preachers, with accounts of experience.

"Jesus our teacher asked his listeners to cut through what they'd been taught," Donald wrote in an essay about preaching at St. Gregory's, ". . . and all their careful doctrinal constructs and formulations, to meet God in the wildness and immediacy of life. . . . We follow that pattern: we're not telling one another how to look at life . . . but to listen to our lives as they are."

Sometimes, of course, preaching failed or was tedious: Preachers made corny jokes; the sharings by the congregation after the sermons were rambling and self-absorbed; and glibness trumped authenticity. I worried that my own vanity and tendentiousness would be even more exposed in preaching than in writing, my own awkwardness harder to edit out. I wasn't sure I wanted to expose myself that much, but I took the dare. You can't make an omelet without breaking eggs, I reminded myself.

Whenever I was scheduled to preach, I'd begin with that

day's assigned text from the common lectionary—a regular cycle of Bible readings, used by churches all over the world, through the seasons of the Christian year—and turn it over in my head, praying and free-associating as I walked or watered my garden or drove to the Food Bank. I didn't have any scholarly background, but I'd read whatever I could about the passage.

Preaching, I realized, wasn't just about me or my experience; it wasn't a neatly packaged "lesson." It was a handmade connection between Word and flesh: text and bread. It was more than anything else a way to point to the Table, use language to set it, lead people to it.

It turned out that preaching the Word—at least, from that chair, gazing at the Table, anticipating the bread and wine to come—would be not only as satisfying as writing but almost as much fun as cooking for people. I wasn't telling them to eat their vegetables or lecturing them about the "right" kinds of food. I was offering them the same words from the lectionary that millions of people were having for breakfast that day and showing them how my life, their own lives, were Gospel, too. "Here," I was saying, as I salted and spiced a section of Scripture for the people at the early-morning service, "try this. It's so good, it's going to be the best thing you've ever tasted."

I was hoping, through preaching, to discover where the words of the Bible and the act of feeding people intersected, and where they were going. I was trying hard to understand the religious and political significance of our work at the food pantry.

"I think," I said slowly once, looking out at the Sunday worshippers, "that we're being called to something harder than being conventional 'Good Samaritans.' To understand ourselves, individually and as a church, being rescued by strangers and foreigners, by the wrong people. To understand ourselves, individually and as a church, as beaten, hungry, hurting, lost at the side of the road. Called to touch the parts of ourselves that are strange and damaged and needy. Called to receive love from people we don't know and have no reason to trust. And only then, in turn, being called to the second part: to go and do the same thing—knowing it will change us in ways we didn't plan and may not like.

"And both receiving and giving mean really opening ourselves to strangers—in whose bodies we find, and upon whose being depends, our own salvation."

Chapter 17

The Desert

The sense of chosen-ness, of a special society of the initiated, is pervasive among Christians. I remember being shocked when I discovered that the phrase "the people of God" was churchspeak for "churchgoing Christians of our denomination"; I'd thought, naïvely, that it meant *all* God's people, all humanity.

As the food pantry entered its third year, I would spend more time among conventional Episcopalians and come to appreciate St. Gregory's great openness. But it would take complete outsiders to make me grasp how large and generous and out of control God's work really was. Strangers helped break open the door for me again. In the wrecked, poor Potrero Hill projects, they challenged me to see what was missing from our food pantry; at my own pantry, they changed what I thought church was for.

The more I read of Scripture, the more it began to occur to me that Jesus, if the stories had it right, was singularly uninterested in church. Everything I'd yearned for when I first tasted that bread was never going be found neatly wrapped up inside the comfortable rituals of religion, the pretty spaces I'd come so quickly to associate with holiness, even my own routines at the pantry. I was going to have to hunt in what the Bible called "the rough places," "the lonely places," "the desert"; among people who'd been cast out, in one way or another, from the church. And I'd have to stumble through the kind of grief and violence I thought I'd mostly left behind in Central America.

Just six blocks from St. Gregory's, on the other side of the Hill, was the food pantry in the Potrero Hill projects I'd visited with Anne Quaintance when I was first starting up. The Potrero pantry, in an unused apartment the Housing Authority had grudgingly made available to the women who ran it, couldn't have looked more different from the one in our gleaming rotunda with its spacious windows and gold-haloed icons. This pantry was set at the far end of the whole dilapidated housing complex, in a battered row of boarded-up, pale blue barracks; to get there, I had to drive down a narrow, unpaved road, park in an empty lot, then clamber up a steep dirt footpath. As I approached, I'd sometimes see a ragged line of dark-skinned people walking away through the field, carrying bags of groceries. It was like the pantry at the end of the world.

I'd started helping the women there by delivering groceries to project residents who couldn't make it up the path themselves, were housebound, or were too scared to go out alone. Each Friday, before opening St. Gregory's own pantry, I'd drive to the Hill, sometimes with Steve Hassett. Ty-Jay would come out and greet us—"Sister's here!" Ty-Jay would shout—and load up my trunk with plastic bags full of food.

"Richard, Mrs. Carter and her kids, Mrs. Robinson, Mr. Yancy, Marlene and her son, Mrs. James, Samuel Brown," Gloria would count, ticking their names off. "I think Mrs. Robinson is at the doctor, but leave the bags with her neighbor if she's not there." We'd cruise past the omnipresent gang graffiti and piles of trash and start knocking on doors. "Food pantry!" I'd call out.

The stale air would hit me in the face. Behind me, the shimmering San Francisco light played over the eucalyptus and made the broken windows glitter. Inside the project hallways was always what a friend who'd grown up with a junkie mother described as "the unforgettable mingled odors of Raid, pet feces, and cigarette smoke."

I'd hand Richard a bag of oranges and potatoes. He was obese, in his early forties, white, and badly sick: His legs, like the legs of his wife, were covered in diabetic sores. "Hey, hi," he'd say, hitching up his boxer shorts. Richard and his wife smoked pot nonstop; they kept a constantly shrieking parrot and several cages of hairless rats. A very unhappy twelve-year-old boy sometimes stayed there as well, sharing the dirty sofa and television with an old man. I never saw what they ate, except for once when I saw the kid hungrily spooning up a bowl of cereal.

The apartment next door to Richard's was fantastically clean, but the oven was always on, and the kitchen stifling. Even the air felt poor, secondhand, inside these rooms. Mrs. James's husband would look up from the plastic-covered couch when I brought the bags of food in, his eyes deeply tired and his face puffy. "How're you doing?" I'd ask, setting down the groceries. "Okay," he'd say. "We're hanging in." The couple ate cooked food—there was often a pot of stew or spaghetti sauce on the stove—but he was dying of cancer and didn't seem able to keep any weight on.

Outside there'd be a sweet breeze, green grass blowing, and brilliant orange poppies waving between cracks in the walkways. Random laundry flapped on a line, above a wrecked barbecue grill. I'd walk past a pile of empty cognac bottles and bedraggled teddy bears and balloons—a makeshift altar commemorating someone who'd been killed—and knock on Mr. Yancy's door. He was a bent-over, toothless, ninety-year-old man from Louisiana who'd once tipped Steve off that he should rub hair conditioner all over his body if he wanted to drive girls wild. "The ladies love it," he whispered slyly, and winked. "That's the stuff, now." As far as I could tell, Mr. Yancy only ate soup from the cans we brought; the rest of the food was commandeered by the stone-faced teenagers who occupied the back room of his apartment.

Ty-Jay came with me sometimes to help carry the bags. He was twenty-three, had a steady girlfriend, no kids, and had never been in jail. With all that, and his part-time job at the pantry, I calculated he was doing better than 90 percent of the men his age living in the projects. Ty-Jay was heavyset and strong, with a dry sense of humor, and carried deep scars on his face and neck. He asked me to stop at the corner store once, so he could pick up some spicy Doritos, a bottle of sweetened ice tea with ginseng, and a couple of cigarettes. "I didn't have breakfast," he explained.

Once in a while, when I was alone, a neighbor would look hostile or threatening, assuming that any white lady up on the Hill must be a probation officer, looking for trouble. But after a while, people recognized the car, the aprons, the cross around my neck. "Hey, Foods on Wheels!" one guy would always call out in greeting. The thuggy boys endlessly fixing their cars and listening to music in the street mostly tried to be polite when I walked by carrying groceries. I was an outsider, marked as clearly as I'd been in South Africa or the Philippines. And yet I was drawn to the Hill, powerfully, and found myself welcomed.

Being in the projects was sort of like being in a war again, and I went there with some of the same combination of dread and excitement and purpose that I'd felt in places such as El Salvador. It may have been partly the omnipresence of automatic weapons that felt familiar—Potrero Hill had more than its share of homicides, and I knew people who'd been shot there—or the adrenaline rush that came from watching stoned, probably armed teenagers in patched-together cars career wildly up the streets, radios blasting. There was the same bad food and the same hunger. There was a familiar aura of edgy all-outness, and I wondered again about my own tendency to romanticize such desperation.

I wasn't particularly afraid up in the projects, though Steve would get jumpy when we heard gunfire or when a fight broke out. But I was often just scared enough, as I had been in wartime, to see things more clearly. I saw that there was church—feeding, communion, love amid suffering—outside the walls of church.

There were all kinds of outsiders who were helping me build a bigger sense of church, and what it was for.

One evening I got a phone call at home from Eddie, the Food Bank worker. "Listen," he said, "I have a favor to ask. Me and my girlfriend want to get married, and we want you to do it. I told her you were kind of like my pastor, and how you'd blessed my hands that time."

Eddie brushed away my protest that I wasn't an ordained minister; like any other citizen, I could get a temporary license from the city to perform a civil ceremony, but it wouldn't be an official church wedding. No, no, he said, the Catholic Church had disappointed them, and they weren't going back. Eddie was set on having the ceremony at a waterfront rented hall run by a drug-rehab organization; his buddies from the Food Bank were going to be his best men, and he wanted me to read the vows. "And then we'll all have dinner," he said. "What do you like, salmon or chicken?"

Another night I picked up the phone to hear a stranger's voice. It was a Mexican guy who'd phoned St. Gregory's office and gotten my number from Steve. He was a day laborer whose friend had been injured when the two of them were working on a roofing job. The employer had washed his hands of the men; there wasn't going to be any workers' comp, any disability pay, anything to cover the rest of the month's rent. Now the two men were living in a motel, trying to scrape together money, one friend looking for work while the other healed his broken leg.

We talked for a while, and I tried to be helpful to the man, though I didn't really know what to say. I didn't recognize his name, though, and I finally asked if he'd been at the pantry that week. No, he said, sounding surprised, he'd never even seen our church. So how did you wind up calling us? I asked, and he paused. "Oh," he said, as if everyone knew this, "some guys on the street told me St. Gregory's was a cool place."

And then, one evening in St. Gregory's kitchen, after everyone else had left, I'd heard a confession from a pantry volunteer, who'd brought me what she said was a "secret" in a shopping bag. She had a cast on her leg and kept looking over her shoulder anxiously, and she made me close the kitchen door. Her boyfriend, who beat her up regularly, had been threatening to kill her, she said, swallowing hard.

"I thought, this is a church, it'll be safe here," she said, unwrapping a dirty dish towel from around a huge .357 Magnum revolver. "I took out the firing pin."

That's what church was for, I realized: a place to bring the ugly, frightening secret you couldn't tell anyone else about. I checked that the gun was disarmed and stuck it in a cookie tin in a locked closet beneath the pantry shelves. I didn't mention it to anyone from the Sunday congregation. The woman moved away, to stay with a sister in Sacramento. A month later, I did tell Steve.

"You must be kidding," he said.

"Isn't this what church is for?" I said.

"Uh, yeah," said Steve. He looked scared, and as if he wanted to laugh at the same time. "Whoa, that's a really big gun." We drove down to the local police station, and I walked up to the officer on duty. I was wearing a crucifix and a fairly respectable sweater. "Excuse me. I found this in our churchyard," I lied. "Can you please take it?"

There's nothing like being a middle-aged white lady, I told Steve as we drove back. The cops had gathered around the officer who unwrapped the package. "Holy shit," said one of them. "Excuse me, ma'am." They passed it around, gingerly, and let me leave after I insisted I didn't want to make a report or get a receipt. "Can you imagine if we'd been two black teenage guys walking in with that?"

"You just made the high point of my career as a parish administrator," said Steve. "I never imagined I'd show a cop something that could make him say 'Holy shit.' "

"Yeah, well," I said, "I guess this is what you call the Christian life."

And yet the Christian life looked very different in other places. "Do you think you would have ever become a Christian if you'd walked into some other church?" my friend Jose asked me once. I'd been telling him about preaching and serving communion at St. Gregory's, and he was remarking on how few barriers the place seemed to have to participation.

"Sure," I said glibly. Then I hesitated, remembering those early visits to check out other churches and how sitting meekly in pews had left me cold. "I don't know," I said. "I don't really know what other churches are like."

I didn't have to go very far to discover how the Christianity I'd acquired through St. Gregory's and my work at the pantry could appear strange to other believers. Even within the Episcopal Church—the liberal wing of the Episcopal Church, at that—I'd often feel like an outsider.

I'd agreed to help Donald and Rick lead worship, St. Gregory's–style, at a conference at Kanuga, an Episcopal retreat center in the North Carolina hills. I would deacon, along with Steve Hassett, and preach; we'd get help from Paul Fromberg, a priest and a friend of Donald's who'd later become my kitchen partner at St. Gregory's. Together, we'd demonstrate to the several hundred mainstream Episcopalian clergy in attendance how experimenting with liturgy could revitalize their congregations.

It had seemed like a good idea. But now we were having lunch on a wide, pleasant porch, surrounded by 150 church people sipping ice tea, and I'd seldom felt so out of place. It was another world: so many nice ladies, so much official Christian-speak, so much polite fellowship. I was wearing what I thought of as my religious camouflage—a pair of khaki pants and a black T-shirt—but I still looked messy and bohemian amid the sea of blouses and skirts. "Yikes," I whispered to Steve. "If these are the people who want to hear about experimental liturgy, what are the conservatives like?"

A tall, open-faced blond man in his early forties ambled up to us.

"Hey, pumpkin," he boomed at Steve, and kissed him.

"Dude!" cried Steve in delight.

Paul Fromberg, who had about the widest hands I'd ever seen, took mine. "So, what's for lunch?" he said. It was a question I'd hear from him a hundred times in the years to come.

Paul was an outsider who looked, at first glance, like an insider: the model of a bright and successful young Episcopalian rector, an artist and intellectual.

Paul's interest in religious architecture, liturgy, and art was not just academic, though, but passionately spiritual, and it put him at odds with the church. "Most people live in a visually impoverished environment," he explained to me once, "and most people in church are satisfied with dismal, mind-numbing stuff from a stock catalog. Their religious art is smooth and sexless, like their liturgy, and says visually, 'I do not believe any of the stuff I'm saying here, the world in which God became incarnate doesn't matter, so we'll just trot out the most banal crap we can.' Meanwhile, the general culture is trying to anesthetize people to buy stuff, so actual art, high or low, is dangerous because it makes them unsatisfied."

Like Rick and Donald, Paul wanted to reform the church— "not by being a policy wonk," he hastened to point out, "or pushing resolutions through some committee, but by changing people's experience of worship." Unlike them, he came of age in the 1980s and had a relentless, wisecracking sense of humor. Raised in Texas's conservative Church of Christ and trained as a therapist in psychology and religion at an evangelical seminary, Paul had endured years of unrequited crushes on his straight roommates and several failed attempts at "reparative therapy" before he came out. "I sort of had hysterical blindness around homosexuality," Paul recalled. "I couldn't see gay people, just the straight ones, the popular beautiful guys, and of course I fell madly, madly in love with them all."

While at Fuller Seminary, he began attending the early service at All Saints in Pasadena—a left-wing Episcopal parish
where he saw a woman preside at the altar for the first time—and
started rethinking his vocation. "It was clear to me that a lot of
suffering was chemical, not just psychological. I felt, as a talk
psychotherapist, I'd be fooling people and not giving them what
they needed. At the same time, I was beginning to believe that
Word and sacrament might have something to do with healing."
He got confirmed as an Episcopalian, took a job at the cathedral
in Houston, and began the process of ordination for the priest-
hood. "Of course," he said thoughtfully, "the bishop wouldn't
have ordained me unless I lied about myself."

What Paul found in the Diocese of Texas was one facet of the
Episcopal Church that St. Gregory's had set itself to change: the
Anglophile church of "society" and the ritualized status quo.
"There I was," said Paul, "working in an affluent parish, being
formed as a company man. I was made a canon of the cathedral,
learned the rules and how to perform. You basically smile; ask a
lot of interested, polite questions; and say 'hmm' a lot."

And yet Paul's art, and his faith, reflected something bigger,
more full of suffering and passion. Still closeted at work, he
began a series of monoprints, one eventually shown at the cathedral, for which he'd painted his body with red paint and lain
down on big pieces of paper. "Then I'd write secret words on the
paper and paint over them," he said. "It was called *In My Father's Image*." Paul winced. "I was so physically disconnected, in
so much pain, and at the same time, I was using my naked body
to make an impression, to say secret things and hide them."

The pain didn't dampen his faith: In fact, Paul said, it made it
brighter. "I had this severe, strong sense of desiring something,"
he said, "and was so keenly aware of the fact that right there was
where Jesus was. All the bullshit of what church life is about,

some of which is very necessary, none of it has ever been able to wash away that love I had for Jesus. It's not about good times only; it's about my bad times and longing and desire when it's not fulfilled." He paused. "I mean, what the fuck does it mean to say that Jesus is in your heart? It beats and keeps you alive. That's how you know it's real."

So finding St. Gregory's, on a trip to San Francisco with his Texas colleague Andy Doyle, had revitalized Paul's belief in the power of liturgy to express authenticity. "I was looking for a way not to become utterly bored with the church," he recalled. "Episcopal worship can be really dismal; you just do it over and over. And I saw something at St. Gregory's I'd imagined but never seen except in a crazy Pentecostal church. There were all these people singing their hearts out, not just spacing out in the back pew. There was this creative power; they were being fed. I wanted to be part of it."

This was what Rick and Donald had insisted on with building worship around open communion. It wasn't just about offering bread and wine to all comers but extending the welcome through what they called "radical hospitality," making the entire liturgy transparent and accessible to strangers every step of the way. It was why Rick badgered the deacons constantly about pitching every announcement and speech to the newcomers and the strangers—eschewing jargon and insider references. And it echoed something I'd heard from Bishop Swing when I talked with him about the food pantry.

"Whenever the church powers get around to feeding," Swing said, "it's usually conditional—you have to be baptized, you have to belong to our club—and it stops being Jesus's meal. Churchly legitimacy gets its hand in rather than crazy hospitality, the open extravagance of the Last Supper. And you get further and further from the power and the genius of that meal."

The power and genius of Jesus weren't on particularly obvious display at Kanuga, I thought. The general sponginess of the "spirituality" reminded me of the call I'd gotten once from a woman who was putting together a fund-raising event for the Food Bank and wanted to find "inspirational" quotes about food to use in her program. Fairly lightly, I'd said, "I guess you don't want something about eating Jesus."

She hadn't been amused. "No!" she'd said, firmly. "That just puts people off."

"Okay," I'd said, "well, there's plenty of stuff about feeding the poor and—"

She'd interrupted me. "No," she'd said again. "Nothing like that. Nothing from the Bible. Just something inspirational."

Kanuga's official liturgies were not even inspirational. I'd tagged along with Donald and Steve to morning prayer, hoping for something like the unpretentious, contemplative half-hour service that Steve and I sang together each day. But morning prayer, in a gloomy chapel, gave me a glimpse of the standard Episcopal liturgy I hadn't experienced before.

An old white man in an alb slumped in a chair on the dais; a silent priest sat facing him beneath a bank of ornate candles. An organist wheezed out a dirgelike hymn, and at some mysterious signal, the congregation stood up, rustling sheets of paper. Steve and Donald, flanking me, gestured at me to stand, and I scrambled to my feet, expecting to sing. In a depressive mumble, the priest started speaking the words to a psalm, and the people around me recited it dully in unison, then sank back into their pews. Steve elbowed me. "Ain't gonna be much singing here," he whispered. "Get ready. Next we're saying the Creed."

The Creed—a statement of belief professed in church by

Anglicans around the world—was deliberately not a part of St. Gregory's service. "It's basically a toxic document," Paul Fromberg would explain to me, "set up to standardize belief and overturn heresies and draw a sharp line between us and them." I recited it dully aloud from the prayer book with everyone, though I missed the cue to sit down and didn't know where to turn next.

"So how did you like that?" Donald asked me, as we filed out to ponderous organ chords.

I was hot and embarrassed. "I didn't belong there," I said. "I felt stupid; I didn't know what to do."

"Exactly," said Donald. "Now you see why we have the deacons explain aloud, every step of the way, what we're doing."

"Why don't they sing the psalms?" I went on. "I mean, aren't they *songs*? And the Creed thing, it's like saying the Pledge of Allegiance in second grade."

"In my old church in Idaho," Donald said, "people loved the Creed, because it was the only time in the service they got to speak. Even if they didn't believe what they were saying, they got to say something."

"Help," I said. "This is church?"

The rest of the day's schedule offered a talk on parish fund-raising, and a New Agey presentation about "healing and the feminine spirit," and a PowerPoint presentation by an earnest church professional wearing a turtleneck. I decided to pass on the after-lunch round of workshops and told my friends I'd see them later, at the ugly gym that St. Gregory's was planning to decorate and transform into a worship space for the closing Eucharist.

I walked away reflecting on all the ways religion tried to

manage and tame God: through compulsive rule-making, magic rituals, good behavior, the sheer weight of church tradition. It was a warm May day, and birds were darting among the rhododendron forests, swooping low over the lake. I had the text for my sermon to consider: the story of Elijah, fed by a hungry woman in Zarephath, and the Gospel about Jesus telling Peter to feed his lambs. And I had a bit of Deuteronomy that Jeff, my spiritual director, had given me to read before I left for Kanuga. "This should be interesting to you," he'd said.

In the verse, Moses foreshadowed Jesus with an unusual emphasis on experienced grace rather than codified religious law. "Surely, this commandment that I am commanding you today is not too hard for you, nor is it too far away," he told his people. "It is not in heaven, that you should say, 'Who will go up to heaven for us, and get it for us so that we may hear it and observe it?' Neither is it beyond the sea, that you should say, 'Who will cross to the other side of the sea for us, and get it for us so that we may hear it and observe it?' No, the word is very near to you; it is in your mouth and in your heart for you to observe."

What was keeping Christians from grasping this very basic idea? It was so tempting to try to turn Gospel into law, I thought; Wisdom into knowledge. But there was Jesus, the Word made flesh. There he was, over and over sweeping away his followers' attempts to codify and regulate their experiences of the divine. He'd spit in men's eyes and stick his fingers in their ears, touch unclean women and corpses, yell at religious authorities, and impatiently demand that people drop their churchgoing and give the poor everything they owned. "Don't be afraid," he said. "It's me. Come on, let's go."

Later that evening, Paul and I played poker, in a humid little cabin with a screened porch. Steve sat rocking nearby in a cane chair, reading a book I'd given him about Pentecostal snake handlers, and the three of us drank tumblers of cheap, warm wine.

"Hear this," said Steve. He read aloud a beautiful passage about a Tennessee preacher who, when he was "in the Word," could not only fling copperheads around but take big swigs of strychnine safely from a Mason jar. "Some folks handle fire, too," Steve added enthusiastically.

"Pumpkin," said Paul, "that's a most unfortunate exegesis of the final parts of Mark's Gospel. Definitely not something I would want to do. Raise you."

There were spring peepers and crickets in the night air, and moths flickered around the porch light.

"Two pair," I said. "But you know, it beats saying the Creed aloud."

"All glory," said Paul, putting down his cards. He had a full house. "Ladies, it's been lovely, but I gotta go. See you tomorrow. And God willing, I'll see you soon in San Francisco."

The next afternoon, I flew alone to Vermont for a long-scheduled visit with my family. My brother picked me up. "We found some chanterelles yesterday up in that pine forest," he told me. "I was thinking I'd just sauté them up with a little Marsala, have them on toast for an app. Ma's coming over for dinner, and we've got a nice piece of tuna."

David and I cooked together, standing side by side in the old, familiar rhythm. My heart filled with happiness. "Whisk?" I asked, and he handed me one for the vinaigrette. "Do a couple of shallots, okay?" Our mother sat nearby, with our sister, drinking wine and talking.

"So, Sara," my mother said, "did you give a talk about the food pantry in North Carolina?"

"I preached a sermon about it," I said. Ellen choked on her wine. David kept chopping. My mother was silent.

"David," she said, after a while, "those mushrooms are just beautiful. Tell me again where you found them."

Paul would soon move to San Francisco and change the way I experienced St. Gregory's as well as the food pantry. My mother would, much later, talk with me about religion over a meal. But first, I went back to my church outside the walls of church.

One Friday it started to pour as soon as Steve and I parked in front of the Hill pantry, a hard, driving rain. I was soaked to the bone in a flash, and the rain was pounding as we staggered down the path with the groceries. "Man, what a day," I said to Ty-Jay, who was helping us. "So how are you?" He smiled at me, with my hair plastered to my head and my face streaming water. "Blessed," he said. "I'm blessed."

We crammed the last of the pink plastic bags into the trunk, and I tried to wipe my glasses dry as Steve turned the car around on the dirt road. I remembered, when I was trying to start our food pantry, that the vestry had asked me how this project fit with St. Gregory's mission. "Physicality of worship," I'd told them earnestly.

I told this to Steve, and he laughed. We pulled up to a block where a bunch of brooding guys in knit caps and baggy jeans were standing, smoking, in a doorway, sullenly watching the rain. I hauled three bags out of the trunk and headed for Mrs. Carter's apartment. One of the men followed me.

"Hey," I said to him.

"Hey," he said back, in a low, angry voice. "What's up?"

I turned. "Blessed," I said.

He jerked, as if I'd given him an electrical shock, and let his breath out in a rush. "Uhnh," he said. "Blessed."

We delivered to ten homes, leaving groceries on Mrs. James's immaculate, linoleum-covered table, chatting with Mr. Yancy, greeting the sick woman who came to her door wincing with pain. I came out of one particularly trashed apartment remembering how Ty-Jay, on another visit there with me, had rolled his eyes and pursed his lips. "Sister," he'd asked, as he slid into the front seat, "did that smell like crack in there to you?"

At the last stop, the rain paused, and Steve parked. I bounded down another path and dropped off a set of bags next to a boarded-up entry. From a car radio, I could hear music: a gorgeous deep bass line, then voices, loud and full. The sky was deep gray, metallic, and I could see all the way out across the water of the Bay, past the docks, the ships, the mountains, the unrolling horizon. Still wet, and shaking with cold, I lifted up my eyes.

There was an outcropping of rock and a muddy set of stairs leading to a row of cinder-block apartments painted a dingy turquoise. And there was Ruth, a woman I'd become friendly with, waving to me from her bedroom window. I came over eagerly and stood at the open window, and Ruth leaned out and embraced me. I gave her a bag of groceries.

Then she groaned. "Look behind you," Ruth said, and I half-turned. A skinny middle-aged guy in an old overcoat darted behind one of the barracks.

"That's my baby," Ruth said, her voice cracking. "He's in and out, in and out of jail. He's mixed up with drugs. I don't know where he lives, he comes around sometimes and then he steals stuff and he's gone. You know, when it gets rainy like this, you think about your baby, and you wonder where he's sleeping. . . ."

"You love him so much," I said. I was crying.

"I love him so much," she said. Tears were running down her cheeks. We held hands, while a guy walked by with a radio and a woman across the street yelled to her neighbor.

All of a sudden, the words I sang every day at morning prayer echoed in my head. "*Send out your light and your truth, that they may guide us and lead us to your holy hill and to your dwelling.* I felt dizzy. *This* was God's holy hill: the Hill. And that apartment, with the broken tricycle out front, next to Ruth's? *That* was God's dwelling. God lived right there, in that actual apartment. God lived in Ruth's hands.

What had I been thinking by praying those words without really paying attention?

They were real. Above me, above the projects and Ruth's tears, above the wrecked roofs and broken doors and every mistake I'd ever made in my life, was the dark sky, luminous in the east. And in my hands were some Cheerios, some lettuce, and a loaf of bread.

I was going to keep giving that food away. What I glimpsed in the projects was the last thing I'd expected growing up: that because God was about feeding and being fed, religion could be a way not to separate people but to unite them.

It wasn't that class and race disappeared in the blinding light of God. It wasn't that the painful cultural splits among believers— over abortion or homosexuality or the role of laypeople—were erased by invoking the name of Jesus. It wasn't even that people on the Hill who prayed with me or blessed me or told me about their churches necessarily shared my own peculiar ideas about God. But something happened when I brought a plastic bag full of lettuce and potatoes and left it on Miss Robinson's table. Something happened when Ruth fixed me a plate of neck bones and green beans and made me sit down to eat it, or Ty-Jay offered me a sip of his ice tea. The sharing of food was an actual sacrament, one that resonated beyond the church and its regulations, and into a real experience of the divine. I wanted more.

Chapter 18

Manna

—

At the food pantry, meanwhile, strangers kept stepping out of the line for groceries and offering to help. They reminded me of myself: I knew exactly how it felt to appear, nervous and hungry, at the Table for the first time, and how it felt to need, inarticulately, to stick around. "I'll give you a hand there," Michael had announced, once, when I was wheeling a trash bin up from the basement; he'd never let go and now basically ran the operation every Friday.

Michael was big, with a broad face, five earrings, tattoos, swept-back silvery hair he cut himself, and significant gaps in his tobacco-stained teeth. I'd never seen him wear anything but jeans, boots, and a black T-shirt. Raised in a working-class Irish neighborhood of London, kicked out of school at fifteen, he'd come to America, joined a nasty little punk band called Our Lady of Pain, worked as a bouncer, learned some Japanese, lived on the streets, and gone through a bad bout with heroin before detoxing, abruptly and excruciatingly, in San Quentin. "When I got out," Michael told me, "I knew I had to stop seeing my old friends, or I'd get sucked right back into the life. And I wasn't going to go through detox again. So I explained to them, Get the fuck away from me or I'll hit you."

His unorthodox sobriety plan apparently worked: Michael had stayed clean and hooked up with a gentle woman with a limp. The two of them lived on one of the worst corners of the city, without official employment. Michael looked tough and knew how to drop a man with one punch. And yet he was a born manager, who knew how to bring out the best in our volunteers through praise and giving them responsibility. I tried to figure out how Michael wound up at St. Gregory's: He had no interest in Christianity or Christians, and no patience with the scammers who were regular fixtures at the pantry.

"I like to work, that's all," Michael told me, looking sheepish. "You might as well do something worthwhile with your life."

Jeff wasn't surprised at all when I told him we now had twenty-three volunteers—only two of them from St. Gregory's, and the rest people who'd come to get groceries.

"Why not?" said my spiritual director. "It feels great to give stuff away. Look what it's done for you." He added, "And if you're poor, how often do you get to give? Here, you hand good food to two hundred and fifty people in an afternoon, and they're all smiling at you and saying 'Thanks.' "

Two hundred and fifty people was an awful lot, though. It was great to have extra volunteers, but we hadn't solved anything about how to run the pantry, just postponed a decision about how big we could get. The arguments continued about how to handle things: Should we give out tickets on a first-come, first-served basis or at random? Should we let kids pick up groceries or limit the pantry to adults? Should we allow two people from the same household to each take food? If some people took more than their share, would we wind up turning others away? I was driving myself to distraction trying to control the process, snapping at the volunteers and pantry visitors as if I were back in a kitchen yelling at waiters and threatening the garde-manger. There needed to be new pantries to take some of the pressure off St. Gregory's. We needed to expand, but I couldn't imagine how.

It took, once again, a stranger. I was at home, working on deadline, and distracting myself by reading e-mail. There was something from the Food Bank about a meeting. There was a memo from the fact-checker at the magazine I was writing for. Steve sent me a note complaining about yet another boring liturgy discussion at staff meeting. "But on the bright side," he ended his note, "some guy just phoned the office and wants to give you twenty-five thousand dollars. Call me."

It took a while to piece the story together, but the basic facts about the man my church friends would, rather cloyingly, refer to as "your angel" emerged. Derek Howard was an aggressive tort lawyer who specialized in suing banks in class-action suits, exercising what his firm's brochures called "a special expertise in business fraud, deceptive practices, and breaches of fiduciary and ethical duties by corporate entities." Derek tended to win large settlements; once all claims by class members in a suit had been filed, and money was still left over, the courts disbursed the extra funds to charities recommended by the lawyers.

The gruff, terse man who finally answered the phone told me he'd decided to make St. Gregory's Food Pantry one of his recommended charities because of the photos he'd seen on our website. He'd seen the website, it turned out, because by chance his wife had been attending some event at Grace Cathedral.

Derek, who had little time or patience for religion, had escaped to the bookstore, where he struck up a conversation with a clerk. "The church doesn't do squat for poor people," Derek said belligerently. The clerk, an amiable man, didn't argue with the lawyer; ringing up the purchases, he just mildly remarked, "Oh, my daughter goes to St. Gregory's. They've got a great food program there. You should check it out."

Apparently Derek had checked us out. And now he wanted me to tell him more about the pantry. "Well," I started, "we give food to everyone who shows up."

Derek pounced. "How do you know they really need it?" he asked. I went through the basics: Most of our pantry visitors are working people with families, they need help making ends meet, it costs just a dollar to feed one family, we can feed about 250 families a week. Then I paused. "You know," I said, "it's just really a drag being poor. You have to wait in line and fill out endless stupid forms, and people always try to make you prove you deserve it. None of us 'deserve' what we have." Derek laughed harshly. "That's right," he said.

So now Derek wanted the court to award me twenty-five thousand dollars. I had to fill out a form with St. Gregory's tax ID number. The day I finally got the check, I was in shock: It hadn't altogether occurred to me that this was actually going to happen. That the power of the food pantry—which, I believed, was the power of Jesus's Table—could pull in not just me, and Michael, and all our crazy volunteers, but a millionaire lawyer who felt the same hunger for communion and yearned to be a part of feeding others.

I called Derek. There was no way I could cling to this money, when it had blown in so unexpectedly. Just as receiving communion had led me to serving communion, receiving such an over-the-top gift made me need to give it away, in turn. "Actually," I said, after thanking him effusively, "we pay for most of our own food from contributions from members—you know, ten bucks here, fifty there. We can cover St. Gregory's pantry ourselves for about seventeen thousand dollars a year. What I'd like to do is give this money away, so other folks can start new pantries." Derek didn't hesitate. "Good, fine," he said impatiently. "I trust you. Whatever you want. Send me a note."

Driving around the Hill, I found what I wanted to do. Starr King Elementary, right across from the projects, had just been rated one of the ten worst-performing grammar schools in the entire state of California. A massive, fenced fortress of a building, occupying a square block, it had been built for 500 students. But, as parents with any kind of ambition or resources pulled out, it had been losing population steadily: There were now about 160 kids left, most poor enough to qualify for free lunch. It looked perfect for a pantry.

It took a few visits to the school office, and some wandering around the echoing halls, before I found Laticia Erving, the parent liaison, who ran after-school programs out of a trailer in the concrete school yard. Young, stylish, fun, and steady as a rock, Laticia was determined to bring order out of the chaos of her kids' lives. The way she'd been raised, that meant, above all, family dinner. "Eating together, that's it," said Laticia. "That's the whole trick."

I knew she was right. I'd seen the studies showing that kids who ate regular meals with their parents were less likely to use drugs or alcohol, more likely to do well in school. It seemed simple, and yet just over half of all families in America said they ate dinner together more than twice a week. Within a month, I'd

taken Laticia down to the Food Bank and finessed some paper-
work so she could get groceries delivered to her trailer as a
"satellite site" of St. Gregory's own pantry. She strong-armed
some mothers into helping out, got some extra folding tables
from the school district, and printed up flyers with little drawings of apples. "Pick up your child and pick up your groceries,"
the flyers said. "Every Thursday, rain or shine." I went back to
St. Gregory's and looked at our books. "We have enough to start
another pantry, too," I told Steve, surprised. There were nearly
six thousand extra dollars left in our account.

"Dude," he said. "I predict you are going to get so sick of
hearing people say 'loaves and fishes' to you."

I told Laticia we'd pay for her first year. And then I went
looking for other places to start pantries.

I met with the Food Bank; I met with the officer for "congrega-
tional development" in the Episcopal diocese; I phoned churches
and community centers and schools. "Hi," I'd say, this time
without hesitation, "I'm Sara Miles, from St. Gregory's, and I'd
like to talk with you about starting a food pantry."

I ran into an old friend from New York who was organizing
around low-income housing in one of the poorest neighborhoods of San Francisco and told her what I'd been up to. An
African American lesbian with adopted twins, she wasn't re-
motely interested in church, though her girlfriend belonged to a
Buddhist group. "Wow, Sara," she said teasingly. "Never thought
I'd see *you* praising Jesus." But food for her was as political—
and as bedrock a moral issue—as housing. "Okay, then," she
said, without missing a beat. "Let's set up a food pantry at this
new housing complex I run."

But when I made the rounds of Episcopal churches, people seemed timid. It wasn't just the familiar fretting I'd heard from my own congregation about cost and mess and dangerous poor folks, though there was plenty of that. It was as if the very habits of churchgoing had stripped away people's capacity to take authority and do things on their own. The priests would refer me to committees, the committees would refer me to the vestry, the vestry would refer me to the priests. "We'd like to schedule a meeting," they'd say to me. And so I'd drive to another bland parish hall on a weekday evening after supper, and three pleasant and worn-out white people would offer me stale cookies and ask me a few questions, while a guy in a collar sat there with his hands folded, nodding until it was time to schedule another meeting.

Just one priest, a middle-aged woman with a no-nonsense air, looked me in the eye. "Sure," she said. "Sounds good to me." I wrote her a check, offered to help on opening day, and two months later, her pantry was serving a hundred families. But she was the exception. The rule was workshops to study the options, and subcommittees to plan the workshops.

"Come on, it ain't that tricky," snorted Steve when I complained to him. Steve had finally decided that he was going to go to seminary and pursue ordination, and the prospect of working in the Episcopal Church for the rest of his life was making him hypercritical and impatient about everything connected with religion. "I mean, you buy a bunch of food, you put it on tables, you give it away. Committees? What is *wrong* with these people?"

"Our people," I said reluctantly. I could taste how much I wanted to be different from them.

"Right," said Steve. "Our people."

That was the first contribution; after the second, another twenty-five thousand dollars, Derek and I spoke for another few minutes by phone, and I sent him a note about the new pantries we'd started up with the money. I could hardly believe it: Nobody I talked to had ever heard of raising money this easily. Checks from the court settlements flowed into St. Gregory's Food Pantry the way excess food flowed into the Food Bank—the incredible waste in the system turning into nourishment for the needy.

I went outside two hours before we opened one day, and there were already eighty people lined up. It was tense and crowded, and there was a simmering argument between two families at the edge of the crowd. The sky was the color of a bruise, of a wet blue iris; it smelled like rain, heavy and close. A tiny, paranoid white woman who always spoke in a whisper was gesturing me over, urgently. I leaned in, and she took my arm, motioning to the skyline, where dark clouds were gathering over the hills of the city. The woman cleared her throat. "Do you ever have days," she whispered, "when you feel like blessings are just being showered down on you?"

I did. I learned a little bit more about Derek Howard. He lived in Marin, had two young daughters, coached soccer, and generally sounded like a rich suburbanite lawyer, albeit with a strong, independent will; a bulldog passion for justice; and a notable lack of patience. He was a cradle Episcopalian, but he thought the church was "too friggin' patriarchal" and "not inclusive"; he also added, as if I hadn't noticed, that he hated being told what to do.

We made several dates to meet, and I kept inviting him to the pantry, but Derek was always either in litigation or on the soccer field terrorizing fifth-grade girls. I didn't meet him in person until Christmastime, when he showed up with his wife, a daughter, and a surprisingly shy smile.

Derek jumped right into the unloading and setup. As we bagged potatoes, he asked me more about St. Gregory's. "This is wild," he said. "I can't believe how open it is." I told him how I wound up in church, and introduced him to the crippled black Pentecostal woman who'd volunteered to hand out candy canes, and showed him how Michael ran the door. Derek's daughter, a slight, extremely polite girl, took over the cereal table; his wife gamely put on an apron and worked doing lettuce.

"I've still got some basic problems with Christianity," Derek told me combatively. "Like virgin birth, life after death, tacking people to the cross, drinking blood. And if you don't believe it all, you're damned. It's like what the fanatic Muslims are doing."

"I hear you," I said. It was strange to be a new convert, approached this way by someone who'd grown up in the faith. I got the sense he wanted me to justify it or give him a reason to believe.

"There are just a lot of principles that are hard for me to explain in the rational world," said Derek.

"Yeah," I said. "There really are."

Chapter 19

Misfits

I'd described the pantry from the beginning as communion. But I'd forgotten that communion was above all a meal. Those first few years at the pantry, the volunteers ate the way cooks do: poorly, in a hurry, carelessly. We worked surrounded by tons of food: stacks of fifty-pound sacks of potatoes, big heaps of peaches or nectarines, three hundred half-gallons of orange juice. But we didn't really eat: I'd pile up some fruit on the altar, open a bag of cookies or crappy snacks, cut up a packaged coffee cake, or spill out some candy. We'd grab whatever was at hand and eat as we worked, until one day when the truck arrived so early there was no setup left to do, and I made a pot of soup.

I had no idea how hungry we'd been. Soon I'd convinced the Food Bank to deliver all our food early, and I was cooking soup for ten, then fifteen, then twenty volunteers. At first, they perched on chairs, bent over individual bowls, or ate standing. Paul Fromberg, who'd moved from Texas to take a job at St. Gregory's, put his foot down the first time he came to the pantry and saw us eating alone. "That is unacceptable," he pronounced. "It cannot be done that way." Paul instantly appointed himself a Friday regular, the first priest to do so. He seemed more at home in the pantry than anywhere else. "Uh, excuse me, this is my job," he said. "My *vocation*. I don't know about you."

Nirmala agreed. "Honey," she said, "Paul's right; let's set a nice table." She showed me a bunch of weedy flowers and some ivy she'd scrounged from the churchyard. "Back in the ashram," she informed me, "when I was the flower girl, I did all the altars. We should have lunch with flowers." Teddy, a cleaned-up meth-head with a severe anxiety disorder, got into the act, picking the prettiest tablecloths. "It should be like family dinner."

Michael snorted. He went outside to smoke. But when he came back in, everyone was seated, somewhat awkwardly, around two long tables, and Lauren, the wispy-haired transsexual from the Bronx, was saying a prayer over the soup. "In the name of the Father and the Son and the Holy Spirit," she rattled off raspily, "God bless this food and all of us. Amen."

In the Gospel, a stranger was revealed as Jesus "in the breaking of bread." And so, as we began to eat together, and as, over bread, I learned more about the lives of our volunteers, I began to pay attention, to see what kind of community these strangers were building.

Martha still referred to the volunteers as misfits, from "the island of misfit toys." We had several ex-junkies, a number of folks living on disability because of mental illness, four guys with varying attention and temper problems who all belonged to the same head-injury support group. And yet these were the people who were solving the problems of the pantry—and also showing me dimensions to the work that I couldn't have imagined when I first started seeing the pictures of groceries around the Table.

Mercedes, a sixty-year-old Mexican housekeeper, came to us

on her day off and swept our floor. She'd left school at eleven and worked as a domestic ever since; she had a fiercely over-developed superego and couldn't stand it when people were ungrateful or complaining at the pantry.

"It's not correct," Mercedes would tell me in Spanish, standing erect, all five feet of her, in a tweed skirt and sensible shoes, monitoring the door. "When people enter the house of God, they need to correct their attitude." I tried to sway her with liberal moral relativism and softhearted we're-all-hungry do-gooderism, but Mercedes was having none of it. "Mercedes," I argued, "who did our Lord die next to?"

"Thieves," she admitted. Then she sighed. As long as she thought I was correcting her, improving her, or putting more pressure on her conscience, Mercedes was okay. I'd seen her kneeling on the floor once, facing the icon of Saint Gregory, praying because she'd yelled at a thief. "When people take more than their share of rice," she'd explained, "and try to cheat the pantry and steal food, it makes me so angry, I can't bear it. I want Saint Gregory to take my resentment away."

Nirmala, who was the most accepting person I knew, came over. She'd befriended Mercedes, and sometimes after the pantry, they'd leave together for the one-room apartment Mercedes shared with her mother, a tiny, demented Indian woman with long braids. "It's so nice and quiet," Nirmala explained. "We eat some radishes and tortillas, you know, and salt, and we just sit there together." Now she took Mercedes's hand. "Honey," she said, "you can't change people; you just have to forgive them."

Mercedes looked at us. "I know I was brought to this pantry for some reason," she said. "What a great school God has given us here on earth."

Like the psalmist who told God "You school my heart, even

at night," Mercedes used her particular brand of religion like a magnifying glass, focusing it on the ordinary things of her life so she could read, better, the lessons meant to bring her to perfection. Her uprightness exhausted me.

The fact was, the pantry and its volunteers were a school for me, too. One day, when Teddy was bustling around in a particularly overbearing way—barking at people from across the room, demanding that all the volunteers stop and listen to him, hounding me with incessant questions—I'd fled into the kitchen, regretting that I'd ever given him a position of responsibility. "Jesus Christ on a crutch," I complained to Nirmala, "Teddy is *so* bossy."

Nirmala shrugged.

I'd had a terrible thought. "Oh shit," I said aloud. "What if God sent me Teddy so I'd have to stop being such a bossy control freak myself?"

Nirmala shrugged. "We're all put here for a purpose, honey," she said.

I didn't believe it, literally. I didn't really think God "sent" anyone or that, as Mercedes insisted, people received "signs" at critical moments to help them make correct decisions. I thought all the signs anyone could ever need were already there from the beginning: food, sky, broken mop handles, breath. If, as the vows in the Episcopal prayer book said, "I believe that the Old and New Testaments contain everything necessary for salvation," . . . well, sure. I believed the *world* contained everything necessary for salvation. It was a matter of keeping your eyes open. Religion for me wasn't believing that God struggled to communicate a preordained plan in clumsy symbols or even in finely crafted sentences written down dutifully by the apostles. Instead, religion was like learning how to see. I was trying to make meaning from things I hadn't previously paid attention to—the events I hadn't bothered to see and the people I didn't want to.

That was the school, and in it, I was getting taught, not always with pleasure, how much I was like each of the volunteers. How, as much as I wanted to separate myself from them—just as I wanted to be different from St. Gregory's members or from other Christians, parsing the distinctions among us and setting myself apart—I'd been drawn to the pantry, and the church, just the way they had, looking for something real.

Now, when we prayed together before the pantry opened, people spoke up. We'd stand holding hands around the altar, around the tables stacked with groceries. "I never said this before," one volunteer blurted out, "but you know, I hear voices sometimes, and I want to pray to have them stop bothering me." He was teary. "Where there's two or three," he said, "that's church, right? And so it's got power, right? Can we pray for that?"

We did.

The volunteers had no romantic illusions about poor people. They were poor, and many of them had been drug-addicted, and they were finely tuned to scams and hustles of all kinds. "You know that old fat Russian guy?" Michael asked me once.

I knew who he meant. He was always grabbing me and saying "God bless" in a deep, scratchy voice, which I found endearing, especially for a Russian.

"Yeah, he's been going around to the other door and coming back in, saying he forgot something. Then he steals a whole other set of groceries, goes outside, and sells it."

Fucking Russians, I thought.

"It's the Chinese I really can't stand," said Michael, broad-mindedly. "I can keep an eye on the Russian guy, but there's like thirty Chinese ladies who are trying to do the same thing, working together."

Wendy, our Cantonese translator, came up. "I'll tell them!" she yelled. Wendy tended to yell when she was excited. "I'll catch them!" Michael and I laughed with her.

There were still plenty of visitors to the pantry who lit up my day: Miss Lola Lewis, the bent-over old black lady; "Love-Ya," the compulsive dancer; the Nicaraguan woman who'd given me a Christmas gift of a Barbie doll dressed in a homemade green tulle ball gown. Valentina, a middle-aged single mother from Moscow who was going to night school at a community college, had offered her services as a translator, and I began to learn more about the Russians. "See that woman?" Valentina said to me one afternoon, pointing at an ancient matron in a shabby blue raincoat, with a shopping cart and a babushka. "She very intelligent woman, very famous. In Baku, she was architect."

There were others, too, who came to get food bringing food: They'd pull open their bags and give me and the other volunteers homemade pork dumplings, salty *pupusas,* red-chile tamales in corn husks, chocolate donuts, chapatis with blistering curried vegetables, sweet purple plums from a backyard tree, Starlight cakes, pecan shortbread, a blended concoction of sour milk and celery, popcorn, gum. One afternoon a wrinkled, bent-over Moldavian woman with a head scarf came hobbling up. She didn't speak any English, but she always talked to me, and we held hands and smiled a lot. She kissed me noisily on both cheeks, then reached in her pocket and handed me two pieces of candy, with pictures of poodles on the wrapper. "When she kisses you," explained Lawrence, who sometimes went to an Orthodox church, "it's the same as when she kisses the icon at the door. She's venerating the Holy Spirit that's manifest in you."

The candy tasted terrible, like a sugary mothball. "Thank you, God bless you," I said.

I tried not to hold a grudge against the bitchy African woman we'd caught stealing or the drunk guy I'd screamed at. I nodded icily at the man who'd spat "faggot" at one of our volunteers, instead of bouncing him. I tried to hold on to the idea of hospitality to strangers, even the ones who threw trash on our doorstep or insulted Michael or whined that the produce was no good. But standing around with Wendy and Susan, right before the pantry opened, and explaining in Spanish and Chinese and Russian and Tagalog over and over again, at the top of our lungs, yes, we will open in five minutes; *please* do not push one another, there's plenty of food; please, sir, let that little girl through; please don't throw your garbage in our neighbor's driveway . . . there were times when all I could remember was Robert, at the restaurant, in his dirty whites, shaking his head over the customers. "The public," I'd pronounce to Michael and Wendy and Teddy and Paul, as if I were instructing them in an important verse of Scripture, "the public is a motherfucker."

There wasn't a clear line between the public and us, though: We had as many as thirty people volunteering on a Friday now. Most of them were great, but a couple of schizophrenics were too unpredictable and jumpy to deal with the stress of a rush; a few of the middle-class neighbors were too self-conscious to set boundaries; and once in a while, we'd get a true sociopath who thought volunteering was the best scam ever. "Hey, if I work, can I get lunch?" they'd ask.

"Sure," I'd say, then point the new volunteer out to Michael or Nirmala. "Just watch, see how it goes," I'd tell them. One skanky guy, a hustler to his core, had started trying to con a retarded girl into giving him extra food, then twenty bucks, then a place to live. I'd gone over and asked, in my sweetest religious voice, if we could talk. He sat down next to me, with a look of expectant piety on his face I was sure he'd practiced for years on church people.

"That girl is precious to me," I told him. "She is precious to all of us." My voice hardened. "So stay the fuck away from her," I said.

His eyes had widened. "I can't believe you're accusing me— what are you saying?—how can you talk like that in a church?" he stammered.

"Don't ever fucking talk to her again," I said. "Stay away."

Michael laughed heartily when I told him what happened. "Good riddance," he said. "I saw bastards like that all the time in jail, and believe me, they're never gonna change." But, he insisted, we had to keep giving people a chance to work if they asked, even if we had doubts. "The thing is," he said thoughtfully, "a lot of people *need* to volunteer. They want more than food."

They wanted, in fact, church: not the kind where you sit obediently and listen to someone tell you how to behave but the kind where you discover responsibility, purpose, meaning. They wanted a church where they could bring their sorrows, their gifts, their entire messy lives: where they could find community.

I wasn't surprised that the volunteers talked about the pantry the way I talked about St. Gregory's. They might have sounded sentimental or fanatical, but I wasn't in a position to pass judgment: I'd been a stunned, babbling convert, too. More to the point, I knew that the volunteers were being honest and finally saying things they'd been unable to say all their lives. It was humbling.

Teddy said he'd hit bottom about two years before he walked

through our doors. "I'd been up for seven days straight on meth," he told me, "and finally crashed under the bridge where I had a little encampment. When I woke up, there were rats crawling on me. That was the moment when something inside me said, Get out of here and start getting help." He smiled. "I asked God for help. You know, I'd been to Sunday school when I was a kid for about ten minutes, that was it. I wasn't a Christian; I didn't think God was in heaven sitting on a throne."

"I know what you mean," I said.

"I didn't plan to go to church at all," he said.

"I know *just* what you mean," I said.

"But," Teddy went on, "I came here to get food, and then I thought I could volunteer, and volunteering changed me. After all those years of being a drug addict, living on the streets, this gave me the sense that there was the possibility of happiness again. Now every time I give out food and make contact and am able to smile at somebody, even if I can't speak their language, I'm just really touched—I'm being fed by it."

Lauren chimed in. He'd grown up in the Bronx, abused by his father, tormented by knowing he was a girl, "back before anyone talked about transgender." As a child in Catholic school, he explained, "I didn't have a great intellect, but I had a great faith. I stayed after school so nobody would make fun of me or beat me up. I remember they'd separate the boys from the girls at recess, and I'd cry all the time. I'd sit out in the playground, by this statue of Jesus, and cry."

Now Lauren had serious health problems; she was indigent, living in subsidized housing, on medication for depression, and the only caretaker for her dying partner, a psychotic brother, and her aging mother. But she came to the pantry every week because, she said, "I need the fellowship."

"Here, I feel accepted as me," she said, in her gravelly Bronx accent. "I give out bags at the door, and I talk with everyone who comes to the pantry. When I say hi, it's like I'm not just giving food but giving of myself. You know, I may not be the happiest person alive. But I'm grateful I'm here. And I have something to give."

Teddy nodded in agreement. "I'm able to perceive beauty in a way I never could before," he said. "I used to walk by stuff and never see it. Now I feel myself connected to the rest of the universe. Giving people food, I can really feel I've done something worthwhile at the end of the day."

This is what gets left out, I was realizing: not just left out of the national political debate but also left out of religious discourse. Politicians talked about welfare—usually to blame and scapegoat—and occasionally made speeches about poverty. There was no shortage of talk about the poor and social service from church leaders of all stripes. But the experiences of people such as my volunteers, the texture and specificity of their incarnate lives, were missing from the story of what Christianity was like now in contemporary America.

And just as I'd looked for the unofficial truth, as a reporter, on the edges of things, I believed I was discovering, at the food pantry, our people's significance to the real story. They were on the margins of society, and often on the margins of the church, but their lives were full of meaning. They threw light not only on the overlooked parts but on how the whole system worked. These poor lives illuminated middle-class life—our anxiety, our reliance on managing and fixing feelings rather than having them, our desire to punish. They made clear the limitations of religions that cast out every member whose reality didn't fit inside church doctrines. Their lives showed the profound re-

sourcefulness and strengths of the weak. The thing that astonished me sometimes—listening to tales of terrible damage, psy-
chosis, loss—was not how messed up people could be but how
resilient; how, in the depths of suffering, they found ways to
adapt and continue.

But in breaking bread with my people, and hearing their stories, I was learning about more than politics or religion. I was
learning something about God: You can't hope to see God without opening yourself to *all* God's creation.

Chapter 20

Cooking with My Brother II

—

I loved my volunteers. I wanted to really cook for them.

It was insane to cook lunch for twenty-five at church: The kitchen, a generous gift from a member, had been designed by someone who obviously liked appliances more than actual cooking. There was a huge restaurant range, big industrial stainless-steel refrigerators and counters, a convection oven, a deep double sink, and about one square foot of usable surface space. The galley was narrow, just about a yard wide, and every single cupboard was crammed to overflowing with the detritus of collective life: a million plastic forks, some sippy cups missing their tops, patens and chalices for communion, chipped platters, coffee cups, plastic bags with sugar packets, someone's unclaimed covered casserole dish, a dozen large bowls for foot washing, a full set of butter plates, a shelf of graham crackers for Sunday school snacks, a closet stuffed with candles and incense, and two drawers full of broken corkscrews, salad servers, measuring cups, and miscellaneous hand tools. St. Gregory's prided itself on its Sunday coffee hour, which soared above the usual church fare of limp pastries and weak coffee, and during the year, the church held regular "feasts of friends," potlucks modeled on

second-century Eucharists in which the congregation gathered
to eat together. At Easter, there was always a fabulous spread,
with ham biscuits and champagne, and I knew there was a bunch
of foodies who hosted spectacular community lunches to greet
newcomers.

But the kitchen was a mess. Then Paul announced he was
going to make lunch every week with me. "I love to cook," he
said. "All I really want to do is cook for people. All the time."

"Hmm," I said. I loved teasing him. "Too bad you're a
priest. . . . Don't suppose you took the job because it had anything to do with food?"

"Shut up," explained Paul.

One Friday we took inventory: Besides the baking dishes,
which apparently reproduced in the dark of their cabinet, the
only usable pots were one six-quart saucepan and a twenty-inch
skillet. "Impossible," I said. "No, it'll be fabulous," said Paul.
He was poking happily through the drawers. "Look, here's a
springform pan! You'll see."

We spent the first few weeks sniffing around each other in the
kitchen, overpolite. "What shall I do?" "That sounds good."
"May I have a spoon, please?"

We tried to figure out what to make. We were cautious at
first—more soups, then stews, chili—until one Friday I couldn't
stand it anymore. "Fuck this," I said. "Why cook if we're going
to cook school lunch? Let's go buy a pork tenderloin." Paul lit
up. "Hmm, what about rubbing it with cumin seed and orange
peel? And I could make some biscuits. And greens. And what
kind of pie?"

I worried that Paul was a show-off. I worried that he was
going to use recipes. But I was promptly humiliated, because he
not only cooked but baked without recipes—and not a big hippie pile of apple crumble either, but a chocolate torte with crème

anglaise. He made his own mayonnaise, he salted enthusiastically, he stirred things with his hands and knocked the refrigerator door closed with his butt and made me laugh hysterically. Paul was good. He was not an idiot. He was not a home cook.

So we started really cooking on Fridays. We bought new pans and a rolling pin to replace the sacramental wine bottle Paul had been using to roll out pastry dough. It was like being home on the range with my brother again. We bumped into each other, gave each other orders, stopped bumping into each other, mastered the rhythm, learned to wordlessly pick up each other's work. Paul and I cooked like crazy, delirious with pleasure. We made chicken and dumplings, scalloped potatoes, roast pork with rosemary and fennel. We made culinary jokes: the deconstructed Boston cream pie; an apparently banal all-white meal of potatoes, cauliflower, and chicken with surprise punch lines of horseradish, white pepper, and lemon.

Our volunteers wandered in and sniffed appreciatively. Mercedes decided we were serious and presented us, seriously, with a wooden *tortillera* so we could make proper *pupusas* with real masa. Teddy, who was in a teeth-grinding, compulsive phase, made coffee about sixteen times a day and carried cups out to the workers on a tray. Paul brought in his grandmother Bessie's cookbook, from the Houston Junior League, and read me aloud the recipes for "Molded Neptune Salad" and "Lamb Hawaii" and "Food for the Gods," which involved saltine cracker crumbs, dates, and whipped cream; we actually baked the "B-Milk Pies" following Bessie's handwritten directions in the back of the book. I hung up a garish Mexican cross over the stove and threw out all the mismatched plastic containers. Meanwhile, we chopped and stirred and talked about food, sex, gossip, politics, and religion.

"Okay, Paul," I said. "So— Shit, do we really not have butter?"

"In the freezer," he said.

"So, okay, tell me what you were saying about the Virgin Mary."

"Yes," he said with enthusiasm. "Right. Here's the radical thing about Mary: She doesn't need a man to have a baby. Her virginity means that her womb belongs to her."

"And that she's willing to be taken over," I said, reaching for a spoon. "To let God move in her and not know what's gonna happen next."

"Exactly," said Paul. "The thing about modern fundamentalists is that they think they can control God like a piece of technology and that they're the only ones who have the secret code."

It was a huge relief to me to have a friend who could get beyond conventional discussions about religion. So many of the arguments between left- and right-wing Christians, fundamentalists and Episcopalians, Roman Catholics and Pentecostals, seemed to hinge on the idea that their own sect had the correct practice, "the secret code," that would save the followers and make God reward them. That was idolatry, as I saw it: magical thinking, pagan religion. I didn't think God needed humans to practice religion at all: God didn't need to be appeased by sacrifices or offerings or perfectly memorized quotations from the Bible spoken in the right order. God was not manageable.

Human beings might want rituals, but it was dangerous to confuse the rituals with an ultimately unknowable God. That led to crusades, sectarian killings, the casting-out of heretics—in fact, to the murder of Jesus, who dared to challenge the religious authorities with raw truth. "The message of Jesus," Paul told me, mixing a black bean salad, "is the only sure cure for religion."

This was a different way to learn theology: not the solitary reading I'd stumbled through, not the instruction I'd received through sermons. There in the kitchen was the physicality at the heart of the story of Jesus. Listening and sautéing, talking and tasting, feeding friends and eating together: It was a stew of words and acts and food.

And through it, I could sometimes grasp the backward, upside-down reality I'd sensed at Christianity's core: the frightening promise that, as the prayer said, echoing Mary's words, "Things which were cast down are being raised up, and things which have grown old are being made new." This was where I found my faith: a faith expressed in the wild conceit that a helpless, low-caste baby could be God. That ugly, contaminated, and unimportant people embodied holiness. That my own neediness and misfitting, not my goodness or piety, were what God intended to use.

And here, at the pantry, just like Mercedes, like Paul, like Lauren, I was finding a message from God. It said the hunger that had drawn us here was so that we could see what the kingdom of heaven looked like.

Some Christians thought the kingdom was about an afterlife, but I believed it was *this* world, just as my parents had, in their secular way, insisted so long ago. The kingdom was the same old earth, populated by the same clueless humans, transformed wherever you could glimpse God shining through it.

Some thought it was about judgment, but I believed that in the kingdom, there was no separation of sinners from saved, righteous from damned. The pantry looked like the kingdom to me precisely because we were all thrown in together—a makeshift community so much bigger and more contradictory than any of us would have chosen. But each of us had come just as we were to this Table, drawn, without planning, to the shores of some lake where we'd heard miracles might happen. And we found the kind of abundance described in parables: food for five thousand, money multiplying like manna; oil pouring out profligately and the lamps burning wildly all night long, blazing through the darkness of our lives.

Steve Hassett would visit us from seminary sometimes. He was getting close to ordination. "I go to the chapel at school, and it's like they're playing dress-up in some fantasy of English life three hundred years ago," he told me wistfully. "I just wish they could look at the pantry and *see* it, you know? Like, it's not about doing charity for poor people. We're bringing people together to share food and praise God. What else do you want? That's church."

"That's communion," I said. "Jesus's Table."

I'd seen it, upside down, when Donald Schell wandered into the pantry one afternoon, looking for a book of hymns, and Michael greeted him sweetly. "Hi," he said to the priest who'd founded the church. He pulled out a chair and motioned Donald to join us for lunch. We were serving flank steak and a big yellow cake. "Welcome to St. Gregory's. Is this your first time here?"

I'd even seen it on the one day of the year when the pantry got no delivery and was closed, Good Friday. The church was stripped of ornament and hung with black; when it got dark, the congregation would gather to chant a funeral liturgy, laying flowers on an icon of Jesus and leaving in silence, taking a hot cross bun to break their fasts.

Around five in the evening, Paul was helping set up. A homeless guy, kind of sweaty and intense, strolled in, and Paul explained to him that the pantry was closed for Good Friday.

"Don't you have any food?" he asked.

Paul turned and saw the trays of hot cross buns, and handed the man a couple. The man lifted them up.

"*Baruch attah Adonai . . . ,*" he began. "*Baruch attah Adonai eloheinu. . . .* Shit, it's been a long time since my bar mitzvah," he said. He was saying the Hebrew blessing for bread: "Blessed are thou, Lord God, king of the universe, who brings forth bread from the earth."

Paul stood there in his black cassock trying to remember the Hebrew prayer, as the homeless guy smiled and took a big bite of the first bun. "*Baruch attah Adonai eloheinu melek ha-alom . . . ,*" Paul began. He couldn't remember it either. "Well, bless this bread," Paul said.

The stranger nodded, took another bun, and walked out. "Okay," he said. "Thanks. Good Shabbas."

"I'm feeling it," said Paul, lifting his hand and bowing his head. "Come, Jesus . . . Yes, Lord . . . Casserole!" he shouted triumphantly, in his best Texas evangelical-preacher mode.

"What, macaroni again?" I said. We were in the cramped kitchen on a Friday morning, figuring out lunch. Sometimes the Food Bank truck would deliver too many pallets of ripe tomatoes or escarole or pears, inspiring a menu because we had to use up the excess, but mostly we argued about what to prepare, then drove down to the Mexican market and bought food. "Mac and cheese? Not exactly seasonal."

"You of little faith," said Paul. "Casserole three ways: I'll make a ham casserole with homemade pasta, a tuna casserole, cabbage with cream."

"Cream and *horseradish*," I said bossily. "And some fresh breadcrumbs. What's for dessert?"

"Oh, I'll fix something light," said Paul casually. He had a sneaky grin.

I was putting on my jacket. "Sounds good," I said. "I'll get the ham. How much cream do you need?"

"Got it already," said Paul, flinging open the refrigerator to show three quarts of heavy cream and some half-and-half.

"You tramp," I said absently. "Have fun."

When I came back to church, with three pounds of ham under my arm, Michael held the door open for me and gave me a rapid-fire briefing. "Teddy's here; he's kind of wound up, but he's got the list," he said. "Mercedes's cleaning. Nirmala's got those Greek pastries. I put the kid on boxes. That tweaker from Polk Street showed up again; he's fucking useless, but I'll get him to bag potatoes so I can keep an eye on him."

"No cereal?" I asked.

"No, but we got enough food for about three hundred, it looks," said Michael. "You won't believe how many watermelons there are. I'll cut the huge ones in half."

Nirmala had tuned the radio to her favorite classical station. "Hello, honey!" she sang out, coming over to kiss me. "Tell me when lunch is ready, I'll set the table, but let me finish unpacking this pastry first."

In the kitchen, Paul was mixing shredded cabbage with his hands in a huge stainless-steel bowl. "Yo, sister," he greeted me.

I started chopping ham.

"Wait," said Paul. "You got to taste this." He wiped his hands on a dishrag and went over to the refrigerator. "Open your mouth."

"Oh my God," I said, swallowing. It was grainy and cold and melting and milky and rich and sweet. "Oh my God, what *is* that?"

Paul tried to keep a straight face. "Just a light little something," he said. "*Tres leches:* You separate the eggs, make a cake, soak it in heavy cream, sweetened condensed milk, evaporated milk. . . ."

"Wow," I said. "That's like, I don't know, being breast-fed by the Wisdom of God."

Paul raised his hand and bowed his head. "All glory."

Chapter 21

Rites

—

The food pantry was our church, and in it, we translated the sacraments, and key Christian rites, in often unorthodox ways. In doing so, I'd come to see that we were sharing in the ongoing work of all believers, and that we were helping make the larger church new, even as we were ourselves being transformed.

In the Episcopal Church, baptism and Eucharist are the two great essential sacraments: "outward and visible signs of inward and spiritual grace." According to church belief, baptism offers "new life"; communion promises a "foretaste of the heavenly banquet" as well as "the strengthening of our union with Christ and one another." Other rites defined by the church as sacramental include confirmation; ordination; marriage; "the reconciliation of a penitent," or confession; and unction. There are also specific rites for healing, anointing, and blessing, at the time of death, and for funerals.

In the Book of Common Prayer, the forms for all these rites are spelled out. In Episcopal practice, though, there's variation among congregations, and St. Gregory's had developed many of its own forms, adapting the prayer book templates.

I had written several liturgies myself—a bilingual Spanish/

English Eucharist for use at the food pantry; a couple of different forms for morning prayer, a noonday service. As a deacon,
I'd become used to long discussions about liturgy: how to take
something as basic as a funeral rite and open it up to reveal its
true purpose; how to take old familiar rituals and express their
meaning more powerfully by tweaking the forms.

At the food pantry, I wasn't consciously planning to observe
specific rites: Instead, I began to notice our people sponta-
neously engaging in sacramental acts, finding their own ways to
express the desires and purposes that had been codified so long
ago by the church. Sometimes these ways looked familiar, as
with anointing and healing prayer; sometimes, as with our
lunches together, it took imagination to see the body and blood
of Christ present in the enchiladas and *tres leches* cake. But I'd
come to see grace in those unofficial rites: They took religious
conventions and played them out with a different cast of charac-
ters but the same crucial themes that had brought me to faith in
the first place.

The whole idea of healing prayer bothered me for a long time: It
seemed not only superstitious but cruel to suggest that God was
listening and deciding, based on human petitions, whether he felt
like curing someone's cancer. Lynn Baird, who'd worked as a
nurse before she became a priest, looked at it differently.
"There's physical healing and a broader healing," she told me.
"Prayer's not about getting the outcome you wish for."

Lynn had entered a new stage in her multiple sclerosis, with
extreme muscle weakness, and couldn't kneel or walk unas-
sisted; sometimes she couldn't even speak clearly. "I look out at
my garden," she'd told me once over the phone, "and every-

thing's overgrown and muddy, and I can't stand not being able to get to it." Lynn had loved digging around in the flower beds; she prayed best, she said, with dirt under her nails. Now she sat at the window or slept, exhausted; she still came to church, but it often meant that she'd have to preside at the altar sitting down, trembling, with deacons holding the cross she could no longer lift. Meanwhile, Lynn's daughter kept calling from the other side of the country, where she was struggling to find a job.

"How do you pray?" I asked Lynn.

"Well," she said, "usually I start off, 'Okay, what the hell is going on here, God?' "

Lynn's approach to healing prayer reminded me of George Schenk, a friend of my brother's, a well-known bread baker and chef who'd given the best commencement address I'd ever heard of. It was also a kind of ordination sermon, such as the ones bishops gave to new priests. Talking to the graduating students at David's culinary school, Schenk said that he believed food could help heal the sick and injured, "not in any complete way" but through incorporating the cook's love "into the broth." By caring for his own family members at the end of their lives, he told the new cooks, he'd learned that delicious food could be "one of the last experiences of physical joy for the dying."

"You have a special trust," Schenk told them. "A lot has been given to you. You've got the ability to feed others with integrity and thus help them heal."

"Food and healing go together," Lynn echoed.

The word *healing* could still work my nerves like a slick of California snake oil. But at the pantry, I had to accept that people came looking for it. They wanted to complain about their sore backs or cry about their sick mother or petition God for a miracle. I didn't believe in miracles.

It turned out, though, that other people did. "Can I talk to you?" Marshall asked me. Marshall was a small, wiry man about my age, with deep-set eyes and a coat too big for him. He had a couple of plastic bags of groceries dangling from his arms. "Can I just talk to you?" he asked again, urgently. "I need healing."

We'd walked over to the chairs beneath the icon of Mary. It was ancient, a faded Ethiopian painting that showed angels swimming around a cross-eyed Virgin, and a huge-headed baby Jesus waving. Marshall couldn't speak for a minute, then I took his hand, and he blurted everything out in a scared rush: He had stomach cancer, and the doctors at the VA hospital had just informed him that he needed an operation within the next few months or he'd die. He was in pain, but mostly he was afraid.

From then on, we'd sit and talk and pray whenever Marshall stopped by the pantry. It was always physical: Sometimes I'd get out the oil and anoint him; sometimes I'd make him a cup of tea. Finally the day came when Marshall said he was going in for surgery. He grabbed me and started to cry. I remember every detail of that moment: Marshall's blue work pants, his funny mustard-colored corduroy coat, the damp warmth of his hands. He laid his head in my lap while I held him, and all thoughts of sickness and operations and cures dissolved. Everything around us slowed and hung there, until there was just God's breath between us, rising and falling in our two chests, not separate at all.

It was an experience of grace. It faded. Marshall sat up, blew his nose, and went off with his groceries. I called the VA hospital the next week but couldn't locate him.

Many Fridays later, someone came up to me outside the church and grabbed me from behind. I turned around. It was Marshall, and he was radiant. "I died!" he shouted. "I died, twice, on the operating table, but I came back each time. They said they thought I was gone for good. You're not going to believe it, but I'm here!"

I didn't believe in miracles. And yet I had begun to believe in healing. I saw that you could be changed, opened to experiencing your life differently, made more whole, even as your body was falling apart. That you could be healed from fear by touch, even when you remained sick.

And I had begun to believe in resurrection. I didn't mean, by resurrection, having Marshall stand up alive from the operating table and walk: I saw no cause and effect between our prayers together and his improbable recovery. Resurrection didn't mean what I still yearned for in my loneliest moments: to see my best friend, Douglas; or Martín-Baró; or my beloved father materialize again, even for just a moment, next to me. I actually couldn't imagine that I would see them again, in the flesh, in a drift of pink clouds in a place called heaven. Resurrection, to me, was mysterious and true in a way I could only glimpse for a second, before my mind refused to stretch that far. It passed, as the Bible said, human understanding. But I sensed it had to do with time, like the time Marshall lay in my lap and we were both completely present and connected. It was about the eternity available in a fully lived instant.

I didn't really believe in marriage either: Never in my life had my relationships with men or women been blessed by church or state. Martha and I, who'd been together for eleven years, hadn't sought a public ceremony of any kind. Officially, my family wasn't legal: Katie was a bastard, and Martha no relative of ours at all. In many churches, our family was an "abomination."

Even liberal churches colluded with the state by having their clergy perform legal marriages for some citizens while offering separate-but-equal "blessings" to others. At St. Gregory's, gay couples were accepted matter-of-factly, but "the blessing of a gay union" was nonetheless an event requiring special permission from the bishop, in order to avoid setting off a firestorm of reaction that could split the Episcopal Church. Meanwhile, conservative churches had thrown themselves into the political fight to "protect marriage" against deviants such as us. I wondered what they would have thought about my performing the wedding of Eddie and his bride.

So I had a bad attitude. And I didn't really understand why matrimony was called "holy" or why marriage rites were, like communion, an essential part of Christianity.

On Valentine's Day 2004, when San Francisco announced that it would offer civil marriages to all, Katie became insistent. She had a strong sense of justice, and something about the idea of a real wedding was powerful to her. "I really, really want you to do this," she said, looking longingly out the car window as we drove past the lines of excited, weeping couples waiting to enter City Hall. "Please, let's do this."

It wasn't a plan, it wasn't a considered act; it was an impulse like taking the bread that first time. Martha and I looked at each other and told Katie yes.

We arrived at City Hall first thing the next morning, three hours before it opened. It was raining a bit, and the line of people waiting to be married was already extending around the front of the domed, ornately gilded building. Over 300 couples had been turned away yesterday because there simply hadn't been enough time to do all the ceremonies, and they'd been given tickets to get in today instead. I had a sudden flash of how much the City Hall line looked like our food pantry, and of how it must feel to wait, with a ticket, worrying about getting inside.

There were people of every race and age, young gay dads with babies, old women holding hands, people in wheelchairs, men pushing strollers, women wearing wedding gowns carrying flowers. Parents were crying and hugging their brides; two elegant guys in pinstriped suits were fumbling with their rings, complete strangers were embracing each other. I thought of the psalm: *Those who sowed in tears are reaping, singing and laughing. They are coming back in joy.*

Hundreds of city workers had volunteered to help: They circulated in the crowd, explaining the process, helping with forms, easing the wait. It was busy and still at the same time. There was a consciousness of history, of people moving together in something huge and collective and unstoppable.

Then all of a sudden we were swept inside. We filled out forms, jammed up against more jubilant, excited people, and stood in the hallways. "On behalf of the sheriff's office," said a teary white man in uniform, "we welcome you to City Hall."

Katie was grinning uncontrollably. We moved into the huge, marble-floored rotunda, where two dozen different city aides, deputized for the occasion, were conducting separate, simultaneous ceremonies. Our marriage commissioner was a portly, dark-haired Irish guy. He took our papers, greeted us, and pulled Katie, our witness, over.

"Okay," he said. "Put down your coats and bags."

We stopped, and everything stopped. "Okay," said the marriage commissioner. "Okay, take a deep breath. This is real. Look at each other."

Martha and I started to cry. We said the vows, exchanged rings, kissed Katie, hugged everyone within reach, signed the papers, kissed some more. As we stumbled down the stairs to the thronged streets outside, a crowd gathered in front of the building burst into applause. A stranger thrust a bunch of red carnations into Martha's arms. People cheered, and a little girl, maybe six years old, dashed up and handed me a folded-up piece of paper. It was a card she'd made. It had pink hearts all over it, and it said, in crayon and Magic Marker, "Congratulations on your marriage."

My mother almost cried with happiness when I called her. My sister, Ellen, yelped with joy. My brother was elated. "We're gonna have to get you a kitchen appliance, now that you're officially married," he said.

The next Sunday, we went to St. Gregory's together, with three other gay couples who'd joined in the historic event. One of the church ladies had prepared an enormous whipped-cream cake, and someone else had brought champagne. Steve and several other straight friends whose weddings I'd deaconed at were there to celebrate with us, along with Nirmala, Mercedes, and half a dozen volunteers from the food pantry.

After communion, before the cake was cut, Donald called the couples forward. "We're going to bless these marriages," he said, motioning the other priests in the room to lay their hands on the eight of us. "Everyone, put your hand on somebody's shoulder, so that we're all touching the newlyweds." A circle of bodies surrounded us. I gripped Martha's hand and bent my head. Donald began to chant a prayer. Light and tulips and a cloud of faces filled the room.

The marriage of a couple, I understood then, was more than personal: It was a rite binding people into community and, beyond that, pointing to the union of all humanity with God. A marriage such as ours prophesied the politically inconvenient but spiritually resonant truth that the unlikely and outcast were part of God's creation, in all ways. It was like communion: When some people were shut out of the rite, the picture couldn't be complete.

Months later, a court would annul all four thousand of the

San Francisco marriages, and the bitter political disputes would grind on. Right-wing Christians would continue to rail against the blasphemous scandal; lawyers would debate the Constitution and the tax code.

But what had happened to us in the blessing at St. Gregory's was outside both the law and the Law. Our marriages had happened on God's time, in God's space. The irregular rites became an icon, a metaphor for the difficult and vital imperative to love others. And they belonged not just to individual couples but to the community—to everyone reaching out a hand for blessing.

A year later, Mercedes would hand me an envelope at the food pantry, apologizing that it had taken her so long to give us an appropriate wedding present. "*Sara y Marta,*" she'd written on the greeting card, which was in flowery Spanish and featured embossed, entwined gold bands. Inside, Mercedes had tucked a Western Union money order for two hundred dollars, which she'd put aside, week by week, from her housecleaning wages. "Your holy matrimony and true love," she'd printed carefully at the bottom of the card, "is a gift from God."

I cried as I read over the prayer from the marriage rite in the Book of Common Prayer. It had new meaning for me. "Make their life together a sign of Christ's love to this sinful and broken world," the prayer said, "that unity may overcome estrangement, forgiveness heal guilt, and joy conquer despair."

The sacrament of baptism, as practiced in churches, initiates believers into a specific denomination as well as into a covenant with God: You're baptized as an Episcopalian, a Roman Catholic—even, well, a Baptist. But at the church of the food pantry, an impromptu baptism demonstrated what I thought was the true meaning of the sacrament, far beyond denominational niceties.

And the rite would reverberate through St. Gregory's, stirring up new questions and insights for believers—as all acts of the Spirit do.

I was unloading groceries one Friday when I spotted Sasha standing out back by the baptismal font, as if she were waiting for someone. Sasha was a very small black girl, maybe six or seven years old, who usually came to the pantry with an impatient, teenage aunt. I'd never met her mother. Sasha's hair wasn't always combed, and this day she had a split lip. "Sweetheart!" I said. I was glad to see her again. "Want a snack? There's some chips inside."

Sasha looked at me, not smiling. "Is this water the water God puts on you to make you safe?" she demanded abruptly, in a strangely formal voice.

I put down my boxes. What was she asking for? Was I being asked to baptize her? My mind raced, flashing back to when I'd stood at the font for my own baptism just a few years ago.

Nothing about that water had made me safe. It had pushed me further out from the certainties and habits of my former life, taken me away from my family, and launched me on this mad and frustrating mission to feed multitudes. It had eroded my identity as an objective journalist and given me an unsettling glimpse of how very little I knew. I was no less flawed or frightened or capable of being hurt than I'd been before my conversion, and now, in addition, I was adrift in this water, yoked together with all kinds of other Christians, many of whom I didn't like or trust.

How could I tell this child that a drop of water could make her safe? I had no idea what Sasha was going through at home, but I suspected it was rough. And baptism, if it signified anything, signified the unavoidable reality of the cross at the heart of Christian faith. It wasn't a magic charm but a reminder of God's presence in the midst of unresolved human pain.

I remembered what Lynn Baird had asked me, when I was contemplating baptism.

"Do you want it?" I asked.

Sasha locked her eyes on me. "Yes," she said. "Yes, I want that water."

There was something so serious in her face that it stopped me cold. I dipped my fingers into the font, and Sasha turned her face up to me, concentrating. I made the sign of the cross on her forehead.

I took Sasha into the church and found Lynn, who was trying valiantly to help out at the pantry, despite her illness. I was so glad she was there. Of all the priests at St. Gregory's, Lynn was the one least fazed by suffering: She was, as the Bible said dryly of Jesus, "acquainted with grief." I told her what had happened, and we walked over to the small wooden shrine by the preacher's chair, where Lynn asked Sasha if she wanted a special blessing.

"Yes," Sasha said again, gravely. "I want that."

From the shrine, Lynn took the small container of oil and showed it to Sasha. The girl stood up, very still, in front of Lynn's chair. "I'm going to put my hands on you and pray now, if you're ready," Lynn said, and Sasha nodded.

Behind us, a crowd was circling around the Table, gathering up rice and beans and Froot Loops cereal. A bunch of other kids were dodging in and out, shouting and punching one another and eating snacks. "Jesus is always with you," Lynn told Sasha, as she finished rubbing the oil on her skin, "no matter what happens to you, even when bad things happen. You're not ever alone." Sasha closed her eyes for a moment, then looked down directly at the seated priest, and I saw something flowing between them: the child, crucified, anointing Lynn with the power of her crucifixion, and Lynn, receiving it, anointing Sasha.

That Sunday, at church, I told some other deacons what had

happened. One of them reminded me of the story in Acts when an Ethiopian eunuch on the road demanded that the apostle Philip baptize him immediately: "Look, there's some water here," said the eunuch, a Gentile, a dark-skinned foreigner, and a stranger. "Is there anything to stop me from being baptized?" Just as the apostle Philip had, in a sense, been converted again to a broader understanding of Christianity by the insistence of the outsider, so Lynn had been converted again, brought to see God in a new way, by Sasha's profound desire for the water.

I was talking about the girl at the font when Lawrence got up suddenly and left the room, crying. "I ran into the bathroom," he said to me later, "and started splashing water on my face, and when I realized what I was doing, that I was rebaptizing myself, I cried even harder."

Lawrence cleared his throat. He took out a handkerchief and blew his nose. His maître d' jacket was draped over his gangly frame.

"Honey," I said.

"Ah," said Lawrence. "It just came to me how much I want God's safety."

"I know," I said.

"I wonder if that water really does protect us," said Lawrence. "I fear not. That's not what it's for."

Two weeks later, Sasha came back to the pantry with her aunt, who was lugging another baby. She ran up to me, leaped into my arms, kissed me, and said, "Let's go find Lynn. I want a special blessing." We anointed her again, and again Sasha received the oil deliberately, with great attention, listening to every word of our prayers. Then she corrected Lynn.

"It's not AH-men," Sasha said, "it's A-men."

I asked her what *amen* meant.

"It means thank you," Sasha said.

"Thank *you*, ladies," said Paul Fromberg. We'd finished washing up the lunch dishes, and there were five minutes left before the pantry opened. Michael went outside for a last quick smoke as Paul took off his apron. "I'd love to stay, but I've got a sermon to write."

I went to dump our meal scraps in the compost bin by the baptismal font. Next to it was the columbarium, where members' ashes were kept behind a door inlaid with a tile mosaic of Jesus levitating from a tomb. I thought about the people inside whose faces I'd kissed around the altar, whose feet I'd rubbed as they were dying, whose ashes I'd sung over with the congregation. The afternoon sun was hot on my neck, and I considered what a visitor to the food pantry had told me about seeing the Jesus mosaic late at night. It was visible through the backyard fence, and always lit up. "When I see him," she said, nodding familiarly at the figure, "I don't feel so alone." She had six kids, she told me, left behind with an aunt in Mexico, and she sent them money and prayed for their safety. "I walk by here to greet him," she said. "Sometimes I tell him to greet his mother for me."

A wave of voices rose up. Michael had opened the front doors, and now a stream of people was entering the church, lugging their shopping bags, tugging their kids by the hand, greeting our volunteers raucously.

I felt dizzy. Sometimes, at the pantry, it seemed as if everything were happening on two planes at once. I was slipping effortlessly back and forth between feeding people and splashing in the waters of new life, taking out the trash and remembering funeral rites. I was watching a regular Friday afternoon, with its ordinary conversations and kidding around, and seeing creation the way God sees it: weak, heartbreaking, and completely beloved.

Paul came outside. He raised his right hand when he saw me standing there. "Sister!" he said. "Am I interrupting a moment of prayer?"

I couldn't always tell when Paul was making fun of me. "What the hell," I said defensively. "Why *not* pray?"

"No, go right ahead," said Paul. "I mean, look at Miss Pollen. You know she asked to pray with me once, and she started speaking in tongues. It was incredibly beautiful." He waved at Miss Pollen, over by the snack table, her bonnet stuck firmly to her hair with a screwdriver-sized hatpin. She was talking with Miss Lola Lewis, who was wearing a raincoat and leaning on her banged-up grocery cart.

The two old women started over to us. Miss Lewis was a regular at the pantry, a tiny lady with gnarled, arthritic hands. Every week she came to get groceries so she could go back to her room, cook on her hot plate, put the meals in rinsed-out plastic containers, and take them down to feed the beggars who lived on her street. She hugged me, and Miss Pollen dropped a cerise lipstick kiss on my chin. "How are you?" asked Paul, beaming.

"Blessed," said Miss Pollen. "I've had a little flu, but I'm blessed."

Miss Lewis smiled at us all. "Are you thirsty?" she asked her friend. "You need to drink plenty of liquids. Wait a minute." She rummaged in her shopping cart and pulled out a bottle of cranberry-grape juice and a Dixie cup.

"Here you go," she said. The sacrament.

I'd been raised to reject religion, but I was finding that people often wanted more of it than the church was willing to give: more sacraments, more rites, more prayer and healing and blessing. Those desires of people formally outside the system of religion could be a force transforming the people inside, just as the visitors to our food pantry were transforming St. Gregory's. What if, in churches that prohibited it, divorced outcasts and gay people asked to be married as well as baptized? What if unprepared kids and nonmembers of those churches asked to receive communion or women offered themselves for ordination?

Most days I thought I was a pretty lousy Christian: mean, self-absorbed, confused. But I knew I was as much a "real" Christian as the Christians who wanted to exclude me. "Real" Christians weren't the ones who happened to control the levers of ecclesiastical power, those who belonged to the biggest churches or the oldest traditions. They could be total outsiders and still perform rites that evoked the Gospel messages of healing, new life, shared food, shared grief, shared peace. They included anyone who, like those first unqualified disciples, got a taste of Jesus and followed him. As Paul Fromberg had said to me once, when I asked him how he had stuck with Christianity when so many wanted to kick him out for being gay, "Honey, I know who my shepherd is." That growing, changing, unruly flock of Jesus's was the only force that could reform the church: When you let the wrong people in, the promise of change could finally come true.

Chapter 22

Multiplying the Loaves

———

At the food pantry, our attendance slowed down and then picked up again, rapidly: 270, 280, 315 people. When it rained, they all packed into the church with their wet clothes and shopping bags. When it was cold and clear, they stood outside for hours waiting for groceries.

We handed out snacks as people waited for the food pantry to open, and I'd see adults squabbling over an extra candy bar or pack of crackers. One old man actually started weeping when he finally got inside to the bread table and there wasn't any left. Newcomers would be furious when I told them we didn't have enough food. "I'm sorry," I'd say. "We're full. We can't take any new people today."

"But I don't have *anything*," a middle-aged woman said desperately. "You don't understand. I DO. NOT. HAVE. ANY. THING. Please."

I took Paul out to the deck one afternoon, where we could see the line forming. We'd just finished serving lunch to our volunteers: fried chicken, mashed potatoes and gravy, coleslaw, perfect little yeast-raised biscuits, and a chocolate layer cake. Nirmala was washing dishes and talking happily to Mercedes, and everyone else was resting, sprawled under the icons and crosses in their pantry aprons.

"*Now* what?" Paul asked. I motioned to the people. There was a hum of voices rising from the crowd, a multilayered chorus of complaint and conversation in five different languages. A bus stopped at the end of the block and discharged another dozen Chinese ladies who scrambled to get a place in line.

"We can't do this forever," I said.

"What," said Paul. "You mean. . . . Oh, Christ, *now* what?"

"You know," I said. "A feast inside the church, for the members, and outside everyone waiting."

"You're not saying we can feed everyone," said Paul, teasing. "I mean, that would be communist. That would be inappropriate. And then"—he made his voice sound stern and bureaucratic—"then everyone would want to come to the Table."

I had to laugh, but it wasn't really a joke. "I know we can't feed everyone," I said. "I'm not saying we should. But I'm telling you, this can't last."

I didn't know what else we could do. Already I'd used Derek Howard's settlement money to launch nine new pantries in schools, community centers, and churches—among them, an African American Catholic parish in the ghetto, a mostly Asian Presbyterian church by the ocean, and a Pentecostal Samoan congregation. It didn't matter that the churches were so different from St. Gregory's; the bread at the core of Christianity could speak to people whose doctrines ostensibly divided them.

The Samoan Assembly of God Church was a long, shabby rectangle of a building on a busy street, with no windows and no ornament. Rena, the pastor's daughter, had come to visit our pantry at the urging of the Food Bank and been, as she told me, "set on fire." A dreamily beautiful, heavyset young woman with long, flowing hair and a soft voice, she started organizing her congregation to feed the hungry.

Rena and a friend were at the front door when I showed up on opening day, eagerly waiting for their first pantry visitors. A few kids wrestled on the dirty green carpet, and in the back of the meeting room, a group of women had arranged groceries on tables. Half a dozen teenage Samoan boys hung around in oversize jerseys, practicing hip-hop dance moves and trying to pretend they weren't in church with their moms.

"Look," said Rena proudly, "we got Spam and everything."

I looked. It was a vision of abundance.

All it took was two or three thousand dollars to get a pantry such as the Samoan Assembly's going. They were opening all over the city, feeding hundreds of new families. Abundance was everywhere; the network was expanding.

But the lines on Fridays outside our doors still weren't dwindling. I called Anne Quaintance at the Food Bank once again.

"Face it, Sara," Anne told me. "You're not particularly conveniently located. You don't give out special food. There are other pantries now to go to. People just like St. Gregory's."

The day the loaves multiplied began, like all my Fridays, with psalms. "*God gives this place to the hungry*," we sang that day; "*the poor shall eat all they want.*" After morning prayer was finished, I propped the church gate open so the Food Bank's truck driver could get in, then put on my pantry vestments: an apron and a dishcloth. I hauled eight heavy tables out of the storeroom, cursing the designer who'd decided chipboard would make a good material for folding tables. I cut up some fruit and a day-old cake and put the food on the altar for the early volunteers, then went downstairs to the office to get the basement key.

There was an envelope from the U.S. District Court in my mailbox, and I skimmed the opening quickly. "This Court issued an order informing the parties to this case and several California charities that under the *cy pres* doctrine and the Court's equitable powers, the Court had determined that over $7 million left over in the First Settlement Fund would be distributed to charities, and listed a number of charities recommended by plaintiff, Bank, or Court itself. . . . Now the Court has determined that the public interest would best be served by distributing the unclaimed funds to charities serving children, families and the elderly." I read on. "The Court was impressed by the charities' work. . . . They serve as an example of what community service is and bring hope to all." Then I saw the news: St. Gregory's Pantry was awarded two hundred thousand dollars. We were going to get an escrow account, disbursed at twenty thousand dollars a year for ten years, because "St. Gregory's Pantry has a tiny operating budget and no staff, but it has accomplished great things."

I reached Derek Howard about an hour later. By this time, I was back up in the church, talking on my cellphone as I unloaded wet pallets of broccoli. Derek kept brushing away my thanks. "No," he finally said, and I finally understood him. "I mean, thank *you*, for giving me the chance to do this." Derek cleared his throat. This was the longest conversation I'd ever had with him. "You know," he said, sounding strangely unsettled, and not at all like a trial lawyer, "I think it wasn't an accident that I met you."

"Yeah?" I said, picking up loaves of bread from a huge plastic bin and setting them on the table.

"I had to go to church when I was a kid," Derek told me, "and they kept telling me what to do—sit still, say this, and . . .

And, you know, I didn't like that. I don't like being told what to do." He laughed. He sounded like my mother, complaining about her childhood.

"Now I take my kids to an Episcopal church," continued Derek, "really rich, everyone's very nice, but you just sit there, it's very white . . ." He paused. "I mean, when I went to your pantry, I saw all the food, and I thought, *this* is what church is for."

I glanced out the back door. Teddy was standing there grinning, motioning to me to let him in. He'd finally gotten new teeth, after a decade of losing them, one by one, to meth, and now he smiled hugely and often. I remembered when Teddy had first started helping out at the pantry: He'd been trying to get his life back together, after his father, his boyfriend, and his dog had all died and he hit bottom with drugs. He was eager to serve, determined to take control, and scraped raw by sobriety. He didn't particularly trust church. "The first time I sang the Lord's Prayer with you guys," Teddy had told me once, reminiscing, "it was awkward. I thought, Is this some kind of a cult I'm being sucked into? And there's this line you sing, 'Make us into your bread.' I thought, What is this, cannibalism?"

It wasn't the Lord's Prayer that had changed him, given him teeth, a new boyfriend, the habit of cooking food at home. It was the experience of being bread. Teddy still had relapses and fights and weeks of almost unmanageable anxiety, but being one of the people in charge at the pantry had become what he called "a kind of spiritual practice." He'd looked at me earnestly. "It's very easy for me to try to control people," he said. "But when I'm not sarcastic or arrogant or egotistical, I see that the qualities in other people that frustrate me are really about me. It's not just about feeding people who come to the pantry with food. It's about nourishing them with my love."

I let Teddy in and kept listening to Derek. "This sounds weird," the lawyer was saying, "but I want you to help me with something."

What did he want? The man—essentially a stranger—had given us a quarter of a million dollars out of the blue. But he was so hungry.

I handed Teddy an apron. "I want you to write out a prayer for me," Derek continued. "I used to say one, but I forget it. Would you write out a prayer, in your handwriting, something I could say, maybe at night, or just something to remind me why I'm doing this?"

"This?" I said.

"The work I do," said Derek, and there was a scratchy noise. "I can't believe I'm sitting here in my law offices," he said, "and I'm going to cry. This is not like me."

"Listen," I said. "Here's the prayer I wrote for the food pantry. We sing it every week with the Lord's Prayer."

I was too wobbly myself to sing, but I spoke the familiar words into the cellphone, pacing around the altar and the boxes of vegetables. They were the same words that had freaked Teddy out. "O God of abundance," I began, "you feed us every day. Rise in us now, make us into your bread, that we may share your gifts with a hungry world, and join in love with all people, through Jesus Christ our Lord. Amen."

"Okay," said Derek. He cleared his throat. "Okay," he said again, brusquely. "That's great. Fax me the court order, and send me the prayer. I'll talk to you soon."

I called Martha first with the news. "You're so nailed," Martha said. "They're going to tell you this comes from the Holy Spirit." I called a slew of people from St. Gregory's, and she was right. But I suspected it might be the Holy Spirit, too. *Blowing everywhere and filling all things. Making all things new.*

—

I wrote excitedly to St. Gregory's congregation, much as I had when the picture of the food pantry first started crowding into my line of vision. "When the Spirit blows," I wrote, "it's not a gentle breeze. We are now challenged by abundance as we were challenged before by scarcity."

We had big program decisions to make, I explained: Although we'd continue to rely on the congregation's donations to support the Friday pantry, we needed to decide what to do with the huge new gift that had landed in our laps through Derek Howard. Should we just keep giving the money away to start more pantries, as we had with the funds from the first two court distributions? Should we look for another place to rent on Potrero Hill where we could provide food for our overflow crowds? Should we try to add one more food pantry at St. Gregory's on another day of the week?

"The food pantry," I wrote, "has always been communion: a Great Thanksgiving for a great love. It's embodied the glorious, disturbing reality at the very center of our church: Jesus's Table, where all are welcomed without exception. If we stand together at that Table and receive the next new thing God is making for us and through us, what will happen?"

I asked Jeff, my spiritual director, what he thought I should do. "Dear one," he said, "it sounds like you need to pray." Jeff suggested discernment based on a Quaker concept called a "clearness committee"—a group of people willing to pray together about the next stage of the food pantry and what we should do with the two hundred thousand dollars. So one morning, Paul and Lynn Baird and I sat in a small room with four others from

St. Gregory's and the pantry in silence, around one of the Sunday school tables. The idea was that they could only ask questions—not discuss or argue or strategize. After I answered, we'd wait together until a picture became clear to all of us. Only then could we start to come up with a plan.

Crap, I thought. *This is so like swami.*

But I was hoping, too. I waited, while the silence stretched on. I'd think about numbers and money, then I'd think about Scripture and the Holy Ghost. I'd wonder about all the fundamentalists I was working with now, then daydream about a storage shed. I looked at our breakfast snacks and some child's forgotten fleece jacket lying on the dirty rug. Daily bread, bread of heaven, daily bread. My head ached. Lynn cleared her throat.

"What are you hungry for?" she asked.

I had no idea how to answer. Suddenly I reached over to the little table where we'd set up our coffee and snacks and picked up a piece of panettone, studded with raisins and citrus peel. I held it out to her. "This," I said, and I knew I meant it. Not just the panettone but the gesture of offering it: my hand reaching out, Lynn's hand reaching out, the sweet bread between us.

This was the hunger that first drew me to the Table at St. Gregory's. It was the same hunger that drew parents to the pantry to get groceries and brought them back to blurt out *help* or *thank you* or some other real word. It was the hunger of the volunteers, with their yearning for jokes, company, lunch, and work to do. It was the hunger of everyone who gave us dollar bills, cans of hominy, apples from their backyard, huge checks such as Derek's. It was a hunger that had to do with the bodies of strangers, with offering everything we had, giving away control, and receiving what we needed to live. Communion. I wanted communion.

Chapter 23

Sunday Dinner

—

We came out of that discernment meeting with a plan: to open up our own pantry one more day a week to feed the overflow crowd. I knew it was important to keep helping new pantries open, but I really wanted to do something else at St. Gregory's. I was proud of the pantry and proud of the church: I couldn't wait to bring everyone together. I suggested Sundays, right after the service, in the time when St. Gregory's usually sponsored concerts and art classes. I figured it would be easy to shift the concerts to late afternoons and open the pantry after the Eucharist. It seemed obvious to me: We could feed more people, offer more of our members the chance to serve, and make explicit the connection between holy communion and free groceries.

"Sunday communion will morph into coffee hour, which will morph into setup for the pantry, then we'll have the pantry, and then we can do another little Eucharist to close at the end of the afternoon, around four," I told Paul enthusiastically. "It'll all finally be in the same place."

"Do you want me to cook lunch?" Paul asked. He sounded a bit wary.

I thought that was a great idea. "Yes," I said. "We'll cook together. And you can preside at the four o'clock service, too." He sighed.

Steaming ahead, I called a meeting of the membership, to present the recommendation of the discernment group that we open a Sunday pantry. I had no clue that I was crossing the line from self-righteous do-gooder to crusading zealot, or how hard the church was going to resist being made new.

"Sunday is too much!" an older woman nearly shouted at me, taking me completely by surprise. "I've been coming here for more than fifteen years, and Sunday is my day of rest." Carol was passionate. "Sunday's for church, art, and beautiful music. Everybody's afraid to say it, but we don't want our Sundays invaded!" Others were equally vehement. Most of them made a point of praising the food pantry, but their message was clear: Feeding the hungry belonged in its place, and "real church" belonged on Sundays.

I was dumbfounded. I believed the food pantry represented the best of St. Gregory's practices and values: its openness, its inclusion, its beauty, and its invitation to participate in creating something together. I'd grown to know the church's members, over years of Lents and Easters, funerals and weddings, sicknesses, stumbling, song. I'd listened to them tell dirty jokes and awkward truths, seen them suffer through the deaths of parents and children, cooked and eaten with them. Everything that had inspired me about this community had wound up expressed in the food pantry, and I'd wanted to return the favor, to give a gift back to the church. I felt as if I'd thought long and hard about a beloved friend, looking for the perfect present that would reflect her values and enrich her life—and then she'd spurned my offer.

Angry notes began to circulate on an e-mail list of members, pitting those who enjoyed St. Gregory's long-standing Sunday-afternoon classical music concerts and painting classes against those who wanted to use that time for a pantry. Underlying the arguments about scheduling, I thought, lurked a deep unease about class, and fear about the difference between the people who came to the food pantry and those who attended services.

"Sunday afternoons are a wonderful, special piece of time," wrote an artist. "If you want to hang out after church, things are quiet. It keeps Sunday sacrosanct somehow. Often there are concerts, sometimes an icon workshop, sometimes an art opening— but all these things are contemplative. If there's a pantry, there would be a rush to get everybody cleared out, and a noisy crowd waiting to get in. It's important not to allow every moment of the church building's time to be programmed for doing good works."

Lawrence, who'd been there at the beginning of the food pantry, was gentle as he addressed her fears. "I'm like other middle-class people," he said, "and I hate being forced to deal with people who are not like me—people who are poor, crazy, who don't behave the way I do in public. They make me nervous. I feel a sense of conflict about this because, on the one hand, I know what the right thing to do is, yet I'm sometimes paralyzed when I try to do it. By the right thing, I mean opening myself to the experience of people who are not like me.

"But," Lawrence continued, his restaurant background showing, "I really want to serve food to the community. I want people who are too tired from a week of work and child rearing and the stress of living in the projects to take their family to lunch without having to cook and do the dishes. And after that, I want them to take a bag of groceries home—so their kids have something decent to eat in the morning before school. I don't care if they ever join our church or not. I don't care if they worship with the Holy Rollers. I don't care if they are against gay marriage. I don't care what they think of me. I just want them to have a little break—to feel my love in what I sometimes think is the best, if not the only, way I know how to show it, with love in my heart and the smell of garlic on my hands. *That's* what the kingdom of God looks like to me."

I tried to argue that a Sunday pantry would bring in new people to volunteer and to get food, and some of them might join the church and change it in exciting and wonderful ways. "Why do we need to grow?" a longtime member challenged me. "We're fine just as we are."

Things heated up. "What am I supposed to do if we have people coming to the door for the pantry and we're still having church?" Carol demanded of me one afternoon when I was lobbying a group of members about my proposal. "And what am I supposed to do if they start talking to me in Chinese or Russian?"

Linda, standing next to me, stiffened. A white woman with a Chinese American husband, she was a devoted Sunday school teacher, and she and her kids volunteered with us at the pantry. "I am ashamed," she hissed, "to bring my kids here on Sunday. They see that nobody in church looks like them, and lots of people on Friday look like them. What does that say about what we believe?"

If I'd understood once that I couldn't be a Christian by myself, I was having my nose rubbed in that idea over and over again: My heart was nearly breaking. I tried to talk with Donald Schell, though, by now, I was suspicious of anyone in authority in the church. I sent him a nasty note when he said that maybe we should wait for a year or so, then try the proposal again. "I wouldn't be so disappointed if I didn't believe you see what's going on here," I wrote accusingly. "You created St. Gregory's with a risky vision of open communion and welcome. You fought with the established hierarchy; made a big, beautiful room; put a Table in the middle of it; and opened the door to everyone. Years and years later, I walked in; you put your hands on me and baptized me and asked me to accept a commission we share: to continue in the breaking of bread. Did you mean that? What the hell did you *think* was going to happen?"

A former Jesuit who sang in the choir took me aside, pointing out that I was hardly the first person to get excited about Jesus, then disappointed in his church. "Get over yourself," he said, not unkindly. "Welcome to Christianity. This is just the beginning."

It was, in fact, the beginning of another story for me. Echoing everything that was wrong with churches and church politics, repeating in microcosm the ugliness of Christianity through the ages, I started to fight fiercely with the people I was supposed to be in communion with, struggled to institutionalize my own dogma, and generally hounded people in the name of the Lord. I felt righteous when I listened to members plead for space for art or music or their own peaceful services. Hadn't St. Gregory's proclaimed that God's Table was open to everyone? Hadn't we announced that welcoming strangers was at the heart of our mission? How could people cling to their comforting, cozy services, rejecting change and newness? Maybe, I told the pantry backers, I should just start a Sunday pantry at another church—peel off, split, find a more open-minded group. The seductive pull of the schismatic impulse grew stronger.

Meanwhile, the larger Anglican Communion was in danger of splitting, as fundamentalists and liberals continued at each other's throats. The endless fights among the faithful had prompted Rowan Williams, the archbishop of Canterbury, to write that "unity is a gospel imperative when we recognize that it opens us to change, to conversion: when we realize how our life with Christ is somehow bound up with our willingness to abide with those we think are sinful, and those we think are stupid." I was moved by his words, but I was stubborn: How could my opponents be so stupid? How could they not see how holy and beautiful the pantry was, how good it would be for the church? I was furious at St. Gregory's and hurt more than I had expected by my fellow members' hostility to our proposal.

Then, one Friday morning, I sat in church with Mark and Steve, watching the sky grow light. As we sang together quietly and let calm envelop us, I thought about the ways that morning prayer had become my sanctuary over the years I'd been at St. Gregory's. It was almost transparent, like drinking water: just a pure slaking of thirst.

We'd just finished the last psalm when I heard the door open, and Veronica, one of the most profoundly psychotic visitors to the food pantry, stomped in. She was a heavyset black woman in her fifties, with a wandering eye, a major cognitive disorder, and a propensity for angry, paranoid rants. She came right over to where I was sitting. "I need to talk to you," Veronica said loudly, "about the hospital board, the lady who gives out the money, there are thirty-three different kinds of vaccines, you know I have people watching, and we need to make sure the children are not up on that lift. . . ."

I motioned Veronica to sit down. "We're praying," I said. She sat down and was quiet for a minute, though she kept digging through and rearranging her plastic bag of newspaper clippings. I heard the Food Bank truck lumbering up the hill to our gate, and a wave of exhaustion came over me. I was going to have to unload the truck, and Veronica wasn't going to shut up, and it wasn't even eight in the morning. I wished her away, and as I did, I saw Carol's angry, anxious face as she argued against the Sunday pantry.

You can't be a Christian by yourself. You can't be more special or holy. I was going to be changed, too, and lose my private church for a new one I couldn't control. I was going to have to work with the people I liked at St. Gregory's, and the ones who irritated the hell out of me, and Veronica, and a bunch of strangers I hadn't even met yet. "In plain words," as the archbishop said, "unity is a gospel imperative to just the extent that we find it hard."

It was hard for me to hear the final decision, which Donald announced as a compromise. The concerts and art openings would continue most Sunday afternoons. Once a month, on the last Sunday, we could schedule a food pantry. Otherwise, things would stay the same at St. Gregory's. "I know I'm being a baby," I told Paul, "but I'm just so disappointed. I really thought this was going to work."

"Let's see what happens," he said. "You never know."

The week before the first Sunday pantry, I called a lot of people and told them not to expect much. "It won't be big," I said. "We'll probably have more volunteers than people coming for food." I felt anxious and hostessy, as if I were preparing a party to bring two sets of friends together, hoping that everyone would be on best behavior, find one another fascinating—or at least show up.

"Yeah, it always starts small," agreed Anne at the Food Bank. "But as you know, word of mouth will spread." I drove around that week to hospitals. A doctor friend met me as she was jogging across a busy street from her maternity clinic to the delivery room. "Babies, babies, babies," she grumbled. "Why don't they slow down and come one at a time?" She took some pantry flyers from me, though, and pushed me up a set of stairs to a shabby little waiting room. "Acute care pediatric's in there," she said. "Lots of people who need food. See you Sunday."

That Saturday, I went to the farmers' market and bought six pounds of asparagus and a huge, glistening bunch of spinach to cook for our pantry volunteers' lunch. The church was empty, but Martha came with me, and I cooked while we waited for the Food Bank truck to show up. I made two large pans of quiche and a couple of flourless chocolate cakes before the dreadlocked driver arrived. "Huh," he said. "So now you're doing it on Sundays, too? Every week?"

"God willing," I said. "But we'll see what happens. We're starting slow."

It was beginning to rain, lightly, and I tied up the pallets with tarps in the churchyard, turned off the oven, and went out to find more poor people. I stopped at the Salvation Army center in the Mission, a black Baptist tabernacle, and the offices of the WIC program. "At the end of the month, do you need more food?" my flyers asked, in English and Spanish. "Come get your free groceries. Open to all, no forms to fill out." I ran into Ty-Jay when I went up to the projects. "Drumming up business," I said. "Tell everyone you know."

It was hard, that Sunday, to sit through the church service. Even as I sang out an alleluia, I was thinking about the kitchen, and how I had to slip away for a minute. Before it was time to bring the body and blood of Christ to the altar, I ducked in and put my pans of asparagus quiche in the oven. "I don't have the slightest idea what God is like, really," preached Rick. "All I know is what I see God doing, in my own life and in the lives of the people around me."

Right before we opened, I grabbed someone from St. Gregory's who had a car. "We're going to the holy hill," I told him. I got out of the car in the projects when I saw a group of people sitting outside and smoking in the watery sunshine; Richard was there, resting on an overturned milk crate. I gave him a flyer and went on to Mr. Yancy's apartment, where the teenage thugs who lived off him were watching cartoons. I gave them flyers, too. "Come on down," I said. "No lines, plenty of food." My church friend hung back, shyly, but laughed when we got back in the car. "You know the parable from Matthew," he said, "when the invited guests won't come to the wedding feast? The master sends his servants out to the crossroads in town, the highways and by-ways, to find all the poor people and invite them instead." We turned past a liquor store, and I slowed down to give the word to one of the homeless guys who hung out on the sidewalk there.

On the next street, I saw Jesse, a skinny woman with silver lamé shoes and a head wrap. She waved at me, and we pulled over. Jesse was sitting on the curb with a woman wearing blond extensions and a lot of blue eye shadow. When I got closer, I could see her beard, as well as the pushed-up breasts straining beneath her tight shirt. "Hi," I said. "Pantry's today. If you're gonna be here for a while, can you hand these out for me?"

Jesse took some, but the tranny looked at me.

"Are you from a church?" she said, in a deep, amused, cigarette-soaked voice.

"Uh-huh," I said.

"Well," she announced, "I want to keep it real. I'd like to say

I'd hand out your flyers, but the truth is, I'm intoxicated, and I'm not going to do it."

"Okay," I said.

"I'm just trying to keep it real," she said.

"Thank you," I said. "I appreciate your honesty."

She blinked and looked at me. She had long eyelashes and heavy foundation the color of an Ace bandage that looked as if it had been put on the night before. "Are you from church?" she asked again.

"Yes," I said.

"Then pray for me," she said.

"I will, absolutely," I said. "What's your name?"

She smiled, fluttering her eyelashes. "Diva," she said.

"I'm Sara," I said. "Diva, come anytime. We're open from two until four today. Thanks for keeping it real. Please pray for me."

"OK, baby," said Diva, waving. "I won't be high at two; I'll see you then. God bless you, now."

Diva never did come that afternoon. Others did, and over the next year, we'd get as many as fifty or sixty people stopping by to get groceries on the last Sunday. But since it happened only once a month, the Sunday pantry stayed small. I enjoyed the order and calm of it, and the little Eucharist service we'd have at the end of the afternoon, when Paul would drape a stole over his apron and hand bread and wine to the three or four remaining volunteers. Once, just as I was chanting the Gospel at the altar— the verses about Jesus telling his disciples to give five thousand people food—there'd been a pounding at the door, as late-comers arrived for groceries. I took a breath and kept chanting, addressing my volunteers: "So Jesus said, 'Donovan, Paul, Elizabeth, give them something to eat yourselves!' " We'd thrown open the doors and given away the last bags of food. There was enough for all.

But Sundays weren't Fridays. The Sunday pantry didn't have the wild energy, the overheated-kitchen sense of rush and grace, the sparks thrown off by so many different lives knocking against one another. Its volunteers didn't need, urgently, to be there. It didn't run out of food; nobody had a nervous breakdown or a miraculous healing. The Sunday pantry was domesticated, more like a wafer than like bread.

I had wanted so badly for St. Gregory's to see and recognize the food pantry as communion, to be transformed by what was happening among us on Fridays, to accept the Gospel of the pantry and make it part of its official theology. I'd wanted to bring the pantry into church—and in a way, I had. It was mildly disappointing to me, in the way that church itself could be, compared to the radical vision implied by Jesus's meal.

Chapter 24

The Cost of Faith

—

Any convert comes—sooner rather than later, if she's lucky—to a crisis of faith or at least a questioning of the meaning that seemed so bright and true at the beginning. My crisis was predictable, but it struck me with the force of newness, just as believing had.

My atheist friends probably thought my doubts must be about the church and its hypocrisies. All they had to do was cite the Inquisition, the Crusades, the cruelties and idiocies of doctrine. How could anyone have confidence in a church that refused to ordain women or a religion that treated them as chattel? How could anyone trust a faith that insisted on ludicrous myths such as the six-day creation of the universe or a virgin birth? How, for that matter, could I reconcile St. Gregory's grand promise of communion for all with its refusal to let me bring poor people into a pantry every Sunday?

But that wasn't my point. It seemed to irritate my friends that I readily admitted church was messed up and still didn't care.

"So how can you be a Christian?" asked Martha.

"Well, you're an unusual kind of Christian," said Jose.

"That's not what most Christians say," said my sister, Ellen.

We were talking past each other. I knew what they thought: Christians were corny, sentimental, vulgar, embarrassing, intolerant, superstitious, dogmatic, self-righteous, do-goody, obtuse, smug, unsophisticated, and dumb. They thought I wasn't like that, so I couldn't be a "real" Christian.

But I *was* like that. I wasn't more enlightened or less enamored of my own piety or purer. Christianity, if it was all I'd come to believe, demanded that I understand exactly how like everyone else I was. And it was this realization that would not go away, even as I battled with the costs of faith.

I still believed. But what was my faith going to cost? The Bible was not reassuring on this point: Everything, it basically answered. "You'll give up home, wife, brothers, parents, children, for the sake of the Kingdom of God," explained Jesus. "You must leave self behind . . . not care for your own safety . . . be lost."

I was okay with being lost. But I wasn't willing to give up my family.

One Friday evening, I came home exhausted, smelling of overripe fruit and unwashed wino, with food stains on my shirt, lipstick smears on my chin, and bruises on my arms. I peeled off my socks and flopped down on our bed. The gauzy curtains blew in the early-evening air, and I could hear doves in the tree outside. "I'm gonna take a shower in a minute," I said. "How was it?" asked Martha. She knew most of the regulars at the pantry and liked to hear news of them. "How many did you do?"

"Two-eighty, two-ninety," I said. "Come here." Martha stretched out next to me. This was bliss, like collapsing at the end of a restaurant shift, dirty and utterly spent and finally able to stretch out. "You're so beautiful," I said. I stroked her forehead.

"This room is so beautiful. Look at those roses." Martha followed my gaze to the jar of fat pink and yellow blooms. "Honey, you're tripping," she said.

Then I added, "Donald came by. I'm going to meet him tomorrow and work on a script for the service we want to do at the pantry."

"Tomorrow?" said Martha.

"Just an hour or so," I said.

"Whatever," said Martha. Her voice was suddenly chilly, and she sat up. I started to apologize. I knew that Martha—and Katie, too—had spells of resentment about the amount of time I spent at church and the way the pantry's demands spilled over into our lives. Last week, when Starlight Wanderer had called me right at suppertime with a long, weepy ramble about her landlord, Katie glared at me. "Mommy," she said, when I came back to the table, "it's not polite to answer the phone during supper."

"I know," I said, "I'm sorry. But she was freaking out."

"Yeah, well what about your *daughter*?" said Katie. She was kidding, and we all laughed, but I knew she often felt jealous. "What about *us*? Tell them to suck it up, get over themselves! Call somebody else! No more crazy-people calls to Sara!"

"Martha," I said now, "I'm sorry." I felt tugged between church and home, the vivid life of the pantry and the no less real needs of my child, my own desire to do more, and my desire just to rest, happily, with my beloved.

"It's like you spend your whole life at St. Gregory's," Martha said. Her face was wounded and angry, and I felt queasy about the speed with which we'd landed in an argument. From bliss on the bed to bitterness, in three minutes. "I'm sick of it always having to be you who volunteers to do everything. It's seven days a week. I didn't sign up to be the minister's wife."

"You're not," I said, feeling hopeless. These were the moments when I wished I had a different kind of Jesus, one who could reveal clear rules for how to be good, evaporate all conflicts with a wave of his holy hand. I wished I could say a prayer and make everything better. Instead, I was stuck with myself and the people I loved: frustrating, disappointing, jealous, sorry, wounded.

"Look," Martha said. She was so beautiful, still. "You know I respect what you do with the pantry; it's great work. Just please don't leave us for the church."

"I'm not," I said. "I won't."

My questions, my doubts, my failures: Everything I lived had been lived by others—from disappointing my wife and confusing my skeptic friends to rebelling against the narrowness of religious dogma. But even more important, according to Christianity, it had been lived by God. When it came right down to it, the God that I'd found was a God who lived on earth, who knew what it was like to walk around in a body, fight with religious authorities, hurt his mother's feelings. *"We walk the road, Lord Jesus, that you trod,"* went one of my favorite hymns. This is what had made my conversion to Christianity possible and what remained true to me. It was humiliating and comforting and yet oddly freeing. It made things so much less lonely as well as less grandiose. Very close to me, right in my hands and in my mouth, as Moses said, was a force drawing me closer and closer to the presence I yearned for. *"Far off yet here,"* said the hymn, *"far off yet here, the goal of all desire."*

And rather than protecting me and sealing me off in a community of shared doctrine and rules, this truth thrust me into the wildness of faith. I didn't need a creed to artificially connect me with other believers: It was the ragged vastness of our different spiritual lives that pointed, for me, to a larger force. It made me even more of a believer to accept that none of us, fundamentalist or radical or orthodox, Muslim or Jew or Christian, could adequately sum God up. If you believed that God had created all life—protozoa and bears, coral and eels, mold and kingfishers and roses—wasn't it reasonable to assume that there wasn't one single template for human belief, one single way to get it right?

My way was through the struggles of the world. It meant wrestling with the unavoidably political Gospel of incarnation and murder, and a Jesus who died poor at the hands of an empire. Yet it proclaimed a risen Christ, alive in what I knew was the repeating, beating heart of the story—that the face of the stranger is God's face, and all people are one body: God's.

My spiritual crisis returned me to the fundamental practices that had stayed central for me, such as just following what Jesus did. Putting the Word into action, in ordinary life, unmediated by religious scripts, raised the stakes. As I'd discovered as a student in Mexico, a reporter in war zones, a cook, learning from experience instead of memorizing a formula forced me to pay attention. Doing the Gospel rather than just quoting it was the best way I could find out what God was up to.

I didn't believe in dragging souls into some special club of the saved. "I mean," I'd told Steve once, exasperated after listening to Donald talk about institutional growth and how to attract new members with our innovative liturgy, "the point of church isn't to get people to come to church."

"No?" said Steve, cocking an eyebrow. "What is it?"

It seemed obvious to me. "To feed them, so they can go out and, you know, be Jesus."

I suddenly was abashed. "I mean, I don't know, I'm new, that sounds pretentious. . . ." My voice trailed off. But I meant it. *You have been greatly loved,* said a piece of the Gospel that had stuck with me. *Go and do likewise.* That seemed pretty damn clear.

My only sense of "mission" now was to show others that they, too, could feed and touch and heal and love, without fear. To catch them up in the desire to see more, taste more, without caring if they got a doctrine right or became a regular at my church. To get them walking, without the safety net of ritual correctness, along the path that Jesus blazed and to share the feast of their lives with others.

Chapter 25

The Heavenly Feast

—

Communion. I chewed and swallowed it. It was at the absolute center of my faith: wheat and water and yeast and heat; grape and sun and time; bread and wine, transformed into life. I ate it up. I kept coming back for more. And yet, even though church was where I found communion, church couldn't, finally, contain it.

Because St. Gregory's offered Christ's body and blood to everyone without exception, I'd been spared the traditional spectacle of argument over who was good enough to receive Jesus's meal. Could divorced people take communion? Murderers? Unrepentant petty sinners? Kids? These questions had divided the church for centuries. I thought the sacraments were a sign of God's grace precisely because they were so over the top: so abundant, so beyond human calculation, spilling over the unprepared and pious alike, feeding the world wildly. "Yeah, well," said a friend dourly, "you know what they say: 'Old men in Rome would ration the ocean.' "

Yet, once I became a churchgoer, I followed church rules, too. In the Episcopal Church, as in the Roman Catholic and Orthodox churches, only ordained priests were supposed to preside over the Eucharist. Not because of biblical precedent—in fact, Jesus made a point of telling his followers that David had eaten the temple bread reserved for priests—but because of tradition: power, institutional arrangements, politics.

"It's kind of crazy talk," said Paul once, trying to explain the official rules of Eucharist to me. "It only happens if the right person with the right stuff says the right words." And yet "rightness" was always more about licensing requirements than about God; the human lines drawn to regulate priestly ordination extended and wrapped round the Eucharist like barbed wire, binding the sacrament to rules about who could be a valid, official celebrant and who could be excluded. "The medieval church said even if a priest's a reprobate, when he says the prayer over the bread and wine, he confects the Eucharist," explained Paul. "No matter how many times a pope is murdering his rivals, he's confecting the Lord's Supper. But a poor, virtuous woman stands in front of the bread and wine and says the same words, and it's dragon meat. Poison."

At St. Gregory's, I joined the whole congregation singing the refrains of the Eucharistic prayer, with its narrative of suffering, exile, covenant, and redemption. I raised my hands when Jesus made his heart-stopping dare to his followers; when, as one version of the prayer put it, "On the night before his friends betrayed him, and enemy soldiers took him away to be killed, Jesus knelt down and washed his friends' feet." I listened as the priest chanted the story of how Jesus told the disciples to remember him every time they ate and drank. I participated in breaking the bread and pouring the wine and serving them to the crowd. But laypeople were never allowed to "celebrate" or preside at the Table, to call down the Holy Spirit on the bread and wine, to speak the "words of institution" at the heart of the ritual.

I had a strong sense of the mystery: I'd seen Donald physically shudder at the altar as the familiar words he was chanting suddenly gripped him. I'd heard my spiritual director say his breath was still taken away every time he celebrated the Eucharist. "The Table's a threshold, a paper-thin place, luminous, where heaven and humans meet," Jeff told me. "It could be anywhere—a room, a jail cell; I could be ego-focused or doing a shitty job remembering the prayers; but I still cross that threshold."

I wasn't particularly eager to deliberately stick my own finger in that socket. Once I'd led an evening Eucharist at St. Gregory's when there was no priest to do it, using "preconsecrated" bread and wine, blessed at an earlier service. There were just seven of us, and I liked the ordinariness of the meal as we quietly passed the bread among ourselves. But I knew our bishop had made a point of asking Donald and Rick, whatever other innovations and experiments they did with liturgy, never to allow laypeople to actually preside.

I was as unprepared to find myself celebrating for the first time as I had been to receive. Other sacraments and rites had migrated beyond Sundays at St. Gregory's to Fridays at the pantry, but Eucharist wouldn't stop. I didn't realize right away what I was doing, because Jesus's meal had left the building.

My old friend and former lover Millie was dying: Cancer had spread from her breasts to her lungs and bones. She'd moved from Brooklyn to Berkeley, and we saw each other frequently. Raised as an Anglican, she'd left religion for decades but, to my total surprise, had greeted my conversion happily. "You believe in God?" she'd said. "That's beautiful! Will you pray with me?"

She still remembered big chunks of the Book of Common Prayer and eagerly took communion now when she visited churches.

But Millie was in almost constant pain and making one last stab at radiation: There wasn't a lot of energy for churchgoing. One day—it was a gorgeous spring day, warm, with blue skies—I was bringing her back from treatment but didn't even make it to her front door. Millie stopped on the steps, under the arbor, which was covered in beautiful wisteria, and bent over, vomiting. I held her up—she weighed less than a hundred pounds by then—and looked at her as she retched and shuddered. She was wearing a thin, soft T-shirt, with stripes, and tiny diamonds in her ears. I stood there as Millie heaved and moaned, and the fragrance of the vines filled the air around us. Her body was almost finished. I could see every line in her face, and the label of the T-shirt sticking up at the back of her neck, and I could hear, by the doorway, a wind chime ringing.

I took her inside. Millie had always been a volatile woman: brilliant and difficult, with a great gift for falling in love, a great laugh, and a harsh, merciless anger. Now, as I helped her undress and lifted her into the bed, a wave of rage swept through her. "Lowlife," she said. "Criminally incompetent." She was talking about the doctors, and as she went on and on in a low, vicious whisper cataloging their stupidity and venality and disrespect, her anger spread, until the litany of people who'd betrayed her grievously included three dear friends who were currently caring for her and her son, Jay. "That's it," she said. "I don't have to see him again."

It was hardest for me to hear Millie attack her son. The three of us had briefly lived together twenty years ago, and though he and I were close in age, I still felt inappropriately maternal impulses toward him. I could look at him now—a grown man,

with a profession and a deep voice—and remember those legs
sprawled out on the sofa or the nights Millie waited up, anxious,
for him to come home. In Brooklyn, black teenage boys hadn't
been safe, least of all from the cops. Every time he was late for
dinner, Millie would pace and chain-smoke and curse the police
and white people; when he showed up, just fine, she'd yell at
him. He'd stand over his mom and hug her hard. "Don't worry
about a thing, little lady," he'd say in his best cowboy voice.
"Don't fret your little head."

Millie retched again. "Oh, honey," I said. "Shh. It's okay."

"It is *not* okay," she snapped. I wiped her mouth, and she
launched into another round of vitriol.

"If you can eat a little toast," I said, "it's time for the pills."

I walked into the bright kitchen trying not to cry. This ugliness at the end was wearing me down: the incessant pain, the
rants, the fear and bitterness coursing like cancer through our
relationships. Jay was flying in from Colorado at the end of the
week, Millie's best friend was coming by in an hour, I had to call
back the doctors and a hospice nurse, and the prospect of more
fighting exhausted me. "I can't do this anymore," I said aloud,
quietly and miserably. I couldn't stand for her to die, and to die
so angry. I was leaning on the counter, tearing the piece of toast
into bits small enough for Millie to swallow. "Help, I can't do
this alone."

What makes the bread into the body of Christ? What makes
words more than words, mortal flesh more than mortal flesh;
what makes a piece of toast into a sacrament?

I broke the bread.

"It is truly right always and everywhere to praise you, Lord
God our Father, Lover of all," the Great Thanksgiving prayer
began. It was chanted every Sunday at St. Gregory's Table, and
I knew the words almost by heart now. "Your wind swept the

waters when our world began, and you spoke the Word that was always your Word. Through him all things came to be, and his life lightened every life with the light darkness could not swallow."

The phone rang, and Millie's answering machine kicked on, her recorded voice happy and girlish. Something was in the kitchen with me, like the sunlight falling on the braided rug, like the piece of bread in my hands, warm and uncompromisingly alive.

"... Now all who receive him have power to become children of God: born from above, they blow through the world with your spirit, bearing witness for the truth of your Word. All who believe in him have left death for new life.

"For on the night he was handed over to suffering and death, our Lord Jesus Christ took bread; and when he had given thanks to you, he broke it, and gave it to his disciples and said: 'Take, eat: This is my body, which is given for you. Do this in remembrance of me.' "

I wasn't alone. This wasn't the end. I took the toast back to the little room, where Millie had propped herself up with a couple of pillows. I could smell the wisteria, faintly, through the opened window, and hear the kids from the school next door yelling in the yard. I pushed away a box of Kleenex and sat down on her bed. "Millie," I said, "this is for you."

She took the sacrament, chewing and swallowing carefully, her dark eyes huge on me. We didn't say anything. She breathed, quieted. Nothing else really happened. In half an hour, I would tuck her in, and set out a glass of water, and drive home across the bridge, stunned and blinking and saying aloud to myself, "Oh my God, it's real."

In a week, I would come back bringing the officially blessed body of Christ straight from the hands of the priest at the Sunday communion Table and offer it to Millie again, officially. But for now, it was like time out of time: each earthly detail incredibly vivid, with the eternal hovering right there in the middle of it, side by side with the suffering, and a huge peace beating slowly like the heartbeat of God.

Millie died a few months later. I drove over the bridge as soon as I got the call. Her body, washed by friends and dressed in a soft gray tunic, was in the little bedroom. I sat there stroking her cold forehead for a while; Millie's dearest friend was in the other room, playing the piano with ferocious concentration. Jay stood nearby, looking as if he hadn't slept for days. A few more people gathered in the bedroom, and I asked one if she'd read something aloud from the Book of Common Prayer. None of them went to church, but they all stepped closer around the body. I got the same oil I'd been anointing Millie with during the awful months of her sickness and touched it one more time to her face. "Give rest, O Christ," I said, making the sign of the cross on her skin, "to your beloved child."

And then I listened to the prayer. It was the same one I'd sung at St. Gregory's in the twilight of September 11, when people had walked together around the altar in shock. It was the one I wished I'd known in wartime, when I was pregnant, and grief and gratitude used to tremble so madly inside me I could barely stand. "All of us go down to the dust," Millie's friend read, slowly, "yet even at the grave we make our song: Alleluia, alleluia, alleluia."

Jay hugged me hard when I left. He was going back to Colorado in a few days. "I don't believe in God," he said. "But sometimes when I'm up in the mountains above tree line, it's like whoa, you know: There's a *big*, big love."

"I know," I said.

Christianity wasn't an argument I could win, or even resolve. It wasn't a thesis. It was a mystery that I was finally willing to swallow.

I was loved by a big love. In the midst of suffering, of hunger, even of death. Alleluia. What was, finally, so hard about accepting that?

My brother David came to San Francisco to visit us, so on Friday, I took him to the pantry. "I'm kind of shy about cooking for a chef," said Paul. "David's probably a little shy about cooking with a priest," I told him.

The three of us made lunch: a chicken casserole from the Houston Junior League cookbook, coleslaw, a spice cake in layers that Paul whipped up without a recipe. David leaned over the counter and meticulously shredded the cabbage, reminiscing about the restaurants we'd worked in. "Remember Jimmy Linen?" he asked. "That Mob guy? Did you know he used to tell me, 'Son, you're young, you're gonna have your own place sometime. Just come to me if you need a hand getting started." David laughed. "Now, that would have been a nice business."

He reached out his hand without thinking, and I automatically put a rag in it. David pulled open the oven door. "Paul," he said, "whaddya think, is this done?"

"You bet," said Paul. He smiled at me.

I remembered Paul telling me about the first time he'd celebrated the Eucharist, at a little noonday service for three people in Houston, and how, despite his nervousness, he'd been filled with eagerness and joy. "It was like that thing Jesus says," Paul had recounted. "You know, 'I have long desired to share this meal with you.' "

I had long desired to share this meal with my brother. I looked at both of them. "Let's eat," I said.

There was no way I could reduce that meal to a religious ritual, even one as lovely and wide-open as the Eucharist at St. Gregory's. I was going to have to take real communion whenever it happened, wherever it found me, in my least prepared and most unfinished moments.

It was like the time I'd been trying to open the pantry while an impatient throng shouted at me and one another in three languages. I'd been unloading crates of oranges as fast as I could and bossing the volunteers relentlessly, but we were still behind schedule. I hated everyone.

The rice needed to be bagged, and a pallet of cereal was still not unpacked. There were a dozen cupcakes on the altar, the remains of the volunteers' lunch, and frosting was smeared on the altar cloth. Teddy was nipping worriedly at the heels of the stragglers, ducking into the kitchen obsessively to ask me questions and check lists.

"Ernesto's back," said Michael quietly, as he walked past me. I looked up. A heavily tattooed Chicano man with huge prison muscles was sauntering in toward the bathroom. "Sara!" he greeted me. "Wassup!"

"Hey, Ernesto," I said wearily. "How've you been?"

"Oh, it was rough," Ernesto said, his eyes darting around. "I had to keep a razor blade under my tongue, you know, to protect myself. Can I have one of those cupcakes?"

I handed him a cupcake from the plate on the altar.

"Yeah," Ernesto said, "you know, I thought of you. Every Friday I prayed for you. Can I get my groceries now, instead of waiting?"

"Gotta wait," I said. "Just like everyone else, wait until we're set up."

Ernesto took his cupcake outside, sulkily. I followed him. On the sidewalk in front of the church, the crowd was gathering. Two old Cuban sisters who always showed up hours early were bickering with each other noisily. Three little kids ran over and started pestering me for candy, and the crazy guy with apocalyptic theories cornered me, wanting to explain the secret messages he'd received. "It's the *end days*," he said urgently.

I could see, over my shoulder, that a visitor was waiting in the doorway, but I couldn't get a minute to talk to him. New volunteers were hovering, asking me what to do, but nothing was getting done. Everything felt hectic and irritating, and my feet were sore. I was sick of poor people, sick of church people, utterly sick of myself.

And then a woman had pushed her way to the front of the crowd. She was Chinese, wearing a quilted jacket, and she was thrusting a package at me. I couldn't understand what she was trying to say, but she kept smiling and coming closer. "Here," she said, and handed me a piece of fish wrapped in wax paper, still warm. "Food, for you."

"You know," Swami Jeff told me once, "God couldn't care less about the church. We don't understand the Eucharist, or that bread and wine live within us, so we ritualize the things that hold the mystery. We focus on the container and formalize the mystery. But you don't have to do that."

So, at last, I came out to my mother. But it turned out I had to cook for her to do it.

First, I set off the smoke alarm. Then, as the room filled with heat and grease, I calmed the large, neighborly stranger who'd rushed into her apartment to help. After he left, and I finished cooking, we opened the windows to the warm Vermont night and sat down. The table was set with bread and wine and lamb. It still didn't occur to me what I was doing, or what a ridiculous pun I was stumbling toward with my pan-seared Lamb of God—much less that I was invoking sacraments. But I broke the bread and lifted my glass and said, "Ma, I have to tell you something. I'm a Christian. I've started going to church."

There are moments in worship described as happening in "liturgical time," *kairos*, time out of time, a kind of suspended, unworldly immanence. I can't remember exactly what the two of us said, but as our conversation spilled out slowly, then in little rushes, I felt fear evaporating—not just mine but hers— replaced by a sort of joined, eager leaning into truth.

My mother was kinder than I ever deserved. "I guess I'm a bigot," she said. "It's just that I had to fight so hard against my parents' religion. It cost me so much. I *can't* believe in it."

I blurted out the stuff I loved about Jesus. "It's about food," I said. "And being with people who aren't like me."

She looked at me. "I get that," she said slowly. I could see the rigid, frightened mother and the rigid, frightened child. "But I told my mother when I was ten I didn't believe in God, and I haven't ever since." She took a bite of her meat. It was dark outside now, the last light gone down over the Adirondacks to the west, and I thought of her listening, unbelieving, to her parents pray in Baghdad, in Damascus, in Baltimore and Ohio and New York, until they, too, were gone, and she was left with her yearning and her refusal.

"I love the hymns, though," she said. "I bet I still know all the verses."

I remembered my mom singing to me, long ago. "Time, like an ever-rolling stream," she'd croon, "bears all our cares away." And the Handel tune about Zion, and "Love Divine," with its amazing flourish at the end, proclaiming that we would be "changed from glory into glory."

"Do you know this one?" I asked. It was a clean, odd Shaker tune. I'd learned it at morning prayer, and I loved the minor, shape-note harmonies. "For happiness I long have sought, and pleasure dearly I have bought," I sang. "I missed of all, but now I see, it's found in Christ the apple tree."

"Jesus Christ the apple tree?" my mother said. "Huh."

She poured me some more wine.

It wasn't official Eucharist. It was real communion, with all the incomplete, stupid, and aching parts still there. Made by human hands, out of meat and hope, incarnate: what the Russian mystics called "a foretaste of the heavenly banquet, where none are left behind."

Sometimes days at the pantry seem to go on forever. Eternal. We'll be unloading the pallets when the fog breaks, midmorning. The two widows from the neighborhood will be sitting in the corner together sorting green apples, Mary in her long black skirt and Amin in her sari and acrylic cardigan. Teddy will be darting anxiously from one table to the next, counting the boxes of cereal and fussing at Michael. Michael will listen patiently and ignore him. Two strangers will be leaning on the altar, scribbling something on a pad of paper.

"What about a little corn bread, too?" Paul will be saying to me in the kitchen, as I beat eggs and sugar over a low flame for the dessert custard. "I mean, why ever *not* make corn bread? It takes only fifteen minutes." Starlight Wanderer will stroll in. "Is there water for tea?" she'll ask. "I'm going to make a pot of tea for everyone. Did you see this book of paintings I got at the library sale?"

Starlight will show Derek the plates of strange medieval saints surrounded by glowing vines, while Paul dumps some cream "for richness" into his batter. "Darling," Nirmala will say, poking her head in, "are we gonna need bowls for lunch or just plates?" As she's setting the table, I'll be pulling out three dishes of arroz con pollo, fragrant with cinnamon and pepper. I'll wonder where Phil is, if he's in jail again, or dopesick and trying to sleep it off somewhere under the freeway. There'll be slamming and chatter, six burners and two ovens going, Mercedes pushing her way over to the sink, upturning a box and standing on it to scrub out the pots. Paul will stick his finger in my mouth. "Taste this," he'll say.

It is so sweet. By the time we're all at the table, sitting and rising and serving and eating and answering the door, sunshine will be pouring into the rotunda, where Donald and Rick and Lynn have joined us under the icons, around the long folding tables that my sister, Ellen, has decorated with ivy and luminous lavender from the backyard. Sasha will run in, lugging her giggly little sister, and grab a piece of corn bread. "Honey!" Millie will scold. "Sit down, eat lunch."

Life, everlasting. Carol will be blushing, as she always does when someone pays attention to her, because the new guy is flirting as he hands her a plate of chicken. Steve will come in with his baby, Elijah, and six Chinese women. Homer will be chewing steadily and sadly. Martha and Katie will arrive, talking and laughing excitedly together with Jose. The room will fill with the intense smell of hops from the brewery across the street and pineapple from the stacks of overripe fruit by the baptismal font. Miss Lewis will serve the salad. I'll be listening to Veronica tell me one more time about her sick mother. My mother will be there, smiling at me. My father will be there, helping my brother David carry out a platter of fish. Paul will reach for the salt.

We're eating together. The door opens. It is never over.

Acknowledgments

A writer's life, like the Eucharistic life, is one of gratitude. I thank all the people who helped make this book possible. I owe so much, first, to the love and example of my parents, Matthew and Betty Miles. I'm profoundly moved by the lifework of my grandparents, Helen and David Baker and Margaret and Max Miles. My mother not only opened the archives of the family but shared her own personal experiences with courage and generosity. My brother David is an inspiration to me about what it means to act with integrity in daily vocation. My sister, Ellen, has been a beacon of sanity and humor about the process of writing. Deb Dwyer, my sister-in-law, did copyedit consults by phone with amazing grace.

My dear friends—among them Christa Aboitiz, Jeanne Carstensen, Susan Evans, Francisco Gonzalez, Leslie Kossoff, Grant Martin, and Gary Wolf—have been extraordinarily patient and loving as I moved toward Christianity, and through this book. I'm grateful to Mark Pritchard, my godfather and partner in prayer, and Cris Gutierrez for giving me space to write. Stacey D'Erasmo turned her brilliant mind and generous heart on an early reading of this manuscript.

Thanks to all my colleagues and friends in Central America and the United States during the war years, especially Deborah Barry, Ruth Espinoza, Paolo Luers, Bob Ostertag, Corinne Rafferty, Joel Rocamora, and Dale Wiehoff. Thanks to Michael Ratner for his continuing example of a righteous life, and for his fearless, principled work for justice.

Much of this book was written on the floor of St. Gregory of Nyssa Episcopal Church, where I worked surrounded by Mark Dukes's icons of the Dancing Saints. I'm grateful to all who guided me at St. Gregory's and who continue to keep my faith living: Lynn Baird, Lawrence Chyall, Hillie and Joe Cousart, Gary Dickinson, Rick Fabian, John Golenski, Tracy Haughton, Will Hocker, Dave Hurlbert, Andy Jacszweski, Barbara Jay, Addie Kugler, Jamie Lunt, Donald Schell, Daniel Simons, Rick Storrs, Leesy Taggart, Philip and Janice Wickeri, and so many more.

For cooking, communion, and living out the Word, I couldn't have a better companion than Paul Fromberg.

My thanks to Bishop William Swing for his example and his conversation. My spiritual director, Jeff Gaines, has taught me, patiently and gracefully, about grace.

St. Gregory's Food Pantry volunteers, over the years, have fed my soul. Special thanks to Tom Benson, Elizabeth Boileau, Nirmala Cadiz, Raymond Conover, Quinton Goodin, Steve Hassett, Elpidia Hernandez, Susan Kellerman, Paul Marshall, Ceatrice Polite, Michael Reid, and everyone who makes up this beloved community.

My thanks to Derek Howard for his unparalleled generosity and to those who started new food pantries with us, including David Brown, Benta Carter, Regina Davis, Laticia Erving, Gina Fromer, Marlene Harris, Rena Ilpaso, Tricia McCarthy, Nina Pickerell, and Ken Reggio.

My thanks to all at the San Francisco Food Bank, including Paul Ash, Anne Quaintance, and everyone who helps bring the food to our table each week.

This book would never have been written without the encouragement and wisdom of my agent, Sydelle Kramer, who brought a skeptic's eye and a missionary's zeal to the project. Danielle Durkin at Ballantine kept the faith and sharpened the prose; I'm grateful for her insights and support.

Mostly I'm grateful for my family: Katie Miles and Martha Baer. They endured my conversion and supported my work on this book over long years. Martha's peerless editorial insights at every stage were matched by her steadfast love. They are my blessing.

Sara Miles
Ash Wednesday, 2006

About the Author

SARA MILES is a writer and an editor. She's the author of *How to Hack a Party Line: The Democrats and Silicon Valley* and an editor of both *Opposite Sex: Gay Men on Lesbians, Lesbians on Gay Men* and *Directed by Desire: The Collected Poems of June Jordan*. Her work has appeared in the *New York Times Magazine*, *The New Yorker*, *OUT*, *The Progressive*, *La Jornada*, *Salon*, and more. She has also written for the website of FRONTLINE/World, and she has written extensively on military affairs, politics, and culture. She lives in San Francisco with her family.

www.saramiles.net

This book is set in Fournier, a typeface named for Pierre Simon Fournier, the youngest son of a French printing family. Pierre Simon first studied watercolor painting but became involved in type design through work that he did for his eldest brother. Starting with engraving woodblocks and large capitals, he later moved on to fonts of type. In 1736 he began his own foundry and published the first version of his point system the following year. He made several important contributions in the field of type design; he cut and founded all the types himself, pioneered the concepts of the type family, and is said to have cut sixty thousand punches for 147 alphabets of his own design. He also created new printers' ornaments.